Spiritual
BOOT CAMP
For *Creators & Dreamers*

**ENCOURAGEMENT, INSPIRATION & BASIC TRAINING
TO HELP YOU ACHIEVE YOUR DREAMS**

Spiritual BOOT CAMP

For *Creators & Dreamers*

ENCOURAGEMENT, INSPIRATION & BASIC TRAINING
TO HELP YOU ACHIEVE YOUR DREAMS

TOM ENGLISH
★ ★ ★ ★ ★ & ★ ★ ★ ★ ★
WILMA ESPAILLAT ENGLISH

RAVENS'
READS
AN IMPRINT OF DEAD LETTER PRESS
BOX 134, NEW KENT, VA 23124-0134

Spiritual Boot Camp
for Creators & Dreamers
First published 2018 by Ravens' Reads
An imprint of
DEAD LETTER PRESS

This edition © 2018

Printed in the United States of America

ISBN-10: 0-9966936-9-6
ISBN-13: 978-0-9966936-9-1

FIRST EDITION
March 30, 2018

DEAD LETTER PRESS
BOX 134, NEW KENT, VIRGINIA 23124-0134
WWW.DEADLETTERPRESS.COM

*This book is
lovingly dedicated to*

Lynn and Nan

For with God nothing will be impossible.
—Luke 1:37 NKJV

*And the LORD blessed the latter days
of Job more than his beginning.*
—Job 42:12 ESV

CONTENTS:

SECTION III: *THE FACTS OF FOCUS & MOTIVATION*

SECTION VI: *NEVER GIVE UP!*

DO YOU HAVE WHAT IT TAKES?

WE ALL HAVE DREAMS: goals we hope to achieve, things we want to accomplish, even relationships we long to develop or repair.

We may be creators working in words, music, graphics, film or other media. We may be innovators or entrepreneurs, trading in better ideas and great inventions; researchers, analysts, or computer programmers, searching for new solutions to life's pressing needs and problems. We may be parents or grandparents, teachers or youth workers, shaping attitudes and training the next generation of pioneers; public servants or spiritual leaders—all working together to build a better world.

Now perhaps you're thinking "My dream is not so lofty." Maybe you just long for a better job, or the opportunity to go to college. Perhaps you're hoping to meet your soul mate, get married, and live happily ever after; or you want to raise well-adjusted children who will honor God and their parents, and become productive members of society.

Hey, don't sell your dreams short. These are admirable goals, well worth pursuing. In fact, whatever you're hoping for, whatever you're working towards, whether big or small, is significant in the eyes of God. (That is, of course, as long as it's good, decent and honest.)

Some people dream of starting a new life; getting out of debt; owning their own home; or simply being the best they can be right where they are. Some pray for a time when their entire family is serving the Lord. Still others look forward to a day when loved ones will be reunited in God's eternal kingdom.

Wherever we find ourselves, whatever we're doing, chances are, we're working toward a goal or dealing with a problem; waiting and hoping for answers and breakthroughs. We may have talent and abilities, intelligence and good looks—and more ideas than we know what to do with. We may have money and connections. Then again, we may possess none of these things!

Regardless, whether we're well on our way to accomplishing great things, or just getting started, the road to pursuing our dreams can be long and arduous. Along the way we can hit speed-bumps and encounter roadblocks. And often, when "life happens," we're forced to take detours or, worse, pull over and park for a time. So it's easy, and also very tempting —while struggling to achieve our goals, or waiting for a promise that seems to be taking forever—to mutter "Enough!" and give up. To throw in the towel and just walk away.

Please don't give up. You are not alone on this journey called life. God is *with* you and *for* you! And we're here, too— with insights and practical tips, words of encouragement and inspiring anecdotes ... and solid spiritual training.

When it comes to hopes, dreams, and creative endeavors, talent and tenacity always help. However, for the "long haul," such things are rarely enough. Life always demands more— and takes more. It's never enough to chase a dream. We need a plan ... and stamina ... and still something more. If we want to stay the course and fulfill our destinies, we'll need the backing, encouragement, comfort, strength, and reassurance that comes from One greater than ourselves: "the everlasting God, the Creator of the ends of the earth" who "knows what you need before you ask Him" and who "bestows favor and honor; no good thing does He withhold from those whose walk is blameless." (Isaiah 40:28; Matthew 6:8; and Psalm 84:11 NIV)

To receive this Divine support, we'll need some basic training on how to take several important spiritual steps toward reaching our goals and realizing our hopes and dreams. We want to share these steps, as well as many practical tips and strategies, in *Spiritual Boot Camp for Creators & Dreamers*. And we promise to stick with you as your personal trainers, encouraging you every step of the way, inspiring you to aim higher and hang tough, no matter how difficult the circumstances, or how long the journey takes.

We want you to succeed—because we understand how demanding the creative process can be; how lonely and *lengthy* the winding pursuit of goals and dream; and how great the obstacles that litter the course of life. We've been there. Actually, we're still there! We're still pursuing our own hopes and aspirations, and facing the challenges that frequently arise. As we stated, YOU are not alone.

Spiritual Boot Camp for Creators & Dreamers is not just one more book written by someone who realized his dreams years ago. Often the authors of such books are "celebrities" who are now out of touch with the difficulties involved—and hence, out of shape for "the chase." These dream coaches mostly share their own personal success stories, offer a few examples from the Bible, and then do their best to encourage their readers. Many of these books are worthy additions to any library, but again, it takes far more than a "rags to riches" story to help people achieve their dreams and destinies.

We creators and dreamers need hands-on training in the spiritual steps and principles that lie *behind* success. We need to know *how* and *why* things often work the way they do, and to master the spiritual and practical strategies necessary to overcome everyday obstacles and disappointments. And this takes discipline and drilling ... to become lean, mean goal-getting machines ... to weather the storms of life and complete the journey no matter how long and arduous!

Join us now for this basic training. We'll share truths from the Word of God and the battle tactics needed to live a victorious life while working, growing, creating, and realizing your dreams—tactics and truths we've learned from decades in the trenches. The training won't be *too* tough, and we'll share plenty of inspiring anecdotes and analogies to keep things lively, and enough encouragement to keep you motivated throughout.

So, *fall in!* We promise to whip you into tiptop shape, so that you, too, can triumph in life, liberty and the pursuit of your dreams!

SECTION I:
BASIC TRAINING

My heart is overflowing with a good theme...;
My tongue is the pen of a ready writer.
—Psalm 45:1 NKJV

Welcome to Spiritual Boot Camp for Creators
and Dreamers. Please follow along and take notes.

Seriously? Notes? As in, write stuff down?
The way our teachers made us in high school?

Relax. We're not taskmasters, but we do wish
to make a point. So please read on.

WORDS.

Life is all about them, both spoken and written. In fact, life started with a few spoken words: "God said, 'Let there be light'; and there was light. ...Then God said, 'Let Us make man in Our image....'" (Gen 1:3, 26 NASB)

Have you received a greeting card or letter from a friend? Did you get a text from a coworker? Have you checked your email today? Did you obey the traffic signs on the way to work? Did you follow the instructions on the packet of instant oatmeal? Such things demonstrate our dependence on the written word.

Do you have a favorite book, short story, or poem? Do you enjoy music while you're working? Do you watch television or go to the movies? All of our entertainment media begins as words thoughtfully recorded by dreamers and creators. Thank

God these people—who often are no different than you and you and *you*—had the foresight to capture their ideas, their insights, their inventions, their wildest imaginings ... on paper. Otherwise, because life and ideas are fleeting, we'd all miss out on a lot!

WORDS. We can't get enough of them! Okay, full disclosure: we are bibliophiles! Yes, we love books. In fact, our passion for bound paper and printed words borders on *bibliomania.* When we're not busy reading—or dusting the bookshelves occupying several rooms of our home—we're apt to be out scouring secondhand shops for new treasures, all the while muttering "So many books, so little time...."

Why do we collect books? For one, we appreciate the orderliness, clarity, and permanency of the printed word. But also, we must confess, because we are "information junkies"! We like having the facts at our fingertips.

Which is why we appreciate the Internet—while being mindful that the "Information Superhighway" is often congested with opinions, misinformation, and faux facts frequently copied and reposted until they achieve the status of urban legends. So we surf the net with prudence, just as we watch television with discernment. But when we do watch telly, we do so with a notepad and pen handy, ready to jot down useful info or to capture ideas inspired by our viewing.

Books, television, and the internet can be wonderful media for feeding our dreams; but our chief source of information, motivation, and inspiration lies elsewhere. It's within easy reach, and yet it's quite literally out of this world. It's the natural choice, and yet it was supernaturally conceived—because it's author is the supernatural Creator of the Universe: the God of Abraham, Isaac and Israel.

This divine fount of strength, knowledge and wisdom is the Bible, the best-selling book of all time ... and the most enduring. Throughout history it has weathered Bans and book burnings, censorship and suppression. At times its commands have been neglected and its truths all but lost, and yet God's Word has miraculously survived.

Its Author is often ignored, misunderstood and even misrepresented. Nevertheless, His Word has withstood the test of time, bringing hope, encouragement, inspiration, and wisdom to each new generation—and PRACTICAL solutions to the problems we all face. The Bible is the operator's guide for life on earth. It's also the training manual for this Spiritual Boot Camp for Creators and Dreamers.

Incredible? Judge for yourself. Here is the first of several important spiritual steps—taken directly from the Word of God Himself—to help YOU reach your goals and fulfill your dreams. Are you ready?

ARE YOU READY!?! Then muster for Basic Training.

WRITE THE VISION

[Your hopes, dreams, goals, and creative ideas]

WHEN IT COMES TO FORMULATING and solidifying your dreams and goals, writing the vision is extremely important. Ideas and inventions, the seeds of great plots and plans, all begin to take shape and grow when properly recorded. In their book *Chicken Soup for the Soul: Living Your Dreams,* writers Jack Canfield and Mark Victor Hansen state, "The more you write about it and talk about it, the more clear and believable it will become."

Sounds like so much hocus-pocus, and yet God also admonishes us to do this—and He would *never* lead us astray. He commanded one of His prophets to "Write the vision; make it plain on tablets, so he may run who reads it. For still the vision awaits its appointed time; it hastens to the end—it will not lie. If it seems slow, wait for it; it will surely come...." (Hab 2:2-3 ESV)

There's so much truth in this scriptural passage, about *being prepared*, *focused* and *determined*. But for now, let's simply concentrate on the phrase, "Write the Vision." Authors Canfield and Hansen explain that, "Just writing them down [ideas, goals, plans, and dreams] will set into motion an amazing process of bringing these things into your life."

How? Well, Words have *spiritual* power, to encourage, to create, or to destroy. In fact, according to Proverbs 18:21, the *spoken* word holds "the power of life and death." The *written* word, however, has even more influence! That's why legal contracts are rarely based on verbal agreements; words on paper carry far greater weight—and are far more binding.

But from an entirely practical standpoint, writing down information and ideas aids the learning process (the mental acquisition of these ideas)—which is why teachers encourage students to take written notes; writing down information and ideas helps us to focus and refine them. Hence, the creators of the Chicken Soup books state, "The more you write about [your dream and/or creative goals] and talk about it, the more clear and believable it will become."

So, fellow creators and dreamers, grab a notebook and label it your Dream Book. If necessary, go out and buy one, they're cheap. Pick a color and design that inspires you—and keep it handy. Your first entry?

Write down your vision/hopes/dream/goals/desires. Be specific, or at least as specific as you can be at this moment in the pursuit of your dreams. Whenever you get a new idea, a fresh insight, or a clearer picture of where you're headed (what you want to accomplish and where you want to be) then WRITE IT DOWN! When it comes to formulating and solidifying your ideas, plans, and goals, writing the vision is extremely important.

Don't edit. At least not at this point. Just put your thoughts down on paper as they come to you. (Yes, typing these spurts of inspiration into a computer or personal data device is fine, but revelations recorded in electronic "notebooks" always look a little cold and impersonal; unlike the vibrant declarations you make on paper—in your own handwriting! (Not to mention, computers harbor built-in distractions. Log on to type up an idea and you may get sidetracked by an email, text, etc.)

Make a habit of curling up with your Dream Book. Find a comfy spot and JOURNAL. **Record your thoughts, breakthroughs, triumphs and even disappointments.** This helps you keep track of your progress. "Taking notes" (the act of writing down facts, tips, ideas, etc.) has two major benefits: First, our notes serve as a tangible record of what we've read, heard, witnessed ... *or imagined.* Notes help us to remember. Second, writing down these experiences helps us to stay focused and make better sense of them. Notes help us to clarify and organize our thoughts. And thus, taking notes (writing stuff down) is one of the greatest strategies that we creators and dreamers can implement—which is why "...The Lord said to Moses, 'Write this for a memorial in the book....'" (Exod 17:14 NKJV)

Whenever possible **find a Bible verse, story, or promise that specifically speaks to you** and your dream/vision/goals. (We'll help you with this in succeeding sessions.) Here's a few of ours which we encourage you to include in your Dream Book:

"God began doing a good work in you. And he will continue it until it is finished...." (Phil 1:6 ICB)

"For God's gifts and His call are irrevocable. [He never withdraws them when once they are given, and He does not change His mind about those to whom He gives His grace....]" (Rom 11:29 AMPC)

"A person's gift opens doors for him and brings him before the great." (Prov 18:16 CSB)

"...Lord, you bless the righteous; You surround them with Your favor as with a shield." (Ps 5:12 NIV)

Now do yourself a favor: **WRITE IT DOWN!** Put your dreams, goals, plans and ideas on paper. Doing so will help you *stay focused, encouraged, and motivated!* "Moreover, the Lord said to me, 'Take a large scroll, and write on it with a man's pen....'" (Isa 8:1 NKJV)

And, getting back to where we started, please consider taking notes during this Boot Camp. Most if not all good teachers encourage students to take *written* notes; because seeing things in written form gives actual shape and substance to our ideas—and *reality* to the abstract thoughts formerly locked away within our brains. Do you want your hopes, dreams, goals and creative pursuits to begin taking on reality? It all starts with WORDS.

Once you've recorded the vision [your hopes and dreams, plans and goals] you'll be ready for the next spiritual step in the journey ... along the path to *fulfilling* the vision!

HAVE FAITH

In the beginning God created the heavens and the earth.
—Genesis 1:1 NIV

THE ABOVE VERSE IS, as far as we're concerned, a simple statement of fact. No, we don't care to debate the age of the earth or the validity of Carbon-14 dating. Science is wonderful and plays an important role in our lives, but it has little affect on our spiritual beliefs. (Besides, we stopped dating over three decades ago—once we were married.)

Are we close-minded? *Nah.* But we do understand the difference between science and faith. Science deals with the systematic study of the physical and *natural* world based on experimentation and *observation*; "Faith is the confidence that what we hope for will actually happen; it gives us assurance about <u>things we cannot see</u>." (Heb 11:1 NLT) Such as the existence of our *supernatural* God and the fulfillment of His promises.

Faith is the Anchor of the Soul. Faith is the food that nourishes our dreams and creative pursuits. Faith is the ember that keeps the flame of hope alive. Faith is what sustains us in the midnight hour, when nothing seems to be happening in the natural and it *looks* like we'll never reach our goals or fulfill our dreams; when we feel stuck ... lost and forgotten on the backside of nowhere.

Face it, dedication, perseverance, and hard work are rarely enough. Faith, on the other hand, is the raw material for miracles to happen. Got dreams? Then it pays to have faith for the journey!

Faith in the truth of God's Word (and specifically, the above verse) reminds us that EVERYTHING begins with the Creator of the Universe. And understanding this, the journey to realizing all our hopes and dreams—and enjoying an abundant life—should begin by enlisting His help.

Will He help us even in the pursuit of our dreams and creative endeavors? Yes! "He is the Rock; His deeds are perfect. Everything He does is just and fair. He is a faithful God who does no wrong; how just and upright He is!" (Deut 32:4 NLT) So, after writing the vision, you're ready for the next step:

Have FAITH that God is able to accomplish the vision —and will bring it to pass

A key to the success of this, however, is to seek first the One who placed the dream in your heart, not just the dream itself. In other words, always keep your relationship with the Lord as your #1 priority. All creative people and great dreamers need a reminder of this, because it's so easy to get caught up in fulfilling the vision, consumed by the creative process, or even simply preoccupied with other "stuff." The Lord must always remain your First Love. (Rev 2:4)

Jesus said, "You must love the Lord your God with all your heart, all your soul, and all your mind.' This is the first and greatest commandment." (Matt 22:37-38 NLT) And concerning all the things in life we need and hope for, He added, "[God] will give them to you if you give Him first place in your life...." (Matt 6:33 TLB)

The essential ideas of *faith* and *making God your #1 Priority* come together in the verse, "...Without faith it is impossible to please God, for whoever comes to Him must believe that He exists and that He rewards those who diligently search for Him." (Heb 11:6 ISV)

But how can you *truly* love someone you don't know? You can't, really. Which is why we must first learn *who* God is and *why* we need Him in our creative corner. So, here's a brief character profile:

He is the ultimate creator. In fact, as recorded in the first chapter of Genesis, He created the entire Universe and every thing within it. "Every good and perfect gift is from above, coming down from the Father of the heavenly lights, who does not change like shifting shadows." (James 1:17 ISV) And speaking of good gifts (visions, dreams, talents, and abilities) ...

He passed this creativity trait onto each of us! First, God created man (and woman) in His own image. (Gen 1:27)

Then, the Lord "filled him with the Spirit of God, with skill, with intelligence, with knowledge, and with all craftsmanship, to devise artistic designs...." (Exod 31:31-33 ESV)

His Love for you is limitless. After all, "...God so loved the world, that He gave His only Son, that whoever believes in Him should not perish but have eternal life." (John 3:16 ESV)

He always makes good on His promises! Concerning dreams, visions, and creativity, God says, "Do I bring to the moment of birth and not give delivery? ... Do I close up the womb when I bring to delivery?" (Isa 66:9 NIV) Indeed, "He is Faithful and True" (Rev 19:11 NKJV); because "He is not a man that He should lie." (Num 23:19 NKJV) "For all the promises of God are yes in Him, and in Him Amen...." (2 Cor 1:20 JUB) No matter how difficult the situation, or how great the odds...

Remember the Christmas Story from the Book of Luke? The Angel (God's Heavenly Messenger) announced to the Virgin Mary that she would *supernaturally* give birth to the Christ child, the Messiah of Israel and the Savior of the world: "For with God nothing will be impossible." (Luke 1:37 NKJV) Absolutely NOTHING is IMPOSSIBLE. The flip-side: ALL THINGS are POSSIBLE—including your fondest hopes and dreams! But ya gotta have faith!

We'll stop here. We could fill a fat book with God's wonderful thoughts, qualities and abilities, but we don't need to—because we already have the complete and final Word on the subject, the Bible. It's must reading for creators and dreamers alike.

Crack the spine on this best-selling book of all time. Learn about the great Creator of the Universe, the author and finisher of our faith (Heb 12:2 NKJV); who "bestows favor and honor. No good thing does he withhold from those who walk uprightly." (Ps 84:11 ESV) Doing so will bring understanding during tough times, and fuel you to pursue your dreams.

Got a vision? [hopes, dreams, plans and goals] *Write it down* and *have faith!* Meanwhile, cling to this truth and the promise it holds (declare it, memorize it, and meditate on it throughout the day): "'...I know the plans I have for you,' declares the Lord, 'plans to prosper you and not to harm you, plans to give you hope and a future.'" (Jer 29:11 NIV)

FEED YOUR FAITH

W E'VE ALL HEARD IT at one time or another. When we meet a seemingly insurmountable obstacle or suffer a bitter defeat, when things seem to be taking forever or our best-laid plans suddenly fall to pieces, some well-meaning optimist will say, "Keep the faith." This is actually sound advice, not only for moody creative types, but also for *anyone* struggling to achieve a heartfelt goal or fulfill the dream of a lifetime. But you can't *keep* what you don't already possess.

Got faith? Actually, we all have faith—in something. Many of us have faith in our own flawed characters, strength, and abilities. What a let down this kind of faith must be, as we continue to make mistakes and come up short again and again. After all, that's what humans do, and that's why it's important to have faith in One greater than ourselves.

Spiritual faith is what it takes for the long haul. But where on earth (pun intended) does it come from? Unfortunately, you can't grab it at Walmart or order a monthly supply from Amazon. No, faith in God comes from one place only. Um, *God!* In fact, He endowed each of us with this faith when He created us. How else could we ever put our trust in Him, or believe in *anything?*

Babies have faith the moment they're born. How else could they survive the shock of coming into this strange new world, gazing up at the doctor and seeing for the first time someone who appears to be trying to hide behind a mask— as though anonymity were the best way to cover up their latest foul deeds? And why else would babies cry when they're hungry, or want the squeaky toy daddy's playing with? What makes them believe they'll get either? Because, by faith, they already know mummy will take care of their needs.

Yes, we all come fully equipped to pursue our dreams. In His wisdom, "God has allotted to each [man, woman and child] a measure of faith." (Rom 12:3 NASB) A "measure" is a good starting point, but—because the harder things get, the more faith we need—it's important to increase and strengthen our faith; to make it grow big and strong by FEEDING IT.

Spiritual faith only thrives on one kind of food, the Bread of Life which is the Word of God. As we devour the Word, our own faith in God's goodness and His ability to fulfill His promises will grow—*better ... faster ... stronger.*

"So then faith comes by hearing, and hearing by the word of God." (Rom 10:17 NKJV)

Okay, spiritual food to feed spiritual faith. But is this food both tasty and nutritious? Judge for yourself: "How sweet are Your Words to my taste! Yes, sweeter than honey to my mouth!" (Ps 119:103 NASB)

"The Scriptures say, 'People do not live by bread alone, but by every word that comes from the mouth of God.'" (Mathew 4:4 NLT)

"Every Scripture passage is inspired by God. All of them are useful for teaching, pointing out errors, correcting people, and training them for a life that has God's approval." (2 Tim 3:16 GW)

"Your word is a lamp to guide my feet and a light for my path." (Ps 119:105 NLT)

Unlike little babies, spiritual faith won't cry when its hungry. So you need to remember to give it regular feedings, even if you don't think these feedings are necessary.

"Blessed is the person who ... delights in the teachings of the LORD and reflects on His teachings day and night. He is like a tree ... that produces fruit in season and whose leaves do not wither. He succeeds in everything he does." (Ps 1:1-3 GW) How's that for building strong faith?

Yeah, and what's my faith gonna look like when it gets bigger? Relax. Your faith isn't like "The Blob" or those alien pea pods in the sci-fi flick *Invasion of the Body Snatchers.* Fully developed, your faith will look like ... well, what do your hopes and dreams look like? We ask because "...Faith is the substance of things hoped for, the evidence of things not seen." (Heb 11:1 KJV)

Reading God's definition of faith helps us understand why *having* faith (and feeding it regularly) is essential in the pursuit of dreams and goals: faith allows us to "see" the finish line—long before we get there—encouraging us to stay on track and not give up, even when (to our physical eyes) our circumstances and chances begin to look bleak.

Whether we're expressing our creativity, or chasing our dreams, or just coping with life, the Apostle Paul admonishes us to "walk by faith, not by sight." (2 Cor 5:7 NKJV) When we do this, we stop focusing on the situation or the problem, while keeping our spiritual eyes on God the Problem-solver, who is able "to accomplish infinitely more than we might ask or think." (Eph 3:20 NLT)

Faith can strengthen and equip us in many ways. We'll discuss several in future Boot Camp sessions. For now, however, we submit the following:

Faith can feed your dreams and nurture the vision. It fuels the flames of hope, enabling you to believe in what would otherwise seem impossible. And during the midnight hour, in the barren wilderness of despair, when your "impossible dream" seems to be getting *further* away than ever and you're tempted to believe all is lost, faith can reassure and sustain you for the long haul. As Corrie Ten Boom wrote, "Faith sees the invisible, believes the incredible, and receives the impossible."

Do you have an "impossible dream"? Are you wrestling with the creative process or struggling to succeed? Are you dealing with a bad situation or facing an uncertain future? Feed your faith and your dreams. Read the Word. Accept its truth. Own its promises. Fully expect to see God's favor, blessings, and the fulfillment of the vision.

COMMIT YOUR EFFORTS TO GOD

ONE OF THE WISEST MEN OF ALL TIME, the Biblical King Solomon, once wrote, "Commit your work to the Lord, and your plans will be established." (Prov 16:3 ESV) These words of wisdom are as fresh and as relevant today as when they were first recorded, nearly 3000 years ago. And, this advice is vital to creators and dreamers alike—actually, to every last one of us.

The word *commit* has several connected and related meanings: "to send, to consign, to entrust, or to place in the care and keeping ... of something or someone. The word *work* applies pretty much to everything we do in life, whether we're pursuing a dream, mowing the lawn, or taking a covered dish to a sick neighbor. In fact, it applies to life itself.

Rather than further explain what Solomon meant, we've decided instead to share two *alternate* but highly *accurate* translations of the same Proverb: "Commit to the Lord whatever you do, and he will establish your plans." (NIV) "Entrust your efforts to the Lord, and your plans will succeed." (GW) No, we couldn't express this any better.

Committing all our efforts (creative or otherwise) to God, and then entrusting Him with both the process and the outcome, requires us to do two interrelated things:

Lean on the Lord!

Have you ever been overwhelmed by the magnitude of your vision? Have you felt that fulfilling your dream is far beyond your capabilities? Perhaps you have the talents and abilities but lack the right connections or sufficient resources (finances, knowledge, background) to achieve your goals. Perhaps you even feel like you're in way over your head, drowning in a sea of challenges and problems, fear and doubt.

Try this: "Turn all your anxiety over to God because he cares for you." (1 Peter 5:7 GW) "Give your burdens to the Lord. He will carry them. He will not permit the godly to slip or fall." (Ps 55:22 TLB)

In other words, lean on God! With all your *weight* (spiritual, emotional, intellectual). "Pile your troubles on God's shoulders—He'll carry your load, He'll help you out. He'll never let good people topple into ruin." (Ps 55:22 MSG) His shoulders are infinitely strong and broad, and He delights in carrying us as much as we delight in carrying a beloved child or a favorite pet.

It's a humbling experience, but what's wrong with a little humility in the face of overwhelming odds and obstacles? What's wrong with placing (committing) total dependence on the Creator of the Universe? The Apostle Paul had to do just that, and he was a pretty savvy fellow: smart, well educated, well-connected, competent, capable and independent. But Paul wrote, "[God] said, 'My grace is all you need. My power works best in weakness.' So now I am glad to boast about my weaknesses, so that the power of Christ can work through me." (2 Cor 12:9 NLT)

Grace is the power to endure, overcome, triumph, and succeed. It's the supernatural patience, stamina, and strength God imparts to us, after we become *totally* dependent upon Him, trusting Him *totally* with our fondest hopes and dreams, and relying totally on *His* goodness, *His* guidance, *His* ability, *His* answers, *His* resources—and His faithfulness to keep *His* promises!

This leads us to the second aspect of "Committing our efforts to God":

Abide in the Lord!

Humility in the face of God is acknowledging that *without* Him, we can accomplish nothing worthwhile. Jesus said, "I am the vine and you are the branches. Those who stay united with me, and I with them, are the ones who bear much fruit; because apart from Me you can't do a thing." (John 15:5 CJB) *Ouch!* The image the Lord uses is clear: God is like a grapevine laden with ripe fruit. But we're like the thick gnarly branches of a tree. If someone looks at us and sees us laden with juicy grapes, it's only because we've allowed ourselves to become entangled in the fruit-bearing vine of our God.

Now, with human effort, we *can* accomplish stuff ... on our own ... in our own strength, in our own way and timing. But if we act independently of God, we'll never fulfill His perfect will and divine purpose for our lives. Hence, we'll never get to see just how amazing things would have turned out— *if* we'd allowed God to be the architect and builder of our dreams and artistic endeavors. And we'll never realize the incredible heights of achievement or see all the wonderful places God wanted to take us—because we refused to let Him drive! And navigate us through the road of life.

In our own strength and wisdom, we can accomplish "great things." But such things carry little if any spiritual weight. They lack eternal value and they'll always pale in comparison to what God can accomplish THROUGH us! We just need to trust Him enough to let Him steer, remembering what God declares about His wonderful plans for us, in Jeremiah 29:11.

Getting back to John 15:5, some Bible translations use the phrase "whoever abides in Me," but the idea is the same. To *abide* means: to dwell and to rest; to remain or stay; to be firm and unmovable. God wants us to dwell with Him, to rest in His strong arms, and above all, to stay connected to Him, the source of our strength and creativity. We can do this by making Him our "First Love," by keeping Him as our #1 Priority, by allowing Him to guide us in all things, and by seeking to obey Him in all areas.

The act of "Abiding in the Lord" doesn't simply happen. It's a discipline, expressed by one's attitude and actions, which must be sought and developed. We begin by believing in God's Word and His promises; by entrusting Him with our lives, as well as our hopes and dreams; and by banking on His infinite love, mercy, and faithfulness. Then, instead of focusing on the problems and challenges of life, we must keep our focus on God's Divine nature and character, and His ability and willingness to meet each and every need—always remembering that "God has said, 'I will never fail you. I will never abandon you.'" (Heb 13:5 NLT)

Learning to *abide* will also require spending some quality time with God each day, during which we fellowship with Him through Bible study and *prayer*.

TAP INTO
THE POWER OF GOD

I have been driven many times upon my knees by over-whelming conviction that I had nowhere else to go.
—Abraham Lincoln

THERE ARE COUNTLESS BOOKS AVAILABLE on the subject of prayer, with more being published each year—and the number of volumes should indicate just how important this spiritual activity truly is. We'd like to offer a shorthand account here, that demystifies prayer and zeroes in on how it can aid creativity and help us to achieve our dreams.

Prayer is actually vital to the discipline of Abiding in the Lord. You can't stay connected to a friend or family member without keeping in touch; and you can't abide in God without staying connected and, hence, in constant communication with the source of your strength and creativity. Communication with God is called prayer. For many people, the act of *praying* is clouded in mystery, seemingly arcane and ritualistic. And yet, Jesus told His disciples that people should pray *often*. (Luke 11:8)

Prayer is just a fancy way of describing a heart-to-heart chat with God. We should talk to our Lord as freely and as easily as we'd talk to a best friend or soulmate, open and honest. No incense or Olde English required. Just open up to the Creator of the Universe; share your concerns, problems, fears, hopes and dreams. Bear your soul and spill your guts. Rant if you need to. The Lord is a good listener, and He takes in every word. And He loves you and wants the best for you, which is why He invites us to dialogue: "Call to Me, and I will answer you, and I will tell you great and mighty things, which you do not know." (Jer 33:3 NASB)

If you can talk, then you can pray. If you have laryngitis, you can *still* pray, silently, with your thoughts. Unfortunately, many people remain timid about approaching God in prayer. They act like a shy schoolboy who's trying to find the words to talk to the new girl in class. These folks are rarely at a loss for words; but once the "big moment" arrives, they suddenly don't know what to say. Even the disciples weren't sure about what to say. They asked Jesus, "How should we pray?"

Prayer is Not Rocket-Science. Nevertheless, Jesus gave His followers some simple guidelines in the form of "The Lord's Prayer" (Matt 6:10-12); which still provides a nice blueprint for conversing with our Heavenly Father. If you not sure how to begin a conversation with God, this "sample prayer" is an excellent icebreaker. It's a good idea to memorize it, along with Psalm 23, another handy Biblical prayer.

Actually, all of the Psalms make great prayers. Because King David wrote each one as a sort of "open letter" to God, in which he poured out his heart to his Lord. Within these "written prayers" David the Giant Slayer expressed his love and gratitude for God. He also shared his problems and fears. And he often cried out for help. David was both a creator and a dreamer who faced the same types of problems and challenges we all face, so *his* psalms can be recited to God as *our* own prayers.

Furthermore, David's attitude toward God and his habits concerning prayer provide us with a model for this important spiritual discipline. The Psalmist is described in Acts 13:22 as a "man after God's own heart." Was David perfect? No, but he was careful to keep God as his first love and #1 Priority. And he daily demonstrated this deep affection and commitment by also making prayer a priority.

Prayer Should *Always* Be a Priority. That's why King David wrote, "Early will I seek Him." (Ps 63:1) The Psalmist knew that—in the course of leading an army, running a government, and overseeing the various needs of a kingdom—he was bound to get busy ... and sidetracked ... and forget that he had made ...

A commitment to talk to God. Meeting with his Lord "early" in the day was David's way of ensuring he made time for prayer, *before* he got involved with other concerns.

What's "early"? Well, "early" is relative to your schedule; it's not so much an hour of the day as it is a slot near the beginning of your personal routine. If you work nights and go to bed around the time most people are having breakfast, then your "early" could be sometime in the afternoon—right after you wake up and before you get involved in other matters. Whether early in the day or early in your schedule, the meaning is the same: "first thing"!

Making prayer a priority (*the* priority, because it's about meeting with God) means setting aside a special time for it, and making it the first thing we do, before we have breakfast, check our email, or tune in to the local news and weather. Never put off prayer till later, because "later" never comes.

Furthermore, prayer helps set the tone for the entire day: it empowers you, improves your outlook, sweetens your disposition, and jumpstarts your creativity. Skipping prayer is worst than going to work without a good breakfast, especially on those days when you wake up feeling anxious or apprehensive: "Do not be anxious about anything, but in every situation, by prayer and petition, with thanksgiving, present your requests to God. And the peace of God ... will guard your hearts and your minds...." (Phil 4:6-7 NIV)

Pick a Prayer Place. Just as we need a "creative space" (a quiet little corner in which we can work and dream without interruption), we also need a specific and similar spot where we can daily meet and chat with the Lord. Your "prayer place" could be at the kitchen table (before the kids wake up), or a nook in the den, or even a folding chair set up in the laundry room. What's important is that you designate a single spot where you're comfy—but not comfortable enough to fall back asleep—and have relatively peaceful surroundings.

If possible, stash your Bible (and any devotional materials you use) somewhere in or near your Prayer Place. This can save you time and frustration, because you won't be hunting for it every morning. Another good idea, especially for dreamers and creative people, is to keep a notebook (or prayer journal) because God will give you new ideas and insights. You'll probably want to jot these down.

Although it's possible to pray in a variety of places and at different times, designating a special spot in your home—*and* a special spot on your schedule—will help you to develop a routine. And having a routine is vital to creating healthy habits, whether the habit is going to the gym, eating a sensible diet, or spending quiet time with God. Such habits, according to experts, require about three weeks to really stick—so stick to a routine of daily prayer!

Keep the Prayer Lines Open. The Word of God admonishes us to "Pray without ceasing." (1 Thess 5:17) A different translation renders the phrase as "Continually be prayerful." (NIV) Being *prayerful* is to be *involved* in and *characterized* by prayer. Meaning? God wants us to stay in touch throughout the day, uttering prayers and making requests whenever and wherever the need arises. Which means you can chat with God on the way to work, at your desk in school or the office, and even while standing in line at the movies. We do suggest, however, that you keep these conversations a little on the quiet side—just between you and your Lord.

Tapping into the power of prayer will bring comfort, joy, peace, answers, and understanding. It can also energize your creativity—and with God's help, you can fulfill even the most "impossible" dreams. Just remember, "I am the LORD, the God of all the peoples of the world. Is anything too hard for Me?" (Jer 32:27 NLT)

TIPS ON PRAYERS
FOR CREATORS & DREAMERS

PRAYER IS JUST A FANCY WAY of describing a heart-to-heart chat with God, and it's vital if we want to stay connected to the source of our strength and creativity. As we discussed, it's a good idea to memorize key Scripture verses, such as Psalm 23, a handy Biblical prayer—as an easy "icebreaker" to get the "dialogue" rolling. Doing so will ensure we'll never be at a loss for words when we address the Creator of the Universe.

Also, we highly recommend that anyone who is pursuing a dream or involved in creative activities follow the Apostle Paul's instructions concerning prayer: "Don't worry about anything; instead, pray about everything; tell God your needs, and don't forget to thank him for his answers. If you do this, you will experience God's peace, which is far more wonderful than the human mind can understand. His peace will keep your thoughts and your hearts quiet and at rest...." (Phil 4:6-7 NIV)

So, don't waste time and energy fretting over *why* your dreams haven't been fulfilled yet, or *when* God is going to open that special door, give you a breakthrough, meet your needs, or solve your problems. Instead, ask and trust God for everything, and then cast your cares upon Him. Again, God admonishes us, "Call to Me, and I will answer you, and show you great and mighty things, which you do not know." (Jer 33:3 NKJV)

Jesus Christ furthered this wisdom by saying, "Keep on asking, and you will receive what you ask for. Keep on seeking, and you will find. Keep on knocking, and the door will be opened to you." (Matt 7:7 NLT) In other words, BE PERSISTENT—both in prayer and in the pursuit of your dreams.

Never, *ever* give up!

Now, why should we believe that God actually wants to answer our prayers? First, because He *said* so (in the preceding verses). Second, because of His Divine nature—His essential qualities of love, goodness, and generosity, and His ability "to do far more than we would ever dare to ask or even dream of—infinitely beyond our highest prayers, desires, thoughts, or hopes." (Eph 3:20 TLB)

God illustrates this truth by providing an earthly reference point: "...Parents—if your children ask for a loaf of bread, do you give them a stone instead? ...Of course not! So if you sinful people know how to give good gifts to your children, how much more will your Heavenly Father give good gifts to those who ask Him." (Matt 7:9-11 NLT)

To help get you started—in the practice of asking your Heavenly Father for some of these "good gifts"—here are a few short Biblical prayers you can read and/or memorize and recite.

To prepare yourself for His blessings: "Create in me a clean heart, O God. Renew a loyal spirit within me." (Ps 51:10 NLT)

> "May all my thoughts be pleasing to [my God],
>   for I rejoice in the LORD." (Ps 104:34 NLT)

"As the deer pants for streams of water, so my soul pants for you, my God. My soul thirsts for God, for the living God. Why, my soul, are you downcast? Why so disturbed within me? [I] put [my] hope in God, for I will yet praise him, my Savior and my God." (Ps 42:1, 5 NIV)

To receive comfort and reassurance: "You are my hiding place and my shield; I hope in Your Word." (Ps 119:114 NKJV)

"Keep my soul, and deliver me; Let me not be ashamed, for I put my trust in You." (Ps 25:20 NKJV)

"In You, O Lord, I put my trust; Let me never be put to shame. Be my strong refuge, to which I may resort continually; You have given the commandment to save me, for You *are* my rock and my fortress. Do not cast me off in the time of old age; Do not forsake me when my strength fails. *You,* who have shown me great and severe troubles, shall revive me again" (Ps 71:1,3,9 NKJV)

To request His blessings: "Stir up Yourself, and awake to my vindication, to my cause, my God and my Lord." (Ps 35:23 NKJV)

The Prayer of Jabez: "[Insert your name] called on the God of Israel saying, 'Oh, that You would bless me indeed, and enlarge my territory [my readership, my viewers, my listeners, my clients, my customers, my influence, my outreach, etc.] that Your hand would be with me, and that You would keep *me* from evil, that I may not cause pain!' So God granted [me] what [I] requested." (1 Chr 4:10 NKJV)

The Aaronic Blessing: "Then the LORD said to Moses, 'Tell Aaron and his sons to bless the people of Israel with this special blessing: May the LORD bless you and protect you. May the LORD smile on you and be gracious to you. May the LORD show you his favor and give you his peace.'" (Num 6:22-26 NLT)

TRUST GOD FOR GUIDANCE

NOW THAT YOU HAVE FAITH that God will empower your creativity and fulfill the vision He gave you, and now that you're daily communicating with God, it's time to follow His lead—*wherever* it takes you. Even if the direction in which He's leading you doesn't seem the right way to go; even when God's counsel seems foolish, perhaps outlandish; even when His advice goes against conventional wisdom, it's vital that you trust your Heavenly Father and follow His good guidance. Doing so will depend on your obedience to …

"Trust the LORD with all your heart, and do not rely on your own understanding." (Prov 3:5 GW) In other words, when pursuing your goals and dreams, you need to **LET GOD STEER!** Simple? Hardly. Once you're accustomed to being in the driver's seat, it's difficult to move over to the passenger side. And even after you do, you may find yourself wanting to go faster (or slower), or to turn "here" instead of "there"; and there's a good chance you'll also spend a lot of time looking in the rearview mirror, still contemplating many of the places and opportunities you've passed.

It's usually hard to deviate from the plans we make, or act in ways that are contrary to our own ideas and desires. But that's where faith comes into play. We need to believe that God knows exactly what's right for us: *where we need to go, who we need to meet, how we need to proceed.* And how long it should take to reach our goals. Nonetheless, faith demands that we trust our Heavenly Father in *all* things, knowing that *His* way is the perfect way:

"A person's steps are directed by the LORD, and
the LORD delights in his [or her] way." (Ps 37:23 GW)

"After He has gathered His own flock, He walks ahead
of them, and they follow Him because they know His voice."
(John 10:4 NLT)

"And if you leave God's paths and go astray, you
will hear a voice behind you say, "No, this is the
way; walk here." (Isa 30:21 TLB)

Remember, every great invention or innovation, every brilliant idea or achievement, and every masterpiece of creativity or engineering, was accomplished by someone who was willing to think outside the box. The "box" is built from preconceived notions, old ideas, and a narrow point of view. Its walls are reinforced by rigid thinking, stubbornness, and the fear of failure. Unfortunately, most people find the box a comfortable and secure place, so that's exactly where they stay.

The Apostle Peter stepped out of the box—and the boat—when His Lord, Jesus Christ, beckoned His disciple to join Him for a walk across the water. (See Matthew 14:29.) Simon Peter had to shrug off fear and logic, and leave comfort and security, to step out onto the Sea of Galilee. Once he did, he out-distanced the other disciples who remained behind. Yes, the apostle eventually started to sink, because he again allowed his narrow-minded view of life and its circumstances to weigh him down, but God applauded his faith and courage to break away from the ordinary and follow His lead.

Although none of it ever made "good sense" or seemed like the right way to proceed: the Patriarch Abraham and his wife Sarah left behind everything they knew, to blindly follow God into the wilderness, where they inherited a fertile land of milk and honey (Gen 12-17); Moses paved an unlikely path for his people to escape the bondage of Egypt, when he parted the waters of the Red Sea (Gen 14:16); and a young shepherd named David took the first step on the road to being a king, when he toppled the gigantic and previously undefeated warrior, Goliath, with a single stone hurled from a crude slingshot (1 Sam 17:40-51). Challenges met and obstacles overcome, dreams fulfilled and history made, all were the result of trusting God and following His lead.

So, are you searching for a fertile land? Do you have a "Red Sea" that needs parting? Are you facing giant challenges and struggles? Step out of the box of what's comfortable and familiar, safe and sound; step out of the box of following the wisdom of the world, or stubbornly doing things your own way. Instead, listen to God. Follow the course He sets for you—especially in the pursuit of your dreams and all your creative activities.

Walk in harmony with the Lord, always trusting in His faithfulness and sound guidance. Determine in your heart and mind, "...I am trusting you, O LORD, saying, 'You are my God!' My future is in your hands." (Ps 31:14-15 NLT)

SEEK AND TRUST GOD FOR SUPERNATURAL FAVOR

Surely, LORD, you bless the righteous; You surround them with Your favor as with a shield.
—Psalm 5:12 NIV

YOU DON'T HAVE TO BE A SUPERSTAR or even an especially gifted person in order to receive God's supernatural favor. In fact, you can be the low man on the totem pole, the last in your class, or "one of the least of these my brethren" (Matt 25:40) and still have confidence that God is in your corner. The Creator of the Universe is all about finding, loving, saving, and upholding the lost, the weak, the oppressed, and the underdog. Furthermore, He's not a respecter of persons, regardless of their experiences, circumstances or background.

The Apostle Peter stated, "...How true it is that God does not show favoritism." (Acts 10:34 NLT) To the contrary, the Bible is filled with examples of very ordinary people who—with the help of God—accomplished extraordinary things. God's only requirement is your willingness to obey and your availability to be used. You just need to be a "whosoever"—as in the verse, "...God so loved the world, that He gave his only begotten Son, that whosoever believes in Him should not perish, but have everlasting life." (John 3:16 KJ 2000)

Always remember that God strongly supports the *whosoevers*. Thank Him for *also* using people who may not have earthly connections, certificates or titles, a recognized ministry, or an established platform, but who nonetheless have big dreams and something of value to offer. Remember that "God's gifts and his call can never be withdrawn" (Rom 11:29 NLT) and that "He who began a good work in you will bring it to completion...." (Phil 1:6 ESV)

So, what's involved in seeking and trusting God for supernatural favor?

Trust the Lord to Open Doors. These "doors" can take various forms: special appointments, big promotions, unexplored avenues, untapped resources, and incredible opportunities. God asks only one thing—that you keep on knocking! He promises us whosoevers, "...Seek and you will find; knock and the door will be opened to you." (Mathew 7:7 NIV)

Although it takes faith and courage to knock on some of these "doors," especially those that appear to be "barred" and jealously "guarded" by important, influential, and well-known people, the favor of God encourages us to be bold! The Lord reassures us, "See, I have placed before you an open door that no one can shut. I know that you have little strength, yet you have kept My Word and have not denied My name." (Rev 3:8 NIV)

Trust God to Bring Influential People into your Life.
Ask God to bring into your life people who will support your vision and help you to fulfill your dreams. Why? Because we all need help. *Nobody* can make it totally alone. Even the so-called "self-made" successes got a helping hand *somewhere* along the way. According to the Bible, the Apostle Paul had all the right stuff—education and experience, connections and influence—but he eventually reached a place where he needed assistance; a friend and facilitator who could help Paul fulfill the great vision God gave him: spreading the Gospel among the Gentiles.

2000 years ago, Paul had his Barnabas (Acts 9:26-31). What's a Barnabas? A person who's willing to help another complete their "mission" in life. Someone who can open the right door for you, point you in the right direction, and get you started on your way. In the Book of Acts, there was a man named Barnabas who did this for the Apostle Paul, and the Gentile Church owes this facilitator a great debt of gratitude.

The Apostle Paul had a dream and a mission: to begin spreading the Good News of Jesus Christ to all the world—namely, the Gentiles. And Paul was the best person for the job. He had the knowledge, the experience and the wisdom—

and the guidance of God's Holy Spirit. Paul had "the right stuff," but not the right connections. Actually, Paul had no connections, and no friends among the Jewish followers of Yeshua (Christ). What Paul *did* have was an extremely bad reputation. Seems that before believing in the Messiah, the Apostle-Formerly-Known-As-Saul had a track record of persecuting his Jewish brethren, and he'd been responsible for the deaths of many of them. Paul had changed, but in the eyes of Jewish believers, he was an unknown quantity, a liability, perhaps even a risk.

Despite his passion and his qualifications, Paul wasn't going anywhere as far as the Jewish leadership were concerned. "When Saul arrived in Jerusalem, he tried to meet with the believers, but they were all afraid of him. They did not believe he had truly become a believer!" (Acts 9:26 NLT) That's when Barnabas, the quintessential facilitator and all-around nice guy, stepped forward. "Then Barnabas brought him to the apostles and told them how Saul had seen the Lord on the way to Damascus and how the Lord had spoken to Saul. He also told them that Saul had preached boldly in the name of Jesus in Damascus." (Acts 9:26-27 NLT) Not only did Barnabas vouch for Paul, but he also joined the apostle on his mission. Barnabas helped Paul to achieve his objective and to fulfill his dream.

Sooner or later we all need a little help. Sooner or later we all need a Barnabas.

For instance, Christopher Columbus had an incredible dream and the chutzpah to chase it all the way to "The New World"; but until he received the support and financial backing of King Ferdinand and Queen Isabella of Spain, Captain Columbus was going nowhere fast! And more recently, Dr. Phil had his Oprah. To quote the Beatles song, "I get by with a little help from my friends." (We'll further explore this topic a bit later.)

So don't be shy; ask God for a "Barnabas" who can assist you in the pursuit of your dreams, goals, and creative endeavors. After all, one "yes" is often all it takes—and yet many of us are so fearful of rejection we never dare to ask.

But exactly what is there to fear? What's the worst that can happen? Someone says NO and *you* simply say, "Next!"

and then move on. Remember: nothing ventured, nothing gained.

In their book *Chicken Soup for the Soul: Unlocking the Secrets to Living Your Dreams,* Jack Canfield and Mark Victor Hansen write, "As you pursue your dreams, have the courage to ask for what you want. Somewhere out there is a person or an organization that wants to give you what you want and who will be willing to say yes to you. It's simply a matter of asking enough people."

We previously wrote of a young entrepreneur who followed this advice to great success. He sent out 150 letters asking for the assistance he needed to realize his dream. 149 of his requests for help were simply ignored, went unanswered, or were answered with a rejection. But one letter received a "yes" that changed the young man's life. The "yes" came from none other than Donald Trump, years before he became the 45th President of the United States. **Lesson learned:** *Speak up and aim high!*

Trust God to Handle the Details. Yes, it's true, the Devil is in the details. And dreamers and creators can go crazy fretting over them, or just trying to make sense of them. Don't concern yourself with disappointments and delays. Don't try to figure out why *this* person wouldn't help or *that* door didn't open. It's a waste of time and energy, and it will steal your peace. There will always be setbacks, false starts, and crazy occurrences that don't seem to make sense.

Know what? Not everything in life *does* make sense. But it doesn't matter if we're trusting God with the details. Regardless of what happens, we can take comfort in the knowledge that God is in control. "And we know that God causes everything to work together for the good of those who love God and are called according to His purpose for them." (Rom 8:28 NLT) Mistakes? Obstacles? Failures? Rejection? *Ha! No worries!* God knows what He's doing. Trust Him.

Never forget, God has promised, "I will never fail you. I will never abandon you." (Heb 13:5 NLT). "Now thanks be to God, [who] always causes us to triumph in Christ...." (2 Cor 2:14 AKJV)

MANAGE YOUR MIND

NUTRITIONISTS REMIND US, "You are what you eat." But just ask any of the leading motivational speakers and they'll tell you, "No, you are what you THINK." Of course, these highly-paid consultants are simply following in the footsteps of the Biblical King Solomon, who wrote that as a person "thinks within himself, so he is." (Prov 23:7 NASB)

If you think you're a failure, then that's probably all you'll ever be. If you think your dreams will never come true, then there's a good chance they won't. Face facts, it's impossible to have hope when your head is full of hopelessness; or to be positive about life and all the possibilities your future holds if you continually feed your mind with negative thoughts.

Researchers have discovered that the average person processes as many as 50,000 thoughts a day. And, unfortunately, many (if not most) of these thoughts are negative. *Yech!* This unpleasant truth brings to memory a worn-out comedy sketch from an old TV show called *Hee Haw!* Four ragged-looking hillbillies sitting in a dirty barnyard look up at the sky with piteous eyes, and croon woefully, *"Gloom, despair, and agony on me! Deep dark depression, excessive misery! If it weren't for bad luck, I'd have no luck at all—gloom, despair, and agony on me!"*

If *we* had that outlook on life, we'd probably never get out of bed, let alone dabble in the rewarding pursuits of our God-given creativity, or follow all our hopes and dreams. Instead, we'd groan, "Please go away! Wake me when the world's over." And we warn you, dear reader, if you're going to create something of lasting (eternal) value; if you're serious about wanting to achieve your goals; if you simply want to live the "abundant life" the Lord promised (John 10:10), then you'd do well to properly manage your mind. Negative thoughts, such as fear, worry, pessimism, and a critical spirit, can kill hope and creativity.

Keeping your mind free of negative thoughts isn't always easy: because we live in a "fallen"—and hence, *imperfect*—world; and because we inherited from our ancestors Adam and Eve, a predisposition to do all the wrong things in life. It's called the "sin nature," but it's just another way of saying that, when left to their own devices, people will always be selfish, self-centered, and self-serving. Collectively, such people have a tremendous *negative* impact on our world, helping to create a harsh, often cold environment that is hostile to dreamers and their dreams, and critical of just about any creative endeavor.

The best we can do to improve the world is to refuse to contribute to the cesspool of hostility and negativity. But in regards to our own hopes and dreams, we can take steps to keep this cesspool from poisoning our spirits ... and our MINDS. The Apostle Paul admonishes us, "Don't become like the people of this world [cruel, pessimistic, critical, spiteful]. Instead, change the way you think. Then you will always be able to determine what God really wants—what is good, pleasing, and perfect. (Rom 12:2 GW) Another way of putting it: "Don't copy the behavior and customs of this world, but let God transform you into a new person...." (Rom 12:2 NLT)

Want to manage your mind? Then, to borrow an ad slogan from Apple Computers, "Think different." Replace any negative thoughts (including spiritual doubts) with positive (faith-filled) thoughts. Be hopeful (optimistic), not cynical (pessimistic). Flush away the "stinking thinking" (thoughts of fear, failure, regrets, hurts, disappointments, and doubts); stop dwelling on the past; stop replaying unpleasant memories of painful events and disparaging words that were spoken to you (or about you). Stop rehearsing any worst-case scenarios regarding your future. And stop nursing any grudges you may be holding. Such stinking thinking creates toxic emotions that will eventually poison your mind and your creativity, as well as contaminate your relationships

Stinking thinking and toxic emotions is a deadly combination. It will steal your precious time and sap your creative energy. Ultimately these mind-melters will soften your brain and harden your heart; they will sabotage your efforts and derail your dreams. So ... let it go ... all of it. Flush the negative thoughts from your brain with the clean, pure, inspiring, encouraging, uplifting and faith-building water of the Word of God.

This flushing process is called "renewing the mind." Think of it as washing, repainting, and redecorating an ugly room—like the one some of us keep in our heads. First you tear down the dingy drapes, pull up the ratty carpet, and dust every corner; then you bring in beautiful new furnishings that make you feel relaxed, refreshed, and happy to reside there. *Now* you have a wonderful creative space (in your head) where you can *really* think ... and dream.

We renew our minds by reading and meditating on the Word of God (the Bible). Meditating is just a fancy word for carefully considering what you read; mulling over it throughout the day; and allowing it to penetrate your heart and spirit. We can "chew" on the promises of God much the same way a cow chews its cud: slowly, methodically, thoroughly, and with great contentment—until we've extracted all the spiritually nutritious "juice" from it. "Study this Book of Instruction [the Bible] continually. Meditate on it day and night so you will be sure to obey everything written in it. Only then will you prosper and succeed in all you do." (Josh 1:8 NLT)

The process of renewing your mind can be aided by memorizing key verses. Once you do, you can speak out these words of comfort and reassurance whenever you're tempted to entertain a negative thought. For instance, when the thought "You'll never realize your dream" pops into your head, quickly replace it with the truth "I can do all things through Christ who strengthens me!" (Phil 4:13) Keeping your mind filled with "the good stuff" will eventually force out all the "junk." And committing scripture verses to memory *guarantees* that God's Good Word takes up permanent residence in your mind. (By the way, once the Word moves in, It doesn't like messy roomies.)

It's vital that we creators and dreamers continually renew our minds—because our minds are continuously bombarded with bits of bad information that can accumulate and eat away at our ability to live full lives and successfully pursue our dreams. Imagine your brain as a super-computer. Too many junk files can clutter your memory; and also, malware from the outside world is constantly trying to get in. When it does, your "processing speed" slows. You. May. Even. Crash.

Let all these bits of "negative programming" be overwritten with the truth of God's Word. Do it daily—because that's what it takes to keep your creative "hard-drive" running at peak performance. In other words, *discipline* yourself to renew your mind. And *discipline* yourself to think positive, faith-filled thoughts. (After all, this is Boot Camp!)

Here's this lesson in a nutshell (straight from God Himself): "Blessed is the person who does not follow the advice of wicked people ... or join the company of mockers. Rather, he delights in the teachings of the LORD and reflects on his teachings day and night. He is like a tree planted beside streams ... that produces fruit in season and whose leaves do not wither. He succeeds in everything he does." (Ps 1:1-3 GW) "You [God] will keep in perfect peace all who trust in you, all whose thoughts are fixed on You!" (Isa 26:3 NLT)

"And now, dear brothers and sisters, one final thing. Fix your thoughts on what is true, and honorable, and right, and pure, and lovely, and admirable. Think about things that are excellent and worthy of praise." (Phil 4:8 NLT)

MORE ON MANAGING YOUR MIND

W HO'S IN CHARGE HERE? Most of us need to feel we have some degree of control over our lives and destinies. So it's a sobering truth that, according to Denis Waitley, "You are either the Captain or the Captive of your thoughts." (*Chicken Soup for the Soul: Unlocking the Secrets to Living Your Dream*) In other words, do you control your thoughts—or do your thoughts control you?

The Apostle Peter wrote, "...Gird your minds for action, keep sober...." (1 Peter 1:13 NASB) The word *gird* means: to muster [collect, assemble] up one's resources; to equip and make secure; to prepare for action. Peter is admonishing us to collect our thoughts, to stay focused—not wasting valuable mental real estate on negative, unproductive and destructive thoughts—to stay intellectually and spiritually alert, and ready for action. This is precisely the strategy we need to adopt, especially when pursuing a dream or tackling a creative project.

Here's another, more direct translation of the verse: "...Think clearly and exercise self-control." (NLT) *Got that?* Get C.O.N.T.R.O.L. of your thought-life.

The human brain is not unlike a super computer—with a powerful high-speed camera built-in. It records a lot of information (and imagery), and then imbeds it in the mind. Not all of this info is useful. Some of it is even harmful. All of it has an affect on our productivity, as well as how we function (act) and what we say (including some stuff "That does not compute!"). As the old saying goes, "Garbage in, garbage out."

And, like a computer, the brain's "data storage space" is not unlimited. In fact, what God has given us is precious— and will be until someone invents a zip drive that plugs into the side of the neck. So, as with a computer, it pays to frequently peruse old data files, to see what's clogging the system. Taking a Mental Inventory allows us to evaluate the quality (and creative value) of our thoughts.

Try it. Ponder these self-assessment questions:

What's the first thing I think of when I wake up in the morning?
What's continually on my mind throughout the day? (What dominates my thoughts?)
What's the last thing I think about before going to bed?
What am I putting into my mind?
What am I reading, watching, listening to, and engaging in? (Games, social media, etc.?)

Ready to evaluate your test against THE standard? The measuring stick is what the Apostle Paul wrote roughly 2000 years ago: "...Friends, I'd say you'll do best by filling your minds and meditating on things true, noble, reputable, authentic, compelling, gracious—the best, not the worst; the beautiful, not the ugly; things to praise, not things to curse. Put into practice what you learned from me, what you heard and saw and realized. Do that, and God, who makes everything work together, will work you into his most excellent harmonies." (Phil 4:8 MSG)

Dwelling on just the positive stuff in life can be a challenge, since we're constantly being bombarded with images and information, both good and bad. But just because a negative thought pops into your brain doesn't mean you have to welcome it. Nor does it mean you should allow it to linger. As the Great Reformer Martin Luther once wrote, "You cannot keep birds from flying over your head, but you can keep them from building a nest in your hair."

So, when thoughts like "You have no talent" or "You'll never fulfill your dreams" try to take up residence in your head, refuse to accept them. Then, quickly replace them with an uplifting and encouraging promise from God's Word, such as "I can do all things through Christ who strengthens me." (Phil 4:13 NKJV)

Every dream or vision begins life as a single thought. Every new invention, innovation, story, song, book, film, work of art, company, ministry, or organization starts with an idea. But to transform thoughts into realities, good ideas must be acted upon; dreamers and visionaries must make a decision to take the necessary steps to achieve the goal or dream. And the *first* step takes place in the mind: If you think you *can*, then you probably *will*; if you think you *can't*, then you probably *won't*.

"Always remember," Abraham Lincoln wrote, "Your own resolution to succeed is more important than anything else." *Resolving* to do something is also called "making up your mind." What are YOU using to "make up" YOUR mind? Please understand, you'll never achieve your dreams and goals, or see the vision become a reality, if you don't take control of your thoughts. You must discipline your mind to receive and ponder what is good and trustworthy, positive and productive.

The Apostle Paul wrote, "...Keep focusing on the things that are above, where the Messiah is seated at the right hand of God. Keep your minds on things that are above, not on things that are on the earth. (Col 3:1-2 ISV)

Keep a heavenly—*godly*—focus by training your mind: read God's Word, the Bible (the most encouraging book on earth); meditate on it, memorize and proclaim its promises. And stay motivated by thinking positive, faith-filled thoughts; by counting on God's unconditional love; by trusting in the future He has planned for you; and by believing only what God has to say about you—after all, who knows you better than the One who created you?

"This is God's Word on the subject: 'I know what I'm doing. I have it all planned out—plans to take care of you, not abandon you, plans to give you the future you hope for." (Jer 29:11 MSG)

"I tell you the truth, anyone who believes in Me will do the same works I have done, and even greater works, because I am going to be with the Father."   (John 14:12 NLT)

"No eye has seen, no ear has heard, and no mind has imagined what God has prepared for those who love Him." (1 Cor 2:9 NLT)

"For we are God's masterpiece. He has created us anew in Christ Jesus, so we can do the good things He planned for us long ago."   (Eph 2:10 NLT)

ADJUST YOUR ATTITUDE

IF YOU WANT TO ACCOMPLISH YOUR GOALS, tap into your creativity, and realize your dreams, then you'll need to manage your mind. Part of the mind management process is developing and maintaining a positive, faith-filled attitude.

Actually, attitude is everything. Thomas Jefferson wrote, "Nothing can stop the man with the right mental attitude from achieving his goal; nothing on earth can help the man with the wrong mental attitude." Or, to put the truth more colloquially: "A bad attitude is like a flat tire. You can't go anywhere till you change it." (Unknown)

Your attitude shapes your thoughts, emotions, outlook, actions, and words. A negative, bleak, sour, fearful or defeatist attitude will get you nowhere in life. Even if you possess amazing gifts and talents, even if you have brilliant ideas, the people around you—your potential audience, readers, clients, customers, collaborators, teammates, backers, promoters, and facilitators—can quickly detect a bad attitude—*if* that's what you have.

People like to associate with "winners": fun, enthusiastic, lively, can-do men and women who are filled with faith. They are drawn to those who keep a good attitude. But your attitude affects more than just your "neighbors"—it affects your openness to sound opportunities and new ideas, your ability to persevere, and to function at peak efficiency. And it can make the journey—during the pursuit of your dreams—far more enjoyable. The late music publisher Allen Klein put it this way: "Your attitude is like a box of crayons that color your world. Constantly color your picture gray, and your picture will always be bleak. Try adding some bright colors to the picture by including humor, and your picture begins to lighten up."

To overcome rejection, closed doors, setbacks, and other obstacles; to stay the course until goals are achieved, visions fulfilled, and the journey completed, creators and dreamers need to maintain a positive, faith-filled attitude—regardless of their past or present circumstances. However, having such an attitude is NOT secular mind-over-matter "think and grow rich" hocus-pocus; which excludes God, while trusting in and relying on the dubious "power" of the human will. No, having a faith-filled attitude is:

Knowing you have God on your side, working *with* you, *through* you, and on your behalf; and fully trusting Him to work out the details, through each and every step of the way, no matter how many twist, turns, and detours your journey takes.

It's relying on God, *His* strength, *His* abilities, *His* goodness, *His* connections; rather than on yours. As the Apostle Paul wrote, "[God] said, 'My grace is all you need. My power works best in weakness.' So now I am glad to boast about my weaknesses, so that the power of Christ can work through me. ...For when I am weak, then I am strong." (2 Cor 2:9-10 NLT)

It's NOT ignoring the facts (failures, false starts, closed doors, and rejection) or denying your feelings (hurts, disappointments, disillusionment). Dreamers and creators who keep a positive, faith-filled attitude don't have their heads buried in the sand. However ...

It *IS* choosing to see the positive side of any outcome; the opportunities that come with every problem; the silver-lining in every storm cloud; the pluses, not the minuses. It's having a mindset that views the "glass" as half-full, not half-empty.

It's focusing on God's promises, NOT *your* problems. It's "...Being confident of this, that He who began a good work in you will carry it on to completion...." (Phil 1:6 NIV) It's remembering that despite your circumstances, "God's gifts and his call can never be withdrawn." (Rom 11:29 NLT) It's knowing that "A person's gift opens doors for him, bringing him access to important people." (Prov 18:16 ISV)

Your attitude will determine how you view life, and how you respond to various situations and circumstances; your general disposition, and how you interact with others. Your attitude impacts your judgement, your decision-making, your relationships (the most important aspect of life) and even your mental and physical wellbeing. Ultimately, your attitude will determine how your life turns out—including your creative pursuits and any goals, dreams, or visions you're pursuing.

"Attitude," to quote the great Winston Churchill, "is a little thing that makes a big difference."

We don't have control over most of what happens in life. We can't make the traffic move on the freeway. We can't shorten the line at the grocery store checkout. We can't prevent the stock market from plummeting. We have no control over rudeness, insensitivity, office politics, double standards, or how people respond to our dreams, visions, or creative endeavors. But we DO have control over how these things affect us. In other words, we have total control over our own attitudes.

We can either waste our time fuming, pouting, sulking and, perhaps, even spiral into depression; dragging our feet in hopelessness, believing that we'll never fulfill our dreams— or we can choose to live in victory, rising above life's little aggravations (and sometimes big disappointments). We can keep a positive, faith-filled attitude, and never lose that spring in our step—even when circumstances don't look promising, even when we don't seem to be getting any closer to realizing the vision God placed in our hearts.

Victory or defeat? Negative, hopeless, and downtrodden, or positive, faith-filled, and enthusiastic? The choice is ours— just as it was when the Biblical hero Joshua urged his people, "Choose this day whom you will serve." (Josh 24:15 ESV)

Which course will *you* choose? Will you take the high road and follow your dreams and creative pursuits, proclaiming "I can do all things through Christ, who strengthens me." (Phil 4:13 KJ2000)? Or wander aimlessly down the back roads of gloom, doom, and despair? It's all in your attitude: "People may hear your words, but they feel your attitude." (John C. Maxwell)

WATCH YOUR WORDS

A RE YOU WORKING ON THE "CHAIN," GANG? What you daily feed your mind will affect your thoughts; and your thoughts will shape your attitude. Your attitude, as previously discussed, further shapes your thoughts and emotions, your outlook on life, your actions, and your WORDS. Your words can be constructive or destructive; facilitate your creative endeavors and bring you closer to your dreams—or have a negative impact on you and the people you encounter.

A positive, faith-filled attitude will ultimately manifest itself in every area of our lives, especially in how we act and speak. And positive, faith-filled words and deeds are—like love—"what the world needs now."

We're constantly bombarded with **foul phrases, critical comments, words that wound, and toxic talk.** These words of death create a suffocating atmosphere of *spiritual smog,* which can choke our creativity and cloud our dreams and visions. On the other hand, constructive, encouraging, faith-filled "words of life," coupled with acts of kindness, can help clear the air—and make our sojourn on this big blue marble a lot easier. Furthermore, positive words of life help to produce an environment where creativity can flourish and dreams can be shared and pursued.

Of course, not everything we *do* is smart, lovable, or justified; nor can we always be proud of everything we *say.* The good news is, just like our attitudes, we can CONTROL the words we speak. And we can ensure that what spews from our lips will work *for* us, not *against* us.

Words have creative power. In fact, the first words ever spoken—by God, the Creator of the Universe—shaped the cosmos: "God said, 'Let there be light, and there was light.'" (Gen 1:3 NIV) And our Lord continued to SPEAK things into reality.

In a string of "Then God said" moments, He created "all the beasts of the earth and all the birds in the sky and all the creatures that move along the ground—everything that has the breath of life in it...." (Gen 1:29 NIV)

If you ponder the wide variety of these beasts, birds, and "creatures"—their many different shapes, sizes, colors, and characteristics—you'll begin to understand just how wonderfully creative our Lord is! Now, consider this: God made each of us in *His* own image. (Gen 1:26-27). And yes, we inherited the traits of our Heavenly Father.

We share the same God-given spiritual DNA and CREATIVITY.

Therefore, OUR words have creative power.

We can say words that bring peace or division; that either encourage and build people up, or tear them down emotionally. The creative choice is all ours, because "The tongue has the power of life and death...." (Prov 18:21 NIV)

Speaking positive words of faith produces a ripple effect that helps shape our social and emotional environment. When we refuse to gossip about or badmouth our "friends," we're doing our part to break the cycle of negativity (the destroyer of dreams, the killer of creativity). After all, change must start with each of us. Besides, we creators and dreamers should never waste our precious time and emotional energy criticizing others, spouting words of death and despair, or complaining about things over which we have no control. We have better things to do.

How often have you heard one of the world's greatest misconceptions? "Sticks and stones may break my bones, but words will never hurt me." Wanna bet? Tell this to any of the countless adults struggling with deep emotional wounds—left by overly-critical parents who never spoke an encouraging word to their children; who instead uttered harsh words like "You'll never amount to anything!" (By the way, that's certainly NOT what God has to say about you. His Holy Word proclaims, "...Thanks *be* to God who always leads us in triumph in Christ, and through us diffuses the fragrance of His knowledge in every place." (2 Cor 2:14 NKJV)

Family feuds, marital breakups, and fallouts with friends and coworkers all begin with negative, cutting words. Of course, the opposite is also true: not only are friendships and family ties formed and nurtured by positive words of love and affirmation, but a sincere word of peace and kindness can also repair any breach. In fact, one of the secrets of a healthy marriage or relationship is the ability to effectively communicate. Remember, "A gentle answer deflects anger, but harsh words make tempers flare." (Prov 15:1 NLT)

Sure, it's okay to vent once in a long while, to get stuff off your chest. But be careful in whose direction you vent—and for how long. You don't want to take out your frustrations on some poor innocent bystander, such as a loving spouse or loyal friend. It's best to vent to God. He's a good listener and never takes a dreamer's doubts or a creator's rantings personally. However, once you *do* get it out of your system—your fears, doubts, disappointments, disillusionments, and any emotional wounds you've suffered—turn it all over to God. Pray about it. Then leave it in His hands and move on. You have places to go, and things to do.

Maintaining strong, healthy relationships is essential, and a careless word can break even the strongest ties. Words have caused important political elections to be lost, peace treaties to be broken, and even wars to be declared. The author Edward Bulwer-Lytton expressed the power of words best when he wrote, in 1839, "The pen is mightier than the sword." Whether spoken or written, words pack a punch that can help you prevail in nearly every trial.

Even your relationship to God is dependent on your words: "If you declare with your mouth, 'Jesus is Lord,' and believe in your heart that God raised him from the dead, you will be saved. For it is with your heart that you believe and are justified, and it is with your mouth that you profess your faith and are saved." (Rom 10:9-10 NIV) And whenever we fail (or stray from God), we can quickly return to His good graces with a few sincere words: "If we confess our sins, he is faithful and just and will forgive us...." (1 John 1:9 NIV)

Jesus said, "A good man produces good deeds from a good heart. And an evil man produces evil deeds from his hidden wickedness. Whatever is in the heart overflows into speech." (Luke 6:45 TLB) Which takes us back to the importance of feeding our minds (the "heart" of the matter) with the Word of God, and its encouraging, refreshing, and uplifting message of hope. And afterward, maintaining that positive, faith-filled attitude we keep emphasizing.

Get into the habit of speaking out God's Word. Feed your dreams and creativity by quoting His precious promises, such as "God never changes his mind when he gives gifts or when he calls someone." (Rom 11:29 GW) A man's gift makes room for him, and brings him before great men." (Prov 18:16 NKJV)

And to combat those times of weakness we all suffer, when we WANT to give someone a piece of our mind (the piece that's mostly gristle), we need to be "prayed up"; we should daily ask the Lord to help us overcome any loose-lips tendencies we may have to spout off, offer our unwanted opinions, put people in their place, or demonstrate our acid wit. Ask God to "Take control of what I say, O LORD, and guard my lips" (Ps 141:3 NLT) Seek His supernatural grace for your words: "Let the words of my mouth and the meditation of my heart be acceptable in your sight, O LORD, my rock and my redeemer." (Ps 19:14 ESV)

"Successful people," according to Jack Canfield, "are conscious of the thoughts they think and the words they speak —both about themselves and others. They know that words are powerful." This best-selling author and leading success coach goes on to state, "Words can destroy relationships, lose sales and start wars. Words can just as easily be used to build self-esteem and self-confidence, nurture relationships and turn dreams into reality. ...Before you speak, think about what you want to create ... and choose your words accordingly."

IMPLEMENT PRAISE

Mind your speech a little, lest you should mar your fortunes.
—William Shakespeare

NOW THAT WE'VE DISCUSSED how NOT to use our words—by making false, negative, pessimistic, critical, and cruel comments—let's cover the most positive, fruitful, and constructive use of human speech. It's the secret weapon of all people of faith, but of dreamers and creators especially. It's the *supernatural* practice of praising and worshipping God.

By "praising and worshipping" God we mean: glorifying or exalting Him in word or song; giving thanks; honoring and adoring; and reverencing God. We describe the practice as "super-natural" for several reasons. Here are a few of the BIG ones:

Praise "clears the air." Previously we described "words of death" asspiritual air pollution. It's toxic, and certainly not conducive to dreams and creativity. Praise puts our focus on the goodness of God—not on our problems. Hence, it has a refreshing, cleansing affect, for both the speaker and those who hear. "Because Your gracious love is better than life itself, my lips will praise You." (Ps 66:3 ISV)

When you find yourself whining about a missed opportunity or an unfair situation; complaining about a neighbor or a coworker; or griping about the traffic or long lines at the checkout, start praising God—instead of grumbling. As a result, you'll begin to feel better almost immediately. Why? Because ...

Praise creates an inviting spiritual environment that's attracts and ... **welcomes the Creator of the Universe.** In fact, the Biblical King David wrote that God *inhabits* (or dwells in) the praises of His people. (Ps 22:3) Having the "full-strength" presence of God *that* close has several benefits:

Joy: "...In your presence there is fullness of joy; at your right hand are pleasures forevermore." (Ps 16:11 ESV)

Comfort: "Is anyone among you suffering? Let him pray. ...Let him sing praise." (James 5:13 ESV)

Strength: "Seek the Lord and his strength; seek his presence continually!"

Encouragement (and relief from depression): "Why art thou cast down, O my soul? and why art thou disquieted within me? hope thou in God: for I shall yet praise him, who is the health of my countenance, and my God." (Ps 42:11 KJV)

Peace: "Rejoice in the Lord always; again I will say, rejoice. ...The Lord is at hand [present]; do not be anxious about anything, but in everything by prayer and supplication with thanksgiving let your requests be made known to God. And the peace of God, which surpasses all understanding, will guard your hearts and your minds in Christ Jesus." (Phil 4:4-7 ESV)

Perspective: "Because your steadfast love is better than life, my lips will praise you." (Ps 63:3 ESV)

Praise opens the door to blessings: "Blessed are those who dwell in your house, ever singing your praise!" (Ps 84:4 ESV)

Praise reinforces Hope: "I will hope continually and will praise you yet more and more." (Ps 71:14 ESV) Exactly what we need in order to stay the course!

It's the right thing to do! "...Praise and exalt and glorify the King of heaven, because everything he does is right and all his ways are just. And those who walk in pride he is able to humble." (Dan 4:37 NIV)

For these reasons, and others, the Apostle Paul admonishes us, "Therefore by Him let us continually offer the sacrifice of praise to God, that is, the fruit of *our* lips, giving thanks to His name." (Heb 13:15 NKJV) But sticking with this important spiritual practice isn't always easy because, let's face it, sometimes we just don't feel like praising God! Actually, when things aren't exactly going our way, it's downright

HARD! But read Paul's verse again. Note that he likens the practice to offering a sacrifice.

The word *sacrifice* means "to surrender" something of value for the sake of "a higher or more pressing claim." Making a personal sacrifice is never easy, but it *IS* a choice we must often make. Similarly, committing ourselves to continually praise God—despite our circumstances, and especially when facing problems—is something we must CHOOSE to do.

It's a real test of our faith to give God our praises, even when we feel as though we've stalled in the pursuit of the vision; even when the fulfillment of our hopes and dreams seems light years away (and perhaps *impossible* to reach)—and even when we feel abandoned, forgotten, and alone.

Job felt this way. He suffered a tremendous loss—everything he loved in life—and yet, in the midst of his pain, grief, and despair, he cried out to his God: "Even if he slays me, I will hope in him." (Job 13:15 NET Bible) This Biblical icon never stopped trusting and praising God.

"Even though the fig trees have no blossoms, and there are no grapes on the vines; ...even though the flocks die in the fields, and the cattle barns are empty, yet I will rejoice in the LORD! I will be joyful in the God of my salvation!" (Hab 3:17-18 NLT)

Modern application? Even when we just don't get it, we still praise Him—every single day, rain or shine. "Every day I will praise you and extol your name for ever and ever." (Ps 145:2 NIV) Even when things go wrong, remember: "But as for me, I trust in You, O LORD, I say, 'You are my God.' My times are in Your hand" (Ps 31:14-15 NASB)

Start implementing the secret weapon of praise. Discipline yourself to worship God throughout the day—*everyday!* Our declarations of praise and worship are pleasing to God, like a sweet aroma (2 Cor 2:14); but *we* get all the spiritual benefits! To quote Houston pastor and author Joel Osteen, "You can change your world by changing your words... Remember, death and life are in the power of the tongue."

DO STRENGTH TRAINING

DURING **B**OOT **C**AMP we can instruct you in the essential spiritual tactics needed for achieving your goals. We can drill you in several fancy maneuvers guaranteed to help you in the pursuit of your dreams. But it avails us little unless you possess the strength and stamina to implement your basic training. With this in mind, we suggest routine "workouts" designed to whip you into peak spiritual condition.

We dreamers and creators continually need this form of "strength training" in order to climb those mountains which lie before us. We'll need to be tough if we want to overcome the frequent obstacles we'll encounter while chasing our dreams. We'll also need endurance if we want to stay the course. We'll need to be the best we can be—so that we can lick adversity when it rears its antagonistic head. We'll need some *serious* strength training!

The dictionary defines *strength* as (doh!) the quality of being strong; or having the power to perform demanding feats. For us, strength is the ability to accomplish our goals. It's the energy required for creative endeavors such as writing, speaking, performing in the arts, researching, inventing, innovating—you name it. And it's the stamina necessary to pursue our dreams ... no matter how long it takes.

The good news is that spiritual strength training won't cause you to bust a gut or even break a sweat. And, best of all, we're not in this alone: God, the Creator of the Universe who gave us both the dreams and the gifts and talents needed to accomplish them, is right beside us on the training grounds of life—and He wants to accompany us every single step of the way. In fact, God promises "I will never fail you. I will never abandon you." (Heb 13:5 NLT)

During strength training it's vital to have God on hand, because ultimately, He *IS* the source of our strength. *Without*

God, we'll mostly grunt and groan and learn what cream puffs we truly are. However, *with* God, we can boldly proclaim: "God is our refuge and strength, always ready to help in times of trouble. So we will not fear...." (Ps 46:1-2 NLT) We can join the Biblical King David in his triumphant battle cry: "The LORD is the strength of my life; of whom shall I be afraid?" (Ps 27:1 KJV)

Interestingly the Bible links *strength* to *joy*. We dreamers and creators need both! But we need to understand that "joy" is NOT the same thing as being happy. Happiness is generally the result of favorable circumstances, or the positive outcome to a situation. It's natural to be happy when everybody loves us and things are always going our way.

Happiness is dependent on external events and circumstances. Joy, on the other hand, is not dependent on such things. Joy is internal (and based on our spiritual condition) We can experience genuine joy in spite of our less-than-favorable circumstances—and even when things don't go our way.

The Biblical leader Nehemiah wrote, "The joy of the LORD is your strength." (Neh 8:10 NIV) And yet, when he penned these words, he was under tremendous stress from people who opposed his efforts to fulfill his dream of rebuilding the city walls of Jerusalem. Obviously, Nehemiah did *not* allow his circumstances to steal his joy.

Similarly, the Apostle Paul was in a horrible predicament when he wrote, "Always be joyful in the Lord! I'll say it again: Be joyful!" (Phil 4:4 GW)

Although Paul was chained up in a cold, dark, stinking Roman prison awaiting execution, his spiritual and mental wellbeing were not dependent on his situation in life. "The reason for Paul's joy was his relationship with Christ," Dr. David Jeremiah states, in the introduction to his book *Turning Towards Joy.* "If Paul's relationship to his master could bring him joy under those conditions, then surely we who also love the Savior can learn to rejoice in our difficult times as well."

So, when we feel we're running out of steam (in the pursuit of our dreams and creative endeavors), when we feel like we're at the end of our rope (from dealing with problems and disappointments), we can still have God's joy and, therefore, God's *strength.* We can rely on His strength to see us through any situation. Indeed, knowing that God is with us, and *for* us, we can confidently declare with the Apostle Paul, "I have strength for anything through Him who gives me power." (Phil 4:13 Weymouth NT)

How strong are *you*? Paul wrote, "[God] told me, My grace is enough; it's all you need. My strength comes into its own in your weakness. Once I heard that ... I quit focusing on the handicap [or whatever problems we may facing] and began appreciating the gift. It was a case of Christ's strength moving in on my weakness. Now I take limitations in stride, and with good cheer, these limitations that cut me down to size—abuse, accidents, opposition, bad breaks. I just let Christ take over! And so the weaker I get, the stronger I become." (2 Cor 12:9-10 MSG)

We dreamers and creators can tap into the same strength, joy, confidence, and divine perspective Paul found in Christ. Even if we're still struggling to reach our goals, we can enjoy perfect peace and spiritual contentment—by committing all our dreams to God in prayer, and then trusting Him to bring them to pass.

You can bank on His promises, because "...The people who know their God shall prove themselves strong and shall stand firm and do exploits...." (Dan 11:32 AMPC)

Be strong in God; be joyful in the knowledge of His grace and goodness. You start by making a choice: having joy is a decision, just like keeping a good attitude. And, just like our attitude, joy is linked to our thoughts and words, which in turn affect our actions throughout the day. So when you wake up each morning, regardless of how you feel or what challenges you'll be facing, choose JOY.

Declare with us:

"This is the day the Lord has made. We will rejoice and be glad in it." (Ps 118:24 TLB)

"Be strong and brave. Do the work. Don't be afraid or discouraged. The Lord God ... is with you. He will help you until all the work is finished. He will not leave you." (1 Chr 28:20 ICB)

MORE JOY, MORE STRENGTH

In every situation [no matter what the circumstances]
be thankful and continually give thanks to God;
for this is the will of God for you in Christ Jesus.
—1 Thess 5:18 AMP

IN HIS BOOK, *LAUGH AGAIN!,* Charles Swindoll states: "I know of no greater need today than the need for joy. Unexplainable, contagious joy. Outrageous joy. When that kind of joy comes aboard our ship of life, it brings ... enthusiasm for life, determination to hang in there, and a strong desire to be of encouragement to others. Such qualities make our voyage bearable when we hit the open seas and encounter high waves of hardship that tend to demoralize and paralyze. There is nothing better than a joyful attitude when we face the challenges life throws at us."

According to Swindoll, "Someone once asked Mother Teresa what the job description was for anyone who might wish to work alongside her in the grimy streets ... of Calcutta. Without hesitation she mentioned only two things: the desire to work hard and a joyful attitude."

Mother Teresa's two requirements for changing the world in Calcutta are also the two most important secret weapons of successful creators and dreamers: JOY and hard work. Okay, hard work is simply about rolling up our sleeves and doing what needs to be done—whenever, wherever, and however—until we accomplish our goals. But how do we lay in a supply of joy? Furthermore, once we get it, how do we keep our joy?

The short answer: **stay plugged in** to the source of your strength, God, the Creator of the Universe, because—and here's where the similarity to the Energizer Bunny ends—we were never designed to run on battery power. Unlike that pink flop-eared mechanical rabbit, we can and *do* wind down when we're running low on power. But that should never happen, *if* we stay plugged in to the power supply; because "...The joy of the Lord is your strength and your stronghold." (Neh 8:10 AMP)

Now for the long answer, and an explanation of HOW we stay plugged in. Well, our spiritual "Life" is a lot like a board game: we continually have to "Go back to START." That would be God. So, let's take a few steps *back* in our basic training to the part about putting our trust in the Lord:

Regardless of what's going on around you, KEEP THE FAITH. Regardless how aggravating stuff gets, **keep a divine perspective** on life—what happens here is but a moment in eternity (and indeed, if you've entrusted your salvation to Christ, then you do have eternal life.) Regardless how long it takes to reach your dreams, remember that you have friends in high places—three to be exact (the Father, the Son, and the Holy Ghost)—who won't fail you!

"...Let all who take refuge in You rejoice; let them sing joyful praises forever. Spread Your protection over them, that all who love Your name may be filled with joy." (Ps 5:11 NLT)

Joy comes with salvation. It's a package deal. And joy increases with spiritual growth: "...The Holy Spirit produces this kind of fruit in our lives: love, joy, peace, patience, kindness, goodness, faithfulness...." (Gal 5:22 NLT)

Manage Your Mind. **Renew that organic computer of yours each and every day.** (Rom 12:1-3) *Do this* by spending quality time with Him, through prayer, worship, and reading His Word. *Do this* by checking in with God FIRST—before you check your email or turn to the news, weather, and sports. All that stuff can wait until you've renewed your power supply.

Remember, "...In Your presence is abundant joy; in Your right hand are eternal pleasures." (Ps 16:11 HCSB) So, if you find yourself losing your joy, getting grumpy, nasty, or negative, take stock of your devotional time. Are you spending

QUALITY time with God? Is it your #1 Priority? Arc you consistent? And whenever you need a spiritual lift, tap into the power of prayer and praise. God will definitely lift you up: "...Though you do not see Him now, you trust Him; and you rejoice with a glorious, inexpressible joy." (1 Peter 1:8 NLT)

Stop focusing on any unfavorable circumstances, problems, or unfulfilled dreams; and instead focus on the goodness of God, His infinite love, and His ability and faithfulness to fulfill His wonderful promises. Value above everything else your relationship with your Heavenly Father. Do NOT take Him for granted!

"...With my whole heart, I will praise His holy name. Let all that I am praise the LORD; may I never forget the good things He does for me. He forgives all my sins and heals all my diseases. He redeems me from death and crowns me with love and tender mercies. He fills my life with good things. My youth is renewed like the eagle's!" (Ps 103:1-5 NLT)

As we previously stated, having (and keeping) your Joy is a choice. It's not dependent on how well your day went. In fact, when things *aren't* exactly going your way, that's when it's most important to keep your joy: "...When troubles come your way, consider it an opportunity for great joy. ...When your faith is tested, your endurance has a chance to grow. So let it grow ...[and] you will be perfect and complete, needing nothing." (James 1:2-4 NLT)

Maybe times are tough and the going is getting rough. And maybe you feel you're not getting any closer to fulfilling your dreams. You can still stay *strong* in the face of adversity and still have *victory*—EVEN THOUGH things aren't working out as you hoped or planned.

"Even though the fig tree does not blossom, and there are no grapes on the vines; even if the olive harvest fails, and the fields produce nothing edible; even if the flock is snatched from the sheepfold, and there is no herd in the stalls—as for me, I will rejoice in the LORD. I will find my joy in the God who delivers me...." (Hab 3:17-18 ISV)

Take time to encourage and bless others. Be a "Barnabas" —a helper/friend/facilitator—to other creators and dreamers. "Why?" you might ask. "How can this help ME?" Well, in addition to making the world a better place for all concerned, you can tap into the supernatural Law of Reciprocity. That's a fancy way of saying, *What goes around comes around:* "A generous person will prosper; whoever refreshes others will be refreshed." (Prov11:25 NIV)

Besides, you want JOY, right? After all, joy keeps you strong, and nothing brings more joy than giving and serving others—which is why the Apostle Paul wrote, "...We must help the weak, remembering the words the Lord Jesus Himself said: 'It is more blessed to give than to receive.'" (Acts 20:35 NIV) Blessings equate to joy!

Take time to rest—*and get the proper amount of sleep!* Lack of sleep results in mental and physical fatigue, and fatigue (being plumb tuckered out) is one of the most common joy-killers facing people today. That's why God created a day of rest: "Remember to observe the Sabbath day by keeping it holy. You have six days each week for your ordinary work, but the seventh day is a Sabbath day of rest dedicated to the LORD your God. On that day no one in your household may do any work." (Exod 20:8-10 NLT)

Sounds like God really means business with this; not only did our Creator make this whole rest thing one of the Ten Commandments—it's number 5 on His list—but He also set the example for us *other* creators to follow: "In the beginning God created the heavens and the earth. ...Then God looked over all He had made, and He saw that it was very good! And evening passed and morning came, marking the sixth day. ...On the seventh day God had finished his work of creation, so He rested from all His work." (Gen 1:1,31; 2:2 NLT)

Hey, God created you, so He knows what's best for you. Rest and relaxation help to restore our enthusiasm and joy. (There's that word again!) Sleep is as important as food, and yet, when it comes to catching some Z's many of us are malnourished. And of course, no matter how dark things may appear *now*, they always look brighter in the morning ... after a good night's sleep: "Weeping may endure for a night, but a shout of joy comes in the morning." (Ps 30:5 AMP)

So, turn off the TV, close the book, get off the Internet, and go to bed at a decent hour—for the sake of your own creativity!

Stop and smell the roses! Yes, always pursue your dreams with gusto. But remember, the path you take to reach your goals isn't just about the destination.

Be sure to enjoy the journey itself; take in the scenery along the way; laugh, play, have some fun; and nurture the curious and creative "child" within. "A joyful heart is good medicine, but depression drains one's strength." (Prov 17:22 GW)

Look forward, NOT backward. You may have left a trail of failures and missed opportunities behind you—but ahead of you are the promises of our faithful God and endless possibilities. Besides, all your dreams lie in that direction. Move forward, not backward; and watch where you're going, not where you've been.

Keep the same joyful (and hopeful) outlook on life that the Apostle Paul maintained: "...I have not achieved it, but I focus on this one thing: Forgetting the past and looking forward to what lies ahead...." (Phil 3:13 NLT)

Your past may be filled with sorrows and mistakes, but your future is bright and full of joy. Remember, God proclaims, "'I know the plans I have for you,' declares the Lord, 'plans to prosper you and not to harm you, plans to give you hope and a future.'" (Jer 29:11 NIV)

Rejoice in what the Lord is going to do in your life: "Stop being afraid...! Rejoice and be glad, because the LORD will do great things. Stop being afraid ... because the desert pastures will bloom, the trees will bear their fruit, and the fig tree and vine will deliver their wealth." (Joel 2:21-22 ISV)

Develop an attitude of gratitude. This is essential if you want to keep your joy and stay strong. As pastor and author Joel Osteen states, "The seeds of discouragement cannot take root in the soil of a grateful heart."

When you start feeling down and disheartened, don't allow yourself to sink into depression. Instead, change your focus—from what you *don't* have to what you *do* have. Count your blessings. You'll be surprised how much you actually have and how much you've accomplished in life.

When upon life's billows you are tempest tossed...
When you are discouraged, thinking all is lost...
Count your many blessings, name them one by one,
And it will surprise you what the Lord hath done.
    —John Oatman, "Count Your Blessings" (1897)

"Therefore by Him let us continually offer the
sacrifice of praise to God, that is, the fruit of our lips,
giving thanks to His name." (Heb 13:15 NKJV)

SECTION II:
TACTICS FOR SUCCESS

Take a lesson from the ants....
Learn from their ways and become wise!
—Proverbs 6:6 NLT

...Wisdom prepares the way for success.
—Ecclesiastes 10:10 GW

MANAGE YOUR TIME

GOOD TIME MANAGEMENT is an important skill everyone should develop, but it's absolutely essential for creators and dreamers. Each of us is allotted just 24 hours a day to accomplish multiple tasks, so we need to spend our time wisely. And if we're actively pursuing a dream, trying to reach a goal, then we'll always have important things to do, places to go, people to see. So, we can't afford to squander our time on unproductive activities that don't add value to our physical, emotional or spiritual well-being—and which don't get us any closer to our goals.

No, we're not veering off course. *Spiritual Boot Camp for Creators and Dreamers* is all about learning the *spiritual* steps necessary to reach our goals—and properly managing our time is actually a Biblically-mandated and extremely spiritual discipline. After all, time is the single most precious resource we have: when it's gone, it's *long* gone; and we can't beg, borrow, or steal more of it. Hence, God expects us to use it wisely; as with any gift or valuable resource, God wants us to be good stewards of the time He's given us here on earth.

In a practical sense, how we spend our time will determine how much we can accomplish; whether we'll meet our obligations each day, as well as the personal (goal-oriented) tasks we set for ourselves; and ultimately whether we'll reach our full potential and achieve our dreams—*or not.* When we're not careful (and wise) with our 24-Hours-A-Day allowance, we often run out of time before we've completed our creative "To Do" List.

Productive people—those who "find" the time to get things done—know how to wisely budget their time. They rarely squander this important resource. Instead, they've mastered the skill of time management, and they make the most of each and every day. Productive people follow the Apostle Paul's admonishment, "...See that you walk carefully [living life with honor, purpose, and courage....], not as the unwise, but as wise [sensible, intelligent, discerning people], making the very most of your time [on earth, recognizing and taking advantage of each opportunity and using it with wisdom and diligence], because the days are [filled with] evil." (Eph 5:15-16 AMP)

How do we make "the very most" of our time? By using it efficiently: by being productive; by filling our time with sensible and worthwhile activities that bring us closer to God and our goals (or which have a positive impact on our world); by making every minute count; sometimes by multitasking, but almost always by making smart choices about when, where, and how we'll spend our time.

Because there are so many people, needs, responsibilities, and activities vying for our attention and time (yes, *literally*), so it's always important to ask the Lord for discernment and direction. Opting to spend time pursuing your dreams rather than wasting time watching too much TV is a no-brainer. However, other choices may not be so obvious. Prayer can help you to prioritize your schedule and keep you on track. Staying tuned in to God and in touch with *His* priorities can also prevent you from going to the other extreme: becoming mean-hearted and stingy with your time.

We never want to reach a point where we're *obsessed* with

time management, always preoccupied with our schedule and plans—bound by the hands on the clock. We need some balance, a bit of moderation in all things. Proper time management will help us reach our goals more quickly, but it's also important to enjoy the "journey" to fulfilling our dreams. Face it, when you're speeding down the highway of life in pursuit of your goals, all the beautiful "scenery" you pass along the way becomes little more than a blur.

Let's clarify something: we're always careful to make time for friends and family; and we periodically take time to go for a walk, read a book, play a board game, or watch a good movie. We need such diversions to help keep our sanity. But maintaining that balance is essential. We never want to spend ALL of our time hanging out and having fun. If you have unfulfilled dreams, you need to stay focused.

Time is a valuable commodity. Ben Franklin once said, "Time is money." Not *exactly* true, but close enough. Time is a valuable resource you can't replenish. It's easy to turn over an hourglass and restart the flow of sand; but in life, once the real sands of time run out, we can't reclaim a single grain. We *spend* time; and we often describe this time as being *well-spent*. On other occasions we may grumble that we've *wasted* our time. We may speak of time we've *invested* in a person or a project. We might even joke about *stealing* a moment from our busy schedules.

If you view time the same way you *should* be viewing money, then you'll have a better grasp of how important time is, and how to maintain the proper balance. Example: You get paid (you have some time on your hands), but how will you spend your resources? You first need to take care of some nagging debts (social obligations); then you decide to invest for your future (devote time to achieving your dreams); finally, you have something leftover and you decide to spring for a mocha latte and a Cinnabon (you spend some leisure time—doing something absolutely mindless, if you want, like playing tiddlywinks).

Budget your time. Do the math. Spend your hours and days wisely. Make sure you have something to show for each and every "purchase."

Remember, the next time you're goofing off (*excessively* so), that instead, you could be hatching grand schemes and chasing big dreams! (It's our favorite sport!)

Like money, **time is also a precious resource that needs to be shared.** If we're pursuing a dream, working to achieve a goal, we tend to be stingy with our resources, including our precious time. We may begin to give our time more and more sparingly, and perhaps grudgingly. It's easy to get the mindset that we can't *afford* to spend our time on anything or anyone but ourselves. Like a "minute miser," we begin to hoard every brief moment, scowling like Ebenezer Scrooge, over every last second of the day.

But do we really want to get that obsessed with our dreams? Is that truly the ticket to success? Not according to Brian Taylor, a popular author and speaker on self development. Taylor states, "Successful people are always looking for opportunities to help others. Unsuccessful people are always asking, 'What's in it for me?'"

Most importantly, what does God think? The Lord proclaims, "Give, and you will receive. Your gift will return to you in full—pressed down, shaken together to make room for more, running over, and poured into your lap. The amount you give will determine the amount you get back." (Luke 6:38 NLT)

Here's that Law of Reciprocity, again! What we share with others eventually comes back to us—some way, some how, in some desirable form. It's one of life's great mysteries, but it works. And it applies not just to money, but also to love, acceptance, forgiveness ... and time. There are many scriptures that reiterate this law, and unknowingly, even non-believers have embraced it, associating it with the idea of good karma and the phrase "what goes around comes around."

So, it actually *pays* to make time for others. Sure, use your time wisely, but don't be stingy with it, either. Don't get frustrated with well-meaning people who take up your time. People aren't problems, but people often have problems. Help a few of them, and you help yourself. For the good of us all, our world needs more Barnabas's! *(As in Acts 9:26-31.)*

Make your plans. Keep a schedule. But be flexible. Let's stop viewing people as interruptions to our schemes and dreams. Instead, let's view them through God's loving eyes, as precious individuals struggling with problems or dealing with some difficult situation—*as we all do;* people who can use an encouraging word and a sympathetic ear. So share your life. Share your resources: your money, your talents, your time! Ultimately, you'll benefit the most: being flexible (and therefore, relaxed) will enable you to keep your peace and joy, which are essential ingredients to maintaining the positive, faith-filled attitude that facilitates creativity and the pursuit of dreams.

Interestingly, experts on the subject of time-management have found that "busy" people have no problem finding time for the things they consider "important." What's truly important? When Jesus Christ was asked *What is the Greatest Commandment,* the Lord responded, "Love the Lord your God with all your heart, soul, and mind. This is the first and greatest commandment. The second most important is similar: 'Love your neighbor as much as you love yourself.'" (Matt 22:37-39 TLB)

Since relationships and human interaction are the most important aspects of life, we need to make time for them. We must never get so caught up in our creative activities, so consumed by our goals and ambitions, that we forget the God who gave us our dreams and visions, as well as the gifts and talents to pursue them. Similarly, because God treasures all people, we must never neglect those around us.

Sounds like a lot of work to add to an already busy schedule. But if we properly manage our time, we can keep our priorities straight. We can be a blessing to others even as we persevere in the pursuit of our dreams. Ask the Lord to help you use *time* wisely and efficiently ... and with compassion. Take stock in the knowledge that God understands all things, and He knows the value of your time.

Now, declare with us, "...I trust in You, Lord; I say, 'You are my God.' My times are in Your hands...." (Ps 31:14-15 NIV)

THE MECHANICS OF TIME MANAGEMENT:
GET ORGANIZED

THE BEST WAY TO MANAGE YOUR TIME WISELY is to live and work efficiently: to achieve maximum productivity with minimum wasted time, effort, energy, or expense. To be efficient is to get the most bang for your buck (or day). And to live and work efficiently, one must do so in a competent and *organized* manner.

Let's discuss organization: *an orderly, systematic approach to any given task, unhampered by needless clutter, confusion, and chaos.*

All those devil-may-care individuals who enjoy flying by the seat of their pants, please say *Ouch!* Uh, we weren't able to hear everyone's response; next time, let's be *organized,* and take turns speaking.

Organization is one of the greatest tools for good time management. We should all know this—instinctively—because the writing has been on the wall—*er*, cosmos—since the beginning of time. After all, when God created the universe, He did so in an efficient, orderly, and systematic manner:

When God began creating the heavens and the earth, the earth was a shapeless, chaotic mass.... Then God said, "Let there be light." And light appeared. And God was pleased with it and divided the light from the darkness. He called the light "daytime," and the darkness "nighttime." Together they formed the first day. And God said, "Let the vapors separate to form the sky above and the oceans below." ...This all happened on the second day. Then God said, "Let the water beneath the sky be gathered into oceans so that the dry land will emerge." ...Then God named the dry land "earth," and the water "seas." (Gen 1:1-10 TLB)

From the beginning, the Master Creator demonstrated that

He's systematic in His dealings: for instance, He assigned different tasks to different days; He also prioritized His work, taking care of first things *first*—imagine the chaos that would have ensued had God created land mammals *before* He separated the seas from the dry land!

Note also, **God works in an orderly fashion.** On the fourth day of Creation He took steps "to identify the day and the night" by organizing the functions of the Sun and moon. He did this in order to "mark the days and years" and "bring about the seasons." Yes, God essentially devised a schedule for all lifeforms—which *He* faithfully keeps. And, before the fourth day was over, He had *arranged* the stars in the night sky. (Gen 1:14-19 TLB)

You know the rest. On the fifth day of Creation God filled the earth with plants, birds, fish, and animals. (Gen 1:20-25) On the following day, after laying all the groundwork (pun intended), God fulfilled His great dream through His ultimate creation: humankind. (Gen 1:26)

But is God an *efficient* creator? Of course, because He "...Looked over all that He had made, and it was excellent in every way. This ended the sixth day." (Gen 1:31 TLB) That's quite an accomplishment for six short days. God was organized and put His time to optimum use. He literally got the most bang for His proverbial buck.

Efficiency, organization, and proper time-management go hand in hand. But regarding good organization skill, here's a vital truth for all dreamers and creators: God actually expects you to be organized, because *HE* is organized.

"God is not one who likes things to be disorderly and upset." (1 Cor 14:33 TLB) In fact, our Heavenly Father is described in several translations of this verse as "a God of order." And since we are created in His image (Gen 1:27) we have His spiritual DNA. So it's only "natural" that we should follow His example in this. That's why the Apostle Paul admonishes us to "be sure that everything is done properly in a good and orderly way." (1 Cor 14:40 TLB)

Nothing wastes time like being disorganized: having to look for the car keys or find your phone every time you're about to leave the house; wandering through the grocery aisles as you try to remember all the things you need buy—

because you never made a list, or because you forgot where you put it; having to make several trips into town, because you forgot an item, or because you forgot about an errand you had to run—while you were out previously.

Being disorganized can cause you to lose time and be late—or to even miss an appointment or an opportunity. It can also cause you needless frustration, anxiety, and stress. These emotions, and the situations which caused them, are counterproductive; they can steal your peace, joy, and creativity, and thereby sap you of your energy.

If you want to make the most of your limited and precious time, then you simply *must* be organized. There is no way around this truth. And you have to be organized in every area of your life; remember, the Apostle Paul stated that "everything must be done decently and in order." (1 Cor 14:40 HCSB) Is your garage "decent"? How about the kitchen cabinets and the bedroom closets?

Our environment, and in particular the home (and how we choose to live within its four walls), has a direct affect on our state of mind. It can affect our attitude and disposition, and even our outlook on life. Our state of mind will in turn affect our emotions, actions, and decisions. As we previously discussed, attitude is everything—especially a can-do attitude. But a messy house, a disorganized office, and a life generally besieged by "clutter" can be aggravating, depressing, overwhelming, and even mind-numbing. Such things can also KILL our creativity!

Regarding creativity:

Is your "creative space" well organized?

A creative space is any designated area in your home where you can escape, to think, dream, and pursue creative projects. It might be the desk in the den or library, a sewing nook in the upstairs spare room, or a workbench in the corner of the garage. But wherever you choose to study, work, and dream, it's important to keep your creative space organized and free of clutter.

Believe it or not, clutter can impede the ability to think clearly. And from a practical standpoint, you can accomplish more in less time, *if* you're not continually shuffling through drawers, files, stacks of paper—trying to unearth whatever it is you need in order to get something done. So, do you want to work efficiently? Want to make the most of your time? Want to accomplish your goals *sooner* than later? Cut the clutter and get organized.

Easy? Not always, because if you *are* disorganized, and if your house or creative space *is* messy, your messiness and disorganization are no doubt the products of bad habits. But hey, as Jack Canfield and Mark Victor Hansen state in *Chicken Soup for the Soul: Living Your Dreams,* about ninety percent of all behavior *is* habitual. These authors advise us to identify any unproductive habits and then work to replace them with good, productive, and beneficial habits—such as getting your house (and life) in order.

Worthwhile? Always! But remember, it takes 21 days to develop and form a habit; that's three weeks of sticking with it. Give yourself time and don't give up.

"I have the freedom to do anything,
but not everything is helpful.
I have the freedom to do *anything,*
but I won't be controlled by *anything.*"
(1 Cor 6:12 CEB)

THE MECHANICS OF TIME MANAGEMENT:
CUT THE CLUTTER

EVER FEEL LIKE YOU'RE DROWNING in a sea of "stuff"? Too many places to go, things to do, people to see? If we're to find the time, energy and resources necessary to pursue our dreams and accomplish our goals, then we need to live efficiently and manage our time wisely. The first step, as we previously discussed, is to get organized—your home, your kitchen, your office, your desk or creative space.

But your organization shouldn't be confined to physical spaces. For instance: organize your finances, and you'll spend less time wondering which bills are due when, and whether or not you've already paid them. Result: less stress, no surprises, more time and energy to pursue goals. "...God is not the author of confusion, but of peace...." (1 Cor 14: 33 KJV)

Just as organization is key to good time-management, there are several actions we can take that are essential to getting organized. One of the most important is to eliminate anything that's cluttering our desks, our homes, our lives. *Because clutter can impede the ability to think clearly and work efficiently.*

Clutter is a huge problem for just about everyone. And the first step to solving *any* problem is to identify where and what that problem is. *Clutter* can be defined as an excessive amount of "any thing"—but especially of unneeded "stuff" or stuff that's not unnecessary for a given task—which is present in a *crowded* or *untidy* fashion, or located in an *inappropriate* place. For example, a mechanic's tools, although extremely useful and certainly not a problem when properly arranged and stored in a tool chest, become clutter when spread haphazardly around the garage or inside the house.

To further identify the problem of clutter, we'll list four

categories. These groupings aren't intended to be definitive. (They tend to overlap; and you may be able to identify other areas of clutter.) However, simply for the purpose of illustration ... and *organization* ... we have created these four categories: Physical Clutter; Temporal Clutter; Social Clutter; and Emotional Clutter.

Physical Clutter should be obvious: an excessive number of objects littering your surroundings: a mess of a desk; an overstuffed office; a house that's a horror, etc.

You can accomplish more in less time, IF you're not continually shuffling through drawers, files, stacks of papers; looking for whatever it is you need in order to get something done. Think about a cook in a disorganized kitchen, where the drawers are a jumbled mess, dishes are piled on the counter, etc. In the course of trying to prepare a meal, the poor cook will be digging for the right utensils, pushing pots out of the way to free up work space, and running back and forth while accomplishing very little.

Temporal Clutter is trying to do too much with too little time: too many goals, too many errands, too many trips—too many pastimes (ouch).

Simplify your schedule (and life): chances are, you have too many activities planned for too little time. Come on, do you really think you can do everything? You can only accomplish so much in a day, a year, a life.

Decide what's most important—like achieving your goals—and limit your other activities. No, don't become obsessed, but realize your time and energy are precious, and cut the clutter from these other areas:

Reduce your recreations: Sports, hobbies, TV, video games, interests, etc. If you go jogging everyday, followed by a few rounds of golf or a game of tennis with a friend, you'll have far less time and energy to accomplish your goals. *Leisure time and light distractions are good for our mental health, and hobbies are fun, but we need to limit how many pastimes we have and how often we indulge in them, if we intend to get anything else done.* For instance, TV and theatrical movies are entertaining, but trying to keep up with over a dozen weekly shows and take in every new movie could be the death of your dreams.

Order your objectives: Do you want to be a jack of all trades but the master of none? We may have oodles of interests, gobs of goals, and dozens of dreams. However, we need to choose a few and shelve the rest (at least for the time being). No one can be in two places at once, and few of us can attain greatness in more than one arena.

So, decide which is it going to be: the next great singer, actor, writer, artist, inventor, entrepreneur, teacher, missionary, pastor ... (just fill in the blank) ... or: the dude with the best physique; the gal with the most Tupperware prizes; the lady who throws the most elaborate parties; the guy with the coolest matchbook collection. Don't allow trivial pursuits and foolish ambitions to clutter the path to what you want to achieve most in life—and to what's most important. (We'll discuss this more, in "Stay Focused")

Social Clutter. Uh, let's be clear: we love to socialize! And we NEED fellowship! Ahem. But too much socializing can clutter your life to the point where you'll never accomplish your goals. Too much of a good thing is ... well, too much! Too many get-togethers, too many phone chats, too many ... friends. (We'll elaborate, in "Hush Up and Be Hospitable.")

Relationships are vital, but you can actually have too many "friends"! King Solomon writes in Proverbs, "A man of too many friends comes to ruin." (Pr 18:24 NAS) This may sound sacrilegious, but all *meaningful* relationships require time, energy, and commitment. "A friend in need is a friend indeed," so lots of friends eventually equates to lots of needs. After all, friends need time to get together, socialize, catch up, and vent. But how many hours are there in a week—AFTER you subtract work and family responsibilities? Not enough, right?

Limit your friends to a few and you'll also reduce your number of social obligations. *Now, this doesn't mean you can stop being friendly!* Jesus Christ is our example. When He walked the earth He was friendly to *everyone*—but He had only a handful of close "friends."

Limiting your social connections will free you from having to attend too many social events, which cuts the *temporal clutter.* (As we stated, these categories do tend to overlap.)

Social clutter, by the way, can also apply to social media. You can have too many friends and followers on Facebook,

Twitter, and other websites intended to keep you connected. Viewing endless pet photos and goofy videos posted by dozens of people, or pausing throughout the day to read what these "twits" ate for lunch or saw on TV, is distracting and time-consuming.

Conversely, if you're spending hours posting your own junk on the Internet, you may want to consider cutting this clutter from your day. Computers are indeed time-machines, but they can't transport you to that unfulfilled dream waiting in your future.

Emotional Clutter. Do you have hurts, fears, and disappointments cluttering your thoughts? If so, cut the clutter! We actually discussed eliminating these negative and toxic emotions in the lessons on "Manage Your Mind." But as a reminder, we once again point out that your thought life should be ordered by the Lord: "Oh, the joys of those who ... delight in the [Word] of the LORD, meditating on it day and night. They are like trees planted along the riverbank, bearing fruit each season. ...And they prosper in all they do." (Ps 1:1-3 NLT)

Damaged emotions and toxic thoughts will distract you from more important, and *Godly,* matters. *So, cut the emotional clutter by forgiving those who have hurt and wronged you.* Dump your toxic feelings toward these people and move forward. Your mind (and heart) should be preoccupied with positive, can-do thoughts that facilitate your creative efforts and bring you closer to your goals. You never want to have to sift through your emotional clutter to find (remember) your hopes and dreams.

In summary: Want to accomplish more? Then manage your time wisely, by getting organized. One key to organization is to cut the clutter—from your schedule, finances, hobbies and interests, as well as your relationships Too much "stuff," too many "friends," too many interests, too many directions—can leave you confused and dazed, with no time or energy for your dreams and creative pursuits.

"...Martha was distracted with all her preparations; ...But the Lord ... said to her, "Martha, Martha, you are worried and bothered about so many things; but only one thing is necessary...." (Luke 10:40-42 NASB)

THE MECHANICS OF
TIME MANAGEMENT:
TAKE INVENTORY

TIME IS PRECIOUS, because there's never quite enough to go around—at least not when we're trying to achieve our goals while also meeting the needs of friends and family, as well as the responsibilities of work, government, and community. So, here are two more tips for maximizing your time.

Take Inventory: The first step to solving any problem in life is to *identify* the problem ... and when and where it occurs.

Think of time as water, precious and limited; flowing through life the way water flows through a pipe. Is there a leak somewhere? Is time being wasted through a "crack" in our schedules—the same way water drips from a damaged pipe? If so, we want to plug the leak and save our time. Problem is, as any good plumber will relate, you have to first find the leak!

Plumbers sometimes use smoke to locate any cracks in large, complex expanses of piping. We don't need anything so elaborate. We can simply take an honest look at how we spend our days. To determine where all our time is going, we can take an inventory of our activities, and how much time we spend on each one. What we discover can be quite sobering.

Is your time leaking away through too much social media, television, sports, shopping, hobbies, or other leisure activities? Studies reveal that on average, people watch 6 to 8 hours of TV per day. No wonder we know the words to all those advertising jingles! Of course, not everyone is glued to the telly. Some of us are wired to our computer tablets and phones: the same studies report that the average person spends 4 to 7 hours on the Internet! Imagine how much could be accomplished each day if we limited the time leaking—actually, GUSHING—through these and similar "cracks" in our schedules!

Yes, we all need recreational pursuits, but we need to maintain a balance. Most of us, however, will never realize exactly how much time we're wasting ... until we take a serious look at how we spend our days. So, take inventory. Keep track of how much time you spend on any given activity; and then cut the clutter from your schedule.

Keep a Schedule: if we don't create and keep one, then we can't truly organize our activities and our time. In fact, schedules were invented by the human race to keep the world organized, and to help people live more efficiently. Schedules are lists (of appointments, functions, services, activities, and responsibilities), their designated times, and often of their durations. Trains and planes run on schedules, which prevents chaos and maximizes productivity. Doctors use schedules to arrange appointments, and ... well, let's move on.

Schedules are time-dependent. *Yes, the clock is our friend.*

Sure, there are occasions when it's nice to hide the clocks, find a spot of ocean sand, throw down a blanket, and just listen to the surf. But if you do this too often, we doubt you'll fulfill your dreams. People will remember you as a beach bum and not as someone who achieved great goals. Again, balance is key: determine in advance how much of your time will be spent playing video games versus pursuing your dreams.

"For every activity there is a right time and procedure...." (Eccl 8:6 HCSB)

Organized people know well in advance what needs to be done, how long it will take, how to go about doing it, and when to get started. And they are disciplined in regards to adhering to their self-imposed schedules. Hence, they always have an objective, a clear goal. They avoid confusion and get more done in less time, while others appear to wander about aimlessly, while accomplishing very little.

When you sit down to draft your schedule—for the day, for the week, and even *longer* time frames—prioritize your responsibilities.

THE MECHANICS OF
TIME MANAGEMENT:
WRITE IT DOWN!

HERE ARE TWO MORE TIPS for maximizing the precious gift of time.

Keep notes and make lists.

It's hard to remember what needs to be done—and when—if you never write it down. Maintain a few lists to help remind you of things you need, projects you should be working on, pressing responsibilities and deadlines. Don't trust "stuff" to memory—our brains can hold only so much; instead, WRITE IT DOWN!

For example, we always keep a shopping list in the kitchen. It's a long notepad with a nifty little magnet on the back, which allows us to post it on the refrigerator door. We frequently update this list whenever we notice we're getting low on milk or eggs, etc. We learned a long time ago that if we *don't* write it down while we're thinking about it, we tend to forget it altogether. But when we shop for groceries we want to make it count: we don't want to come home without everything we needed. So, before we go to the market, we grab our list containing all the stuff we jotted down during the week. Because nothing is more aggravating than coming home, putting away the groceries, and then starting dinner—only to realize we FORGOT the oregano for the spaghetti sauce!

Lists help us to live efficiently. And keeping a list of things to do is not only smart, it's also Godly. Even our Heavenly Father has His own list—and He keeps close track of it, jotting down our names, so that He will never forget us: God reminds us, "...I have written your name on the palms of my hands." (Isa 49:16 NLT)

"[Lord,] You keep track of all my sorrows. ...You have recorded each one in Your book." (Ps 56:8 NLT)

We suggest keeping a notebook handy. Jot down things you need to accomplish each day. In the morning, following your Quiet Time with the Lord, compose a "To Do List." Include these categories: job responsibilities and deadlines; household chores; social needs and obligations (family, friends, community); steps you wish to accomplish concerning your personal dreams and goals. Then prioritize the items on your list.

Don't be "listless"! Keeping one or more lists of your needs, goals, and responsibilities will remind you of your duties, keep you on track, and give you peace of mind. Lists allow you to keep your mind organized and free of clutter. *Write it down*—and you won't have to stress yourself with trying to remembering it, or having to juggle it with a thousand other thoughts! Lists also facilitate multitasking.

Multitask! Efficient, time-conscious people have learned to work two or more jobs simultaneously. NO! We're not advocating texting while driving! But if you *are* driving into town, check your list: make the trip count, by arranging and scheduling other things you can accomplish while you're out. The last thing you want is to waste time.

Other examples of multitasking: doing the laundry while writing; listening to a recorded teaching while cooking; catching up with friends by phone, while trimming the hedges, etc. And, if you suddenly find yourself waiting, seemingly with nothing to do, you can pull out your "Things To Do" list. Chances are you have calls to make, a bill you can pay on your phone, etc.—or you can spend the time updating your list!

One last point on time-management: Lists and schedules, organization and "clutter cutting" are intended as tools to help creators and dreamers achieve their goals. But we should never become so rigid in our thinking as to allow these tools to control our lives. Be *disciplined* but be *balanced* also. Allow God to guide you in all things. Time is our friend, NOT our master! Which brings us to the most important time-management tool:

Never get too busy to spend time with God.

Among a multitude of duties, the Great Reformer, Martin Luther, wrote his history-changing thesis, composed scores of hymns and catechisms, and even found time to translate the Holy Scriptures from Latin. *He was quite the busy fellow, and yet, Luther once stated,* "I have so much to do today that I'm going to need to spend three hours in prayer in order to be able to get it all done."

It sounds crazy, but scheduling quality time with your Heavenly Father every morning will actually help you to get *more* done during the day—and accomplish far *more* in life. Seeking God in all things is truly supernatural in the way it bends time to God's will:

"Take my instruction.... Counsel is Mine and sound wisdom; I am understanding; power is Mine. ...I love those who love Me; and those who diligently seek Me will find me. Riches and honor are with Me, enduring wealth and righteousness. My fruit is better than gold ... and My yield [increase] better than choicest silver." (Prov 8:10, 14, 17-19 NASB)

HAVE A PLAN

WE'VE ALL HEARD IT: "If you fail to plan, you plan to fail." Say what?! Nobody in his right mind plans to fail. Not intentionally, anyway. But many of us do fail to plan. We fail to set goals, map out what we want to accomplish in life, and strategize how we'll go about doing it.

If you don't shoot for something in life, then you're not living life to its fullest. Or to put it another way, if you don't aim for something, then you'll be ... well, aimless!—just shuffling along with no purpose and no hope. Soon you'll start to shrivel spiritually, emotionally, and even physically.

The writer of Proverbs 29:18 teaches us that "Where there is no vision, the people perish"; so don't keep living aimlessly. **Take aim.**

Once you do take aim, everything else boils down to strategy, your plan of attack. Think of a war. Great wars are won with smaller victories won in battles. Your goals will be achieved in much the same way, through the small victories and accomplishments that move you closer to winning your bigger dreams.

And indeed, achieving a truly big dream is much like waging a war, to overcome the obstacles imposed by time, resources, circumstances, and even people who don't want to see you succeed (for various reasons). You need a plan!

Having a plan means having a strategy: a course of action; the necessary steps you're going to take to reach your goals. For instance, getting organized (along with the other steps we've discussed) will enable you to live more efficiently, maximizing your valuable time, moving further along the road to fulfilling your dreams. Following a plan involves sticking to a schedule and having a routine, disciplining yourself to stay on task—to stay the course.

Keep in mind, however, that occasionally we'll encounter

roadblocks and detours: there *are* situations in life which are totally out of our control; and no matter how well we plan, things won't always work out as we hoped. To paraphrase the poet Robert Burns, *the best laid plans of mice and men often go awry!*

When life happens, be flexible and go with the flow. **Don't allow these "interruptions" to frustrate you.** Refuse to get bent out of shape. Remember, "[God] will keep in perfect peace all who trust in [Him], all whose thoughts are fixed on [Him]!" (Isa 26:3 NLT) But afterwards, take the necessary steps to get back on track with your plans.

A big key to success is developing the discipline to return to your scheduled routine and/or outlined goals as soon as the crisis, challenge, issue or interruption is over. Part of the beauty of having a plan is being able to pick up where you left off—because you've mapped out your course (objectives, schedule, etc.)

As previously discussed, our Heavenly Father is a God of order, and He wants His followers to be a *people* of order: organized, so they can make the most of their time; having a plan, so they can fulfill the destiny to which He's called them, as they fulfill their hopes and dreams. God is therefore actively involved in the plans we make—*and He should be.* He not only helps us to execute the plan, but He also guides us in formulating it! As King David wrote, "The LORD directs the steps of the godly. He delights in every detail of their lives." (Ps 37:23 NLT)

Have a plan. Stick to the plan. **But don't be obsessed with the plan.** The Lord expects us to maintain a balance. He does not want us to become obsessed with our goals and dreams; slaves marching to the ticking of a time-clock; robots blindly following the "programming" of our own intricate plans—while stepping all over the rules, people, and the desires and dictates of God.

We must never put our personal goals and ambitions before the will of God. And we must never put our *plans* above the needs of those around us. Living a godly and orderly life means carefully balancing our dreams and creative pursuits—the stuff that's important to us—with spiritual issues and matters, which are important to the Creator of the Universe. If we do neglect the spiritual things, in a mad dash to reach our goals, we'll regret it at the end. We might make it to the top, but we won't find peace and fulfillment once we get there: "[For] what do you benefit if you gain the whole world but lose your own soul?" (Mark 8:36 NLT)

What's the good of achieving your goals if during the process you sacrifice (upon the "alter of success") your relationship with God? Relationships, both with loved ones and with the Lord, are what make life worthwhile. What's the point of reaching the top only to find yourself alone when (and if) you get there? With whom will you share your hard-won victory? Chances are, even YOU won't be able to enjoy your accomplishments—because YOU (the wonderful person you once were) will probably no longer exist.

Like so many Hollywood celebrities who climbed to the top of the heap by turning their backs on God, sacrificing their principles, and stepping over people, you could find yourself alone and feeling hollow inside. Or, you can avoid this haunting scenario by maintaining the proper balance: pursuing your dreams while putting the Lord first; and following a plan *without* forsaking friends and family.

Make your plans, but follow your dreams *God's* way. You'll eventually find success, and when you do, you'll still have your honor, self-respect, inner peace, and loving people with whom you can share your triumphs. Most important of all, you'll have the approval of your Heavenly Father, who will someday speak these affirming words: "Well done, good and faithful servant! You have been faithful with a few things; I will put you in charge of many things. Come and share your master's happiness!" (Matt 25:21 NIV)

Actually, we can "hear" these words everyday, as we keep our priorities straight and put God first in our lives in all things. We can also sense His pleasure when we use our time wisely (by being organized and having a plan), and with each and every tiny step forward in the pursuit of our dreams.

"Good planning and hard work lead to prosperity...." (Prov 21:5 NLT)

THE PRINCIPLES OF GOOD PLANNING

ACTRESS AND SINGER DORIS DAY belted out the lyrics to a catchy tune called "Que Sera, Sera" in Alfred Hitchcock's 1956 thriller *The Man Who Knew Too Much.* The song picked up an Oscar the following year and soon became Day's signature tune. A decade later the song served as the opening theme to the long-running television comedy, *The Doris Day Show.*

The lyrics contained the following sentiment: "When I was just a little girl; I asked my mother, what will I be? Will I be pretty, will I be rich? Here's what she said to me. *'Que Sera, Sera,* Whatever will be, will be. The future's not ours to see— *Que Sera, Sera.'"*

True enough. We're not fortune tellers. On the other hand, we *can* take an active role shaping our destinies. In fact, we creators and dreamers can't afford to wake up each morning with the laid-back (and lazy) attitude of "Whatever will be, will be"—not if we hope to accomplish anything worthwhile in life. If we're going to realize our goals and dreams we can't sit around waiting to see what's going to happen. We need to *make* things happen, and to do this we need a plan (an agenda, a course of action, a God-given strategy).

As previously discussed, having a plan helps us to manage our most valuable resource, time. It helps us to keep our priorities straight, while working, playing, and living more efficiently and, hence, more wisely. Let's move on to the principles of good planning.

Formulating a plan consists of several elements:

Learn to prioritize your responsibilities, activities, and goals. As we previously stated, the chief priority of all followers of Christ should be to give God first place in their lives, and to keep Him there. Godly plans always include the Creator of the Universe, as well as provisions to do His will. How does accomplishing "God's will" help us to achieve *our* dreams? "He will give them to you if you give Him first place in your life and live as He wants you to." (Matt 6:33 TLB) Sounds like a plan!

Our plans should never exclude people. After all, we can't do God's will if we don't leave room in our plans for "interruptions"; because God loves people and He expects us to love them, too—and to be kind, considerate, and caring. In other words, God expects us to adjust our schedules, and even lay aside our plans temporarily, in order to interact with our neighbors and coworkers, build relationships, and meet pressing needs.

Use the tools of planning. Keeping lists is vital. If you don't write it down, chances are you won't remember it. And if you don't remember it, then you'll definitely fail to do it. "It" can refer to anything from a shopping list to a work agenda.

Write IT down, on your "Things To Do" list, in a journal, on a calendar, or in one of those clever little notebooks sold at office supply stores— called Daily PLANNERS!

Keep a schedule; albeit a flexible one. Schedules promote order and efficiency. And setting self-imposed deadlines serves several purposes. Having a deadline motivates us to buckle down and get to work. Self-imposed goals and deadlines also help us to push ourselves, to accomplish more each day than we might otherwise. And *meeting* one or more of these deadlines helps us to measure our progress—not to mention the sense of accomplishment we'll get, each time we're able to check off an item on our To Do lists.

Make a commitment to accomplish *something* worthwhile—each and everyday. (It's okay to take a day off, however. We all need time for rest, recreation, and relationships) Even something as simple as organizing your desk or creative space, listening to a motivational message, or learning something new in your area of interest, will help keep you on track to realizing your dreams.

Map out each day. This allows us to organize our activities. Yes, this pointer is yet another way of admonishing people to keep a schedule, but it's important to apply the practice day by day. So each morning, after we spend some quiet time with the Lord, we should make notes of things we need or *want* to accomplish. We can also compose this list the night before. Once we have our daily To Do list, we should prioritize our goals and responsibilities, and make every effort to complete at least the top two or three items.

Plan some Dream-Time. Since most of us creators and dreamers have regular "day" jobs, we must discipline ourselves to carve out specific times when we plan to work on our goals, dreams, and creative projects. Whether that designated time is before or after work, during a long bus or train commute, at lunchtime or during a break, dream-time must be planned.

We can't afford to wait until we go on an extended vacation, or retire, or win the sweepstakes and can quit our jobs. We have to be ready to accomplish *something*, no matter how small, whenever we have the opportunity—or we may end up doing nothing at all. Truth is, there will never be enough time for our dreams. We usually have to *make* time—and be ready to make the most of that time, whenever and wherever it arises. This takes planning and discipline.

And even if you *are* retired, or you have the privilege of working at home, you'll still need to schedule WHEN you're going to pursue your goals. Later never comes. Business ventures don't materialize from thin air and books don't write themselves. So, plan your dream-time.

Make the tough choices. All this brings us to another cold hard fact of the creative life: Due to a time crunch, many of us may need to devote a good portion of our weekends and vacations—or any occasion when we...

have a block of uninterrupted time—to fulfilling our dreams. After all, we'll never reach our goals sitting in a La-Z-Boy in front of the TV. But *choosing* to invest part of our weekends (and *any* spare time we chance upon) pursuing our goals, will also take planning.

Ask the Lord for wisdom. Each day you can join other dreamers and creators who pray for guidance: "[Lord,] teach us to keep account of our days so we may develop inner wisdom." (Ps 90:12 ISV) And remember, you can accomplish great things even if you don't have huge blocks of free time.

Thirty minutes here or there, each day, each week, each month, ultimately adds up to an impressive investment over the years. Castles and cathedrals are constructed one stone at a time. Books are written one chapter at a time, and chapters a few paragraphs at a time. Again, plan to do at least a little each day.

Little steps carefully planned each day can take you far along the path to success. The important thing is to have a plan. And while you're making plans, keep in mind that God has a plan for your life: "to prosper you and not to harm you, plans to give you hope and a future." (Jer 29:11 NIV) Cooperate with His plan and He'll help you with yours!

"Careful planning puts you ahead in the long run...." (Prov 21:5 MSG)

EXECUTE THE PLAN

EVERY GREAT DREAM STARTS WITH AN IDEA. It's that passion that never fades—no matter how many years pass; the vision God plants in a dreamer's heart and mind, which continues to shine bright no matter how many challenges and obstacles come.

Once we dreamers write the vision to "make it plain" (Hab 2:2), and concrete, we must plan a course of action that will enable us to achieve our goals. Most people are good at this, but many fail at the next step. They map out a course of *action,* but then fail to *act* upon it.

Planning without action is pointless. In fact, a plan is like a pirate's map: unless someone follows it to the treasure, it's just a scrap of old paper. No matter how much we plot and plan, we won't accomplish much until we put our grand schemes into action. We. Must. Execute. The Plan!

Think about it, buying a cool musical instrument and signing up for lessons won't make sweet music—until a person commits to attending the classes and practicing for long hours. And those nifty blueprints for a better mousetrap will just be gathering dust unless the inventor follows them to construct his new contraption. Similarly, a book outline is meaningless until a writer sits down at the keyboard and taps out the complete manuscript.

In an episode of 1970's TV drama *The Waltons,* the show's protagonist learns the difference between having a plan and executing a plan. During the Great Depression, a budding writer nicknamed John-Boy, struggles to finish his schooling in rural Virginia, while helping his family make ends meet. He dreams of leaving the mountain—where he helps his father operate a sawmill—to become a novelist. To accomplish this, he knows he must work hard, at the mill to save for his college tuition; and every night, after school and work, upstairs in his room, writing and rewriting, until he's filled scores of notebooks. John-Boy is executing his plan.

One day a stranger passes through Walton's Mountain, bound for adventures in exotic places. John-Boy's parents offer this tired and hungry traveler the hospitality of their home, as is their custom, and John-Boy gets an opportunity to hear about the man's "journey." Turns out this dusty fellow is a WRITER. At least, that's what the man claims; and he certainly knows his stuff: he's met many of the great poets and novelists John-Boy has read and admires; and he appears to have mastered all the skills of writing.

This wanderer regales John-Boy with tales of famous authors, gives him practical advice on becoming a novelist, and shares about the lifetime of experiences he's collected from many strange lands—in the pursuit of his own dream of being a great writer. Needless to say, John-Boy is in awe of this man who is actually "living the dream." That is, until he learns the truth about his guest. Despite the stranger's erudition, despite all his literary friends and connections, despite his endless travels hither and yon, the man has never published anything. Far worse, he's never written a single word of fiction.

As this unfulfilled dreamer bows his head in shame, he confesses to John-Boy that he'd always wanted to be a great American author. He'd made plans to that effect, but he'd failed to execute those plans. For decades he'd thought about writing, talked about it, and even prepared for it. He just never got around to *doing* it.

Ironically, John-Boy was more of a writer than this aimless wanderer, who talked a good game but never actually ventured into the field. The poor guy *had* a plan to write, but he never sat down and got to it. He never executed his plans. While John-Boy, on the other hand, spent his nights writing about his family and the simple life he led in the mountains. He *planned* to write. And he did!

The Waltons is based on a book that ultimately grew from John-Boy's impassioned scribblings—only Earl Hamner, Jr. was the writer's real name. Hamner stayed faithful to his plans and fulfilled his dreams. He penned several books, scripted radio dramas, and even wrote several episodes of *The Twilight Zone.* Eventually he created the aforementioned, award-winning television series, which ran for ten seasons.

Fellow dreamers and creators, let's take this cautionary tale as a warning. We can follow all the steps discussed in Boot Camp (and there are more to come), read every motivational book we can get our hands on, and attend monthly seminars on fulfilling our dreams—hosted by the most sought-after teachers. We can have tons of talent, great ambitions, and a solid game plan for success. But if we don't put our plans into action we'll never accomplish our goals or achieve our fondest dreams.

Life is funny that way. So if you're serious about your vision ... make a move. **Get up and get going.** No one will ever care if you *have* a plan—or benefit from it—until you begin to implement it. We all know that talk is cheap, and deeds speak louder than words. Or, as the Apostle James writes, "...What good would your words alone do? The same is true with faith [or a plan]. Without actions, faith is useless. By itself, it's as good as dead." (James 2:16-17 VOICE)

The world wants to see your plan in action! "OK, you have faith [a plan]. And I have actions. Now let's see your faith without works, and I'll show you a faith that works." (James 2:18 VOICE) So, put your money where your mouth is. Make your plans. Then execute those plans.

JUST DO IT!

HERE'S ANOTHER FAMILIAR SAYING: "God helps those who help themselves." But before anyone goes out and steals a new car or robs a bank, we should point out that this little nugget of advice doesn't appear in the Bible. And for good reason. God is actually all about helping the helpless. He "strengthens the weary and gives vitality to those worn down by age and care." (Isa 40:29 VOICE) And regarding personal salvation we're entirely dependent on the Lord to redeem us.

"For it's by God's grace that you have been saved. You receive it through faith. It was not our plan or our effort. It is God's gift, pure and simple. You didn't earn it ... so don't go around bragging that you must have done something amazing." (Eph 2:9 VOICE)

God never said it; and it's hard to know for sure just who did originate this old adage. We do know that Benjamin Franklin popularized the saying when he quoted it, in his *Poor Richard's Almanac,* in 1757. Apparently, God approved, however, because Franklin went outside in the middle of a violent electrical storm to—of all things—fly a kite. And the inventor didn't get struck by lightning, not even once! (That's just a joke, friends.)

Seriously, though, there are many principles in the Bible that support Franklin's oft-repeated motto: God rewards our faith and obedience; and thanks to the Law of Reciprocity (discussed earlier) acts of love, service, and giving always come back to us in the form of God's favor and blessings. But what's all this got to do with creators and dreamers?

It's God who gives us the vision, along with the talents and abilities necessary to create and achieve our goals; so He definitely wants us to fulfill our dreams. But He also expects us to do our part. For instance, God is *probably* not going to make you the next winner of the Publishers Clearing House

Sweepstakes if you don't mail back the entry form! We state "probably" because God created the Heavens and the earth, so nothing is too difficult for Him! (Jer 32:17) But don't count on it, even if you *do* get one of those crazy letters proclaiming "You may already be a winner!"

If we want God to help us get published, we must first sit down and write a book. Oh, and it doesn't hurt to mail the manuscript to a few dozen prospective publishers. Want to paint? Have you even purchased a brush and pigments yet?

If you want to do something fun and creative, if you want to realize your goals and see your dreams fulfilled—and you want God's help—you need to do your part. Make a plan. Then execute the plan. Or, look at it this way: If we're going to achieve our dreams, or be successful at anything, we gotta make the grade. And we should all hope to get a "D"!

Actually straight D's are even better. D is for Dreams ... and *daring* to dream BIG. But D stands for so much more.

D is for Decision. Decide what you want out of life; decide what you want to accomplish in life; decide how you'll achieve these things. Then make a decision to get started. You'll never lose weight, look for a better job, sever a wrong relationship, put a stop to a destructive habit, or achieve any goal until you first purpose in your heart to do so. Doing the right thing starts with deciding what the right thing is! And you'll never follow through on anything until you DECIDE it's something YOU really want to do. Start deciding. Decisions are all about choices. Making them and sticking by them.

D is Discipline. You'll need this if you're serious about accomplishing anything in life. You can't hold down a job, maintain a relationship, stay out of trouble, stay out of debt, stay healthy, stay focused, or stay on track until you get Disciplined. And just like the nutritional supplement Vitamin D, we need more of this "D"; never less.

We all want to achieve our dreams. We all want something. But the unpleasant truth about life is that everything comes with a price, every achievement involves W.O.R.K! The work is always hard. Sometimes the work is no fun. But discipline is about getting the work done, even when your heart's not in it; even when you're tired; even when adversity strikes; even if people criticize you. Muhammad Ali always wanted to box. But staying in the training ring took discipline: "I hated every minute of training, but I said, 'Don't quit. Suffer now and live the rest of your life as a champion.'"

The next "D" works synergistically with Decision and Discipline. But, as with taking big vitamin tablets, it can be the hardest pill to swallow. There are tens of thousands of people who make a decision (and a plan), and who even have discipline—but you'll never hear about these people. You'll never know their names. They're dreamers just like you. But sadly, they never go beyond the dream stage. They never move forward to the next "D".

D is for DOING! After all, nothing ever gets started until someone makes a start.

Be a "healthy" dreamer. Take your dietary supplements, especially vitamin D. But make the other D's an important part of your life. DECIDE what you want to achieve, DISCIPLINE yourself to reach your goal, and then JUST DO IT! Because God wants us to put our good intentions (and plans) into action.

That's why the "Disciple who loved Jesus" offers this case in point: "...Let us not love [merely] in theory *or* in speech but in deed and in truth (in practice and in sincerity)." (1 John 3:18 AMPC) Got it? Then get going! Let's do this!

COUNT THE COST

ALL GREAT ACHIEVEMENTS COME AT A PRICE. In fact, every dream, discovery, invention, business deal, artistic pursuit, ministry, relationship, project, hobby, or activity—each and every great human endeavor—has its own price tag. Whether it's building a lasting marriage, raising great kids, achieving some long-held goal or realizing your vision, if you plan to accomplish anything worthwhile in life then you'll need to count the cost.

Once we understand this truth, we'll tend to analyze and evaluate every goal and situation. We'll start counting the cost *before* committing to something new. After all, would you agree to purchase an item without first knowing its price? Probably not. Because any investment or expenditure must fit into your budget and not overdraw your account.

"Jesus said ... 'No one who puts his hand to the plow and looks back is fit for the kingdom of God." (Luke 9:62 ESV) "...Don't begin until you count the cost. For who would begin construction of a building without first calculating the cost to see if there is enough money to finish it?" (Luke 14:28 NLT)

Once we stop long enough to count the cost in time, energy, effort, sacrifice, patience, love, understanding, and faithfulness, we won't be so quick to enter in to just any relationship or project. Knowing we're accountable when it comes to "paying the tab" might keep us from blindly charging into things. And the things we do decide to commit to, we'll do so wholeheartedly, knowing the cost and being mentally prepared to pay it.

Any noble enterprise, creative pursuit, great cause—*everything* "begins with a dream, a fantasy, a goal that looms on the distant horizon," states Emmy Award-winning comedy writer Gene Perret. (*Chicken Soup for the Writer's Soul)* "But

[we] must realize, too, that every goal has a price tag. Admission to a fantasy [or dream] is never free. There's research to be done, studying to do, practice, practice, practice. The cheapest, and usually the quickest, way to attain any desire is to pay the full price. Do the work."

Hard work, however, isn't always the only "currency" we'll be paying. Some endeavors come at a truly great price and demand far more, in terms of time, energy, and emotional endurance. Therefore, it helps to be psychologically prepared; ready to give it your best shot, so to speak. As the author Charles Bukowski once wrote: "If you're going to try, go all the way. Otherwise, don't even start."

In other words, if you're going to make a go of something, make a "good go" of it. No half-hearted attempts. "And whatsoever you do, do it heartily, as to the Lord, and not unto men." (Col 3:23 KJ 2000) That said, remember it should *always* be the Lord whom we strive to please, not others—and certainly not ourselves, by attempting to fill some personal need to be rich and famous. Instead we should long to become all God created us to be. Yes, He wants to help us fulfill our dreams, but that's just the icing on the cake.

Regardless, before you take on a new responsibility or dive into a new pursuit, you should:

Learn before hand what the price is—and what you're getting into. Spare yourself and your loved ones any unnecessary heartaches. Once you understand the cost of realizing ANY dream, and make a commitment to pay the price, no matter what, you'll be more likely to follow through on every endeavor.

Understand what you're saying NO to. Every time you say YES to new project, pursuit, commitment, etc., you're automatically saying NO to something else.

Achieving a worthwhile goal takes time and energy; and each of us, unfortunately, is *limited* by these precious commodities. Hence, not one of us can ever hope to do it all. When we follow our dreams, we'll ultimately have to leave our comfort zones behind—and abandon some of our more trivial pursuits. This truth applies to every great cause, every noble quest.

Jesus said, "If anyone wishes to follow Me [as My disciple], he must deny himself [set aside selfish interests], and take up his cross [expressing a willingness to endure whatever may come] and follow Me [believing in Me, conforming to My example in living and, if need be, suffering....]" (Matt 16:24 AMP)

A disciple is one who adheres to a belief or cause; who learns discipline, and trains to follow a way of life, or a course of action. In a manner of speaking, all creators and dreamers are disciples: to reach our goals we must learn, train, and practice within our chosen fields of interest; and we must discipline ourselves if we are to complete the journey. And, like Christ's spiritual disciples, we have to bear the cross of our own hopes and dreams.

Christ's cross was made of wood. It was large, heavy—and Christ labored to carry it uphill to Calvary, where He was nailed to it. This sounds like an unpleasant finish, but it was only the beginning. After His death, Christ rose from the grave to take His place next to the Heavenly Father. And through His crucifixion, Christ realized His great dream of redeeming humankind from their sins; thus securing the eternal salvation of all who trust in Him.

The cross of Christ represents our Lord's greatest achievement, but that achievement came at a terrible price—the death of God's only Son. Following Christ wholeheartedly, as a disciple, also comes with a price. It involves bearing a cross of unwavering commitment and self-sacrifice.

Similarly, there are times when even our fondest hopes, dreams, and creative endeavors can feel like a cross. We'll labor to bear the weight, struggling to carry our "burdens" all the way to the finish line, on a journey that's mostly uphill. And, like true disciples, along the way we'll have to deny ourselves many of the comforts and pleasures most people take for granted.

But that's the price we pay to achieve something great, with blood, sweat, and often more than a few tears. The good news is that we *can* accomplish great things. Furthermore, God has promised, "Those who plant in tears will harvest with shouts of joy." (Ps 126:5 NLT)

Got a dream to fulfill? Count the cost. Be committed to give it your best; disciplined in your thinking, attitude, words, habits, and how you spend your time; always ready to foot the bill (without neglecting God—your first priority—or the people closest to you). Then stick with the plan and pay the price.

BE WILLING
TO MAKE SACRIFICES

Great achievement is usually born of great sacrifice,
and is never the result of selfishness.
—Napoleon Hill

WHEN WE LAUNCHED OUR FIRST SERIES of internet articles designed to encourage creators and dreamers, we decided to call it *Diet for Dreamers* (which were later collected in a book of the same title). Our thoughts ran along these lines: to accomplish anything in life, whether it's a healthy body or the fulfillment of a dream, we need the proper food.

A bodybuilder needs extra protein, a runner needs more carbs, and someone wanting to lose weight needs ... uh, less of everything that's truly delicious! This last example seems unfair, doesn't it? But until someone invents a pill that consumes excess fat, a dieter will have to stick to his or her diet—which means sacrificing desserts and other high-calorie foods.

Similarly, anyone who's trying to achieve great things in life also needs a special diet: Inspiration to feed the dreams, encouragement to foster the creativity; organization and strategy to make the most of time, talent, and resources; and steadfast faith and a deep passion for the goal or dream, both of which can fuel a person all the way to the finish line.

And, as with any dietary program, some sacrifices will have to be made, and that's never easy; which is why many people quit—or cheat too often and too much. Diets only work if we're willing to stick with them. Although we do need to give in to a craving occasionally, just to keep our sanity, most of the time we have to resign ourselves to sacrificing the foods we love (in the case of a nutritional diet) or the activities we love (in the case of a dreamer's diet).

The word *sacrifice* means to surrender something of value for the sake of a higher cause, a more pressing need, or a more important objective. If we're cutting calories in order to squeeze into that favorite pair of jeans, we'll need to *sacrifice* sweets or second helpings of our favorite foods. We may even have to leave the table while we're still hungry. In other words, we have to do what it takes to stick to our diet.

Writers, artists, actors, and musicians who achieve a level of virtuosity, entrepreneurs who exceed their goals, researchers and inventors who make great breakthroughs, visionaries who change the world, and even people who build solid marriages and raise well-adjusted kids, all do so because they stick to their diets ... and that usually means sacrificing certain things.

We have friends who, during their spare time, watch tons of television, or play video games almost non-stop, or participate in any number of other leisure activities. And then—every couple of months, it seems—they're taking an elaborate vacation or going away for a long weekend. (Apparently, having fun all the time can be quite fatiguing.)

These people are relaxing and doing what they enjoy most, and there's nothing wrong with that. We, on the other hand, want to achieve our goals and fulfill our dreams—and we have BIG dreams. So we need to make the most of our time. (Personally, we're always working on our books, articles, and stories.) We can't walk away from our day jobs, family responsibilities, and social obligations; and we have to take time to eat, sleep, and shower, so whatever time is left usually goes to pursuing our dreams.

Bottom line? **We sacrifice our leisure time—or at least a good portion of it—which is tough.** Of course, we all know "dieting" has never been easy. But if we want to fit into our pants or achieve our dreams, we *resign* ourselves to making sacrifices.

Full disclosure? We won't lie, sacrificing our down time continues to be a challenge; and sometimes, seeing others at play while we toil away at extra (and optional) tasks can be a little irritating. Frankly, we have to pray about it. We ask the Lord to help us guard our hearts, reciting David's prayer:

"Create in me a clean heart, O God; and renew a right spirit within me." (Ps 51:10 KJV)

Lastly, we keep reminding ourselves that, if we are to accomplish something—*any* thing—worthwhile, we need to stay on our diets and continue to sacrifice activities that could ruin our progress.

Can you relate? Do you find yourself getting a little envious of people relaxing while you're working, training, studying, tinkering, analyzing, researching, practicing, or honing? Remind yourself, if you're pursuing a goal or a dream, then you're simply paying the price. You *need* a certain diet with built-in sacrifices. Stick to it, and stop begrudging the guy next door who's playing video games all day long. Your diet and sacrifices will make you a lean mean dreaming machine, and someday you will achieve great things! And the guy next door? So what if he's happy with his diet of computer games. Perhaps someday he'll be the best Pokemon player in the neighborhood!

Concentrate on *your* "diet," not on the huge servings of leisure time being consumed by others.

It's worth repeating: "counting the cost/paying the price" requires focus, discipline, and sacrifice—just like dieting. And, as with dieting, it also helps to be psyched up; physically, spiritually, and psychologically prepared to stick with it. Face it, some goals and dreams come at a great price and require incredible sacrifice. In addition to the long hours and hard work, we often face failure, disappointments, setbacks, and rejection.

Here's what Charles Bukowski had to say on the subject:

If you're going to try, go all the way. Otherwise, don't even start. This could mean losing [friends] and maybe even your mind. It could mean not eating for three or four days. It could mean freezing on a park bench. It could mean jail. It could mean derision. It could mean mockery—isolation. Isolation is the gift. All the others are a test of your endurance, of how much you really want to do it. And, you'll do it, despite rejection and the worst odds. And it will be better than anything else you can imagine. If you're going to try, go all the way. There is no other feeling like that. ...You will ride life straight to perfect laughter. It's the only good fight there is. (Charles Bukowski, *Factotum*)

Making sacrifices along the way to fulfilling a dream is nothing new.

In fact, it's par for the course. All the great achievements in this world, all the great discoveries, and every great work of art, music, and literature, exacted a heavy price from creators and dreamers who *chose* to pay that price. Men and women such as Thomas Edison, Marie Curie, George Washington Carver, Edgar Allan Poe, L. Frank Baum, Mother Teresa, Abraham Lincoln, Dr. Martin Luther King, Jr.—the list of people who made tremendous sacrifices to realize their God-given dreams and visions would fill countless volumes.

"Do you see what this means—all these pioneers who blazed the way, all these veterans cheering us on? It means we'd better get on with it. ...Start running—and never quit! No extra spiritual fat, no parasitic sins. Keep your eyes on Jesus, who both began and finished this race we're in. Study how He did it. Because He never lost sight of where He was headed ... He could put up with anything along the way: the Cross, shame, whatever. And now He's there, in the place of honor, right alongside God." (Heb 12:1-3 MSG)

Are you pursuing a big dream? Are you willing to make a few sacrifices? Pay the price today, so you can celebrate tomorrow. It's the "diet" we choose for ourselves—the sacrifices we make to succeed.

CONSIDER THE EMOTIONAL INVESTMENT

IN 1899, RUDYARD KIPLING WROTE OF "the institution of the 'free lunch'": a once-common practice in American saloons, where "You paid for a drink and got as much as you wanted to eat." But this seemingly altruistic practice was artfully deceptive. First, the true cost of the free food was usually disguised in the high price of the beer being served. Second, the "free" munchies on offer were extremely salty—ham, pickled eggs, pretzels and crackers—so patrons "wolfing food from a counter" stayed thirsty, ordered more beer, and ended up paying far more than they intended.

You already know the lesson here. Another popular writer, Robert Heinlein, popularized the old adage in his 1966 science-novel *The Moon Is a Harsh Mistress*: "There ain't no such thing as a free lunch." Period.

Nothing in life is free. Somewhere, someone is footing the bill. True, salvation through the atoning death of our Lord Jesus Christ is a free gift to all who believe and trust in Him—but only because Christ paid the price for our sins. (Eph 2:8)

Along with this sobering truth comes yet another fascinating fact—of which many of us aren't aware. At least many of us *act* like we're oblivious to it: No one besides Christ—not your teacher or your neighbor, your boss or your best friend, not even your Aunt Petunia or your Uncle Billy-Bob—is too keen on paying your way in life. What's all this mean?

If you want something in life, you generally have to pay for it. And if you want to accomplish your goals and fulfill your dreams, you'll need to put up some sweat capital. And usually, you'll also need to make some emotional investments.

Let's discuss these emotional investments. God-sized dreams often carry God-sized price tags; and require God-sized sacrifices—especially in the area of human relationships. Not necessarily because we dreamers tend to get caught up in the pursuit of our goals, and end up neglecting those around us. That *can* happen, but as we stated earlier, people who keep their priorities straight will never be guilty of this. On the other hand, however, it's often the creator or the dreamer who feels left out.

Most people don't understand what motivates those of us who have grand visions and chase big dreams. They wonder why we want to create, achieve, accomplish, go higher; why we aren't content to simply maintain the status quo; and why we aren't satisfied being just like everyone else. And yet, God calls us to break out of the mold, to outdistance the pack, to knock the ball out of park.

"Don't let the world around you squeeze you into its own mold, but let God remold your minds from within, so that you may prove in practice that the plan of God for you is good...." (Rom 12:2-3 PHILLIPS) In other words, be like Christ; think, talk, and act differently. Don't be afraid to stand out from the crowd, but in a good way. Breaking out of the mold is how many great men and women achieved their dreams and made incredible contributions to the world. But don't expect the crowd to love you for it.

Don't be surprised if your friends can't understand why you spend your days pursuing what *they* perceive as an elusive dream—while they themselves waste hours of precious time playing video games, watching TV, Tweeting, or posting funny videos to Facebook.

Be prepared to be misunderstood; and to have your actions misinterpreted. Many people will view your desire to create and achieve, or to reach a level of excellence, as sheer pride. And they'll view your struggles as a display of stubborn arrogance. Such attitudes may seem preposterous—*if* you've never experienced them firsthand—but these critical and judgmental attitudes are as old and as familiar as civilization.

Jesus Christ, while working to achieve His purpose on earth, frequently encountered these attitudes. In fact, some people were quite vocal in their criticism: "'He's no better than we are,' they said. 'He's just a carpenter, Mary's boy.... And his sisters live right here among us.' And they were offended!"

(Mark 6:3 TLB) These people were essentially grumbling, "Just who does He think He is!"

Even at that time, our Lord knew *exactly* who He was. But was He prideful? Definitely not!

"Though he was God, He ... gave up His divine privileges; He took the humble position of a slave and was born as a human being." (Phil 2:6-7 NLT) So why would people misinterpret this great Creator's mission?

Sometimes people can't see beyond the familiar. They fail to understand that God has planted the seeds of greatness in every man, woman, and child. So when they consider the average dreamer, they don't see potential; instead, they see a friend, a relative, a coworker, or the person next door. Which is why Jesus states, "The only place a prophet isn't honored [or respected] is in his hometown, among his relatives, and in his own house." (Mark 6:4 GW)

Remember those emotional investments we warned creators and dreamers about? In this brief remark, Jesus revealed the BIG ONE!

What is it? Stay tuned. Until then, take heart, fellow dreamers and creators. You're in good company, because: Jesus Christ was the perfect manifestation of God here on earth; He lived a perfect, sinless life; and everything He did was out of love. And yet, He was misunderstood, judged, criticized, and finally put to death. Our Lord paid the *ultimate price,* but He kept His eyes on *the world's greatest dream:* the redemption of humankind. So be encouraged, because God understands *exactly* what you're experiencing.

God knew what He was doing when He entrusted you with the dream or vision! He's the One who gave you the gifts and talents to pursue it—and He *will* help you to fulfill it! In the meantime, hold onto His promises: "God, who began this good work in you, will carry it through to completion...." (Phil 1:6 GW)

"...The gifts and the calling of God are irrevocable [for He does not withdraw what He has given, nor does He change His mind about those to whom He gives His grace or to whom He sends His call]." (Rom 11:29 AMP)

"...With God nothing [is or ever] shall be impossible."
(Luke 1:37 AMP)

BRACE YOURSELF FOR THE BIG ONE!

IN THE OLD TV SITCOM *Sanford and Son,* young, enterprising Lamont frequently shocked his elderly father with some new scheme or startling news. The veteran junkman, Fred Sanford, would always clutch at his heart, look heavenward, and exclaim to his dear departed wife: "This is the BIG ONE, Elizabeth! I comin' to join ya!"

Jesus Christ got to see the BIG ONE up close and personal. In order to fulfill His destiny on earth, He made a huge emotional investment. No matter how wonderful His accomplishments—He healed the sick, fed thousands, and brought to life the Word of God like no one had before—He nevertheless encountered resistance. Like many creators and dreamers today, Jesus was misunderstood, His actions misinterpreted. He took it in stride, however, commenting that "The only place a prophet isn't honored [or respected] is in his hometown, among his relatives, and in his own house." (Mark 6:4 GW)

What is the BIG ONE?

In many cases, even the people *closest* to you—members of your own family—may not support or encourage you! (—Not even if you have a solid track record of encouraging, supporting, and being there for *them.*)

Ouch! This is undoubtedly the most challenging and painful truth we dreamers must face. But too often it's an ugly situation we all contend with. The people closest to us won't always "celebrate" us, or our achievements. To the contrary, the people we *thought* would be in our cheering section—often end up resenting our efforts to reach our goals, as well as the small victories we win on the road to fulfilling the dreams and visions God gave us. (This can be especially painful if you have a track record of supporting *them* and celebrating *their* achievements.)

Take heart! If you've encountered this absolutely weird reaction from friends and families, you are not alone! Join the club, of which our Lord and Savior is President: "We don't have a priest who is out of touch with our reality. He's been through weakness and testing, experienced it all—all but the sin." (Heb 4:15 MSG)

Like most creators and dreamers, our Lord dealt with misunderstanding, criticism, and lack of support from His family. He also had to deal with the Two-Headed Green Monster of Jealousy and Envy. Regarding Christ's crucifixion, the Roman officials "knew that the chief priests [God's own family] had handed him over because of jealousy." (Mark 15:10 CEB) We'll provide you with a complete dossier on the green monster of jealousy, along with a few other villainous attitudes, when we discuss the pitfalls and "perils" all creators and dreamers eventually encounter. Stay Tuned!

Learn to accept that people are NOT perfect.

Far from it—which means that in addition to jealousy, envy, misunderstanding, misinterpretation, and a general lack of encouragement and support, we'll have to contend with the apathy, indifference, laziness, self-absorption, and preoccupation of other people. This is important, because not everyone who fails to show their support is guilty of harboring ill-feelings. Sometimes the people we were counting on to encourage and assist us with our vision are just too busy, or too tired, or too distracted.

Then too, some people—the ones who've already achieved a modicum of success or notoriety, who have already "arrived"—may be reluctant to help and encourage those still struggling, because ... well, because they've grown too big for their britches. And no, we don't mean they've put on weight. But it's all good.

Whether others respond to our dreams with malice or misunderstanding; or fail to respond due to indifference or inopportunity, we must always guard our hearts, make allowances, and give them the benefit of the doubt. Cut even your most vocal critics some slack—because that's how the

Lord deals with each of us. "Make allowance for each other's faults, and forgive anyone who offends you. Remember, the Lord forgave you, so you must forgive others." (Col 3:13 NLT)

Remember that at the end of the day, God is still in control. We can trust Him to have the situation well in hand. He knows what He's doing, which obviously means:

Not everyone will play a part in God's plan for your life.

Simply put, those who don't support you in your dream (regardless of their reasons) were never intended to play a part in the vision with which God entrusted you. They are not a part of your destiny.

So, if you're not getting support and encouragement from friends and family, don't sweat it. To quote a song from Disney's *Frozen,* "Let it go!" It's all part of paying the price for aiming high—an emotional investment toward achieving your dreams. And if the price seems dear, take comfort in the knowledge that God is on your side: "Even if my father and mother abandon me, the LORD will hold me close." (Ps 27:10 NLT)

Not only is the Lord in our cheering section, not only does He support our efforts, but He also promises us, "God has said, 'I will never fail you. I will never abandon you.'" (Heb 13:5 NLT)

"For the eyes of the LORD move to and fro throughout the earth that He may strongly support those whose heart is completely His." (2 Chr 16:9 NASB) Nothing else really matters, does it?

BE WILLING TO STAND ALONE

EMOTIONAL INVESTMENTS: part of the price we creators and dreamers must be willing to pay if we're to achieve our goals and fulfill God's plan for each of our lives. One such investment is learning to deal with a general lack of encouragement and support. People may fail to see your potential or the value of your dreams. They may even react negatively, due to envy, competitiveness, or a misunderstanding of your motives. The best way to deal with these often-painful disappointments is to:

Allow all invalid criticism to roll off your back the way water rolls off a duck's feathers. And whenever jealousy and envy enter the picture, you can vanquish this Green Two-Headed Monster simply by following the example of our Lord Jesus Christ, by quickly forgiving anyone who wrongs you.

Remember that jealousy and envy usually stem from insecurity or a low self-esteem. People who are hurting emotionally tend to compensate for their pain by trying to hurt others—and dreamers and creators seem to make tempting targets. Nevertheless, we must learn to have victory over any slights and slurs, or over a silent lack of support.

What does victory look like? It's keeping your peace and proceeding with your plans; and learning to celebrate others even if they routinely fail to celebrate you. After all, we're here to please God, and nothing makes Him happier than when we behave like His Son. "Love your enemies [as well as your obstinate friends], do good to them ... without expecting to get anything back. Then your reward will be great, and you will be children of the Most High...." (Luke 6:35 NIV)

Be willing to stand alone. There's another aspect of these emotional investments, a rather frightening one many of us may face: having to STAND ALONE.

Jesus reassures us, "I am with you always, even to the end of the age." (Matt 28:20 NLT) So we're never alone in the *spiritual* sense. However, in the physical world, situations may arise in which the dreamer finds him- or herself abandoned by friends and family; isolated from any support groups; working alone to fulfill a vision. If you find yourself in one of these frustrating situations, take heart. Again, you're in good company. (In a manner of speaking.)

The Biblical King David, who is described as "a man after God's own heart" (Acts 13:22), was a fellow dreamer and creator who knew how to stand alone. He was alone when he faced Israel's great adversary, Goliath. He was alone when he made the hard decisions that affected God's people; and alone when he suffered temporary defeats and setbacks. And yet, even when isolated, abandoned, and opposed in the face of overwhelming adversity, David knew how to:

Stay in faith and draw encouragement from God. More to the point, David had learned how to stand alone for what's important. But where did he get his training?

David had spent *most* of his formative years alone. As a youth he'd endured countless lonely nights as a shepherd, with no company except a few sheep. Remember the movie *Babe*? The hero of this fantasy flick is an intelligent pig who doesn't want to be treated like a pig. He has, in essence, one of the biggest, most impossible dreams ever. But he ultimately finds himself alone in the barnyard with a bunch of "stupid sheep."

Sheep have rather limited vocabularies. So when Babe tries to communicate with his woolly friends, all they have to say is *Baaahhh!* Not too encouraging. Which is why David turned to God during *his* years of isolation. The great Psalmist later wrote, "Whom do I have in heaven but you? I desire no one but you on earth. ...My heart may grow weak, but God always protects my heart and gives me stability." (Ps 73:25-26 NET)

During this time, David found comfort and companionship in God. He also gained tremendous insights into the nature of his Lord, which he shared with the world in the many Psalms he penned. And who can forget David's oft-quoted observation, from his most famous Psalm? "The LORD is my shepherd; I shall not want." (Ps 23:1 KJV) Isolated? Perhaps, but never abandoned, never lacking.

David developed some impressive spiritual muscles while guarding his sheep on the backside of the wilderness, muscles which would later serve him well, in dealing with disappointment, overcoming adversity, and standing alone. He received his greatest affirmation from his Lord, and no matter what he faced—whether it was opposition in the form of people or giants, or heartache from loneliness or a lack of support—he learned to:

Run TO God, not FROM Him. "God is our shelter and our strength. When troubles seem near, God is nearer, and He's ready to help. So why run and hide? No fear, no pacing, no biting fingernails. When the earth spins out of control, we are sure and fearless...." (Ps 46:1-2 VOICE)

Are you going through a difficult season? Remember the example of David, the poet-warrior-king who, with the help of God, overcame incredible odds and defeated fierce opponents. But first he learned to stand alone—WITH GOD! (We'll catch up with this remarkable creator and dreamer later on, because he's got more wisdom to impart to us.)

Standing alone isn't *always* about being abandoned, or isolated, or singled out; but it *is* always about getting our encouragement, support, and affirmation from the Lord.

God created us. He knows us, understands us. He also gave us the vision, the dream, the ideas. And finally, God gave us the gifts and talents needed to execute the plan. Trust us, He gets it. He can relate to whatever we're going through— and He's *for* us and *with* us. Even when we're "standing alone," we don't have to feel lonely.

Feeling a little left out, forgotten by God and the people closest to you—as though you're stuck on the backside of the desert? You are NOT alone. Friends, family, or coworkers may abandon you, but God will never leave you. Whatever you're going through, GOD GETS IT. Run to His loving arms. "God

is your refuge, and His everlasting arms are under you."
(Deut 33:27 NLT)

Like David, we dreamers and creators must learn to stand
alone (with God) for those times when we'll need to. We can't
afford to waste our emotional capital by being overly concerned with people's opinions of us or our dreams. We can't
afford to focus on who *is* and who's *not* on our side. God is on
our side—and that's what matters most!

We have *His* stamp of approval. He loves us more than we
could ever comprehend, and He's in our cheering section for
every step of the way. "What then shall we say to all these
things? If God is for us, who can be [successful] against us?"
(Rom 8:31 AMP)

Need some encouragement? At the end of each day, picture your Heavenly Father: He's smiling; He's celebrating both
you and your accomplishments; He's saying, "Well done, good
and faithful servant [creator, or dreamer]." (Matt 25:21 AMP)

JUST THE FACTS

REMEMBER THAT OLD **TV SERIES** *Dragnet*? If not, google it sometime. It was one of several realistic shows produced by Jack Webb, which included *Adam-12* and *Emergency*. Webb was a talented actor, too. But when when he decided to play the starring role of LAPD Sgt. Joe Friday, he chose NOT to act. Instead, he rarely smiled and recited all his lines like an emotionless robot. It worked, however, because Webb was trying to achieve a documentary style: he wanted viewers to focus on the facts of each case—which were drawn form actual police files—and not on the actors.

Focusing on the facts even played into Sgt. Friday's signature line. And Webb got a chance to say it in nearly every episode. During a criminal investigation, if a witness got long-winded or strayed from the issues at hand, Friday (in a deadpan voice) would remind the person, "Just the facts." Which is excellent advice we should all follow in life.

In Boot Camp, we've worked hard to give you *just the facts*. Sometimes, of course, the facts can be hard to handle. For instance, we realize that all this stuff about counting the cost, paying the price, making sacrifices, and investing emotional capital is a bit daunting to the average dreamer or creator. But trust us, we're not trying to discourage our readers.

Nor do we want to rain on anyone's parade—and we certainly don't want to scare anyone off. We WANT you to pursue your dreams! We also want you to succeed, and not abandon your dreams at the first sign of trouble. That's why we feel duty-bound to lay it on the line. As the Apostle Paul writes, "...We will speak the truth in love, growing in every way more and more like Christ...." (Eph 4:15 NLT)

Big, God-sized dreams demand patience, fortitude, and endurance. They also require a tremendous amount of preparation and planning. Since being forewarned is forearmed, it's always a good idea to have all the facts (truth) at our disposal. Sometimes the truth we share has a sharp edge. We're not being pessimistic, though; we're being *realistic*. Would you want it any other way? Sgt. Friday wouldn't. So we give it to you straight: the lowdown; the plain dope; the real skinny; *just the facts.*

Fact:
First, it doesn't pay to view the world through rose-colored glasses. **We need to see life through the eyes of faith.** "...Faith is the reality of what is hoped for, the proof of what is not seen." (Heb 11:1 HCSB) When we view life (and our future) through the eyes of faith, we get God's perspective on each and every matter, including our hopes and dreams. Then, no matter what challenges we face, we can truly believe that "...With God nothing is ever impossible...." (Luke 1:37 AMPC)

Fact:
God is on your side. He loves you. He's totally committed to helping you realize your dreams. Ultimately that's all that matters. "God is our protection and our strength. He always helps in times of trouble." (Ps 46:1 NCV)

Fact:
We're not called to be people-pleasers. Here's another hard fact of life: trying to please people (instead of trying to please God) can be hazardous to your dreams and creativity.

We should always be loving and respectful of all people, but we should never overly concern ourselves with their opinions of us or our dreams. Paul writes, "Our purpose is to please God, not people. He alone examines the motives of our hearts." (1 Thess 2:4 NLT) Since this is our over-arching goal in life, the only question we need ask ourselves is, "Am I pleasing God?"

Fact:
God is not hard to please. He's neither a celestial tyrant nor a critical, hard-to-please parent. He is our loving and understanding Heavenly Father. "Great is His faithfulness; His mercies begin afresh each morning." (Lam 3:23 NLT) At the

end of life's journey we'll hear Him say, "Well done, good and faithful servant." (Matt 25:21, 23) And that's the key to our relationship with God: He won't say "good and *perfect* servant"—because He understands we're only human.

Fact:
God has NOT forgotten you!

"I have written your name on the palms of my hands...."
(Isa 49:16 NLT)

"God even knows [numbers; counts] how many hairs
are on your head." (Matt 10:30 EXB)

"You [O God] know how troubled I am;
You have kept a record of my tears.
Aren't they listed in Your book?" (Ps 56:8 GNT)

"God is fair. He won't forget what you've done
or the love you've shown for him." (Heb 6:10 GW)

Fact:
God is trustworthy!

"God is not a human being, and He will not lie.
He is not a human, and He does not change His mind.
What he says He will do, He does....
What He promises, He makes come true...."
(Num 23:19 EXB)

"He is like a rock. What He does is perfect. He is always fair.
He is a faithful God who does no wrong." (Deut 32:4 ICB)

"He rewards those who sincerely seek Him." (Heb 11:6 NLT)

Fact:
God has planned a bright future for you!

"I'll show up and take care of you as I promised....
I know what I'm doing. I have it all planned out—

plans to take care of you, not abandon you,
plans to give you the future you hope for."

(Jer 29:11 MSG)

"...The people who know their God shall be strong
and do great things."   (Dan 11:32 TLB)

"...Thanks be to God, who always leads us
in victory through Christ."   (2 Cor 2:14 ICB)

These facts are plain, simple, and straightforward—just the way Sgt. Friday would want them. Memorize them, recite them, cherish them; because "the truth will make you free." (John 8:32 ICB)

BUT DON'T BE
A LONE WOLF

THOSE CLOSEST TO US may not always share our faith, or believe in our dreams and abilities, so we need to be ready and willing to stand alone. This truth can mean the difference between success and failure, giving up or going the distance.

Rest assured, should friends and family ever turn their backs on us, God will always be there to encourage and support us through these difficult times. However, being *able* to stand alone is never sufficient excuse for thumbing our noses at the people around us. In fact, our Heavenly Father never intended for anyone to become a lone wolf.

We were created to interact, encourage, and cooperate with each other. So, although we may experience situations in which we must stand alone, it's always *best* if we can find support and fellowship among like-minded people—and enlist their aid in the pursuit of our goals, dreams, visions, and creative endeavors. (Rom 15:5) Stand alone? By all means, *if* and *when* we absolutely need to; but if we're blessed to have faithful friends, affirming family members, and—we hope—more than a few facilitators, then NEVER!

"...One standing alone can be attacked and defeated, but two can stand back-to-back and conquer; three is even better, for a triple-braided cord is not easily broken." (Eccl 4:12 TLB)

Life is always easier and more enjoyable when we cooperate, network, and team up. To quote an old Beatles song, "I get by with a little help from my friends." Furthermore, even if we're standing alone in one area, regarding a particular issue, a creative project, a business venture, or an impossible dream, we needn't be alone in other areas!

King David faced some of his greatest challenges while

standing alone—but he didn't make a habit of it. He chose *not* to allow the time he spent in the wilderness, hanging out with God alone, to turn him into a hermit; or his solitary confrontation with Goliath to prevent him from seeking assistance with future challenges. Shortly after slaying the giant, David recruited a team of other capable and brave heroes, to assist him in further Biblical adventures. His version of "the Avengers" would go down in history as "the Mighty Men of Valor." (Nick Fury, eat your heart out!)

"And they helped David in his expeditions; for they were all mighty men of valour, and were captains in the host." (1 Chr 12:21 DARBY)

David—long before he took his rightful place as the leader of God's people—also benefitted from the unfailing support and friendship of another Biblical hero, who had single-handedly defeated an entire garrison of enemy warriors; a courageous champion who was beloved by all the people, and therefore had an impressive following. Who was this mystery man? His name was Jonathan, and we first meet him in 1 Samuel 13:2.

During that time, King Saul was ruling over Israel. He had actually been chosen by the people to be their first king. He was a tall, handsome, talented, and extremely capable individual, who nonetheless suffered from low self-esteem—an open invitation to that dangerous Two-Headed Green Monster of Jealousy and Envy. Indeed, Saul's poor self-image marked *his* downfall, and the beginning of David's troubles.

King Saul tended to overcompensate (*to strive to overcome a sense of inferiority through overt, opposite behavior*). In doing so, he disobeyed many of God's directives—and then made up lame excuses. (We won't go into all the details here, because you can read a full account of Saul's rise and fall, in 1 Samuel.) As a result of Saul's shenanigans, God chose an unassuming Shepard named David to replace him as king.

Oh yeah, one more thing. Once Saul heard the news, he grew increasingly preoccupied with his own personal agenda: he spent most of his days chasing David across the desert in hopes of executing God's chosen leader! But the Two-Headed Green Monster of Jealousy and Envy had been nagging Saul since the first day he met David and realized the young man's potential; and upon returning victorious from a fierce battle with the Philistines, King Saul witnessed something which infuriated him, a celebration that led him to open wide the door to his own downfall, and let the monster in: "...The women sang to one another as they celebrated, 'Saul has struck down his thousands, and David his ten thousands.'" (1 Sam 18:7 ESV)

But where does Jonathan fit into all this?

Although Saul was consumed by jealousy and envy, his own son Jonathan—heir to the throne—did the *right thing!* Jonathan realized that God was with David (and for obvious reasons). So, instead of following in the footsteps of his foolish father, **Jonathan vanquished the Green Two-Headed Monster,** and remained one of David's truest and most loyal friends—fully supporting his future king.

What's our point? Both Jonathan and David *knew* how to stand alone, but they also understood the importance of seeking (and offering) a helping hand. We creators and dreamers should follow their examples. We were never intended to handle the challenges of life alone! And God certainly doesn't want us pursuing our fondest hopes and dreams all by our lonesome—at least, not if we can help it.

Don't try to be a lone wolf. Stand alone when and *if* you must, but remember:

"Two people are better off than one,
for they can help each other succeed." (Eccl 4:9 NLT)

"...One person (can) chase a thousand ...
(but) two people put ten thousand to flight...."
(Deut 32:30 NLT)

GET CONNECTED

G OD CREATED PEOPLE TO BE RELATIONAL BEINGS: to have interaction with Him, obviously, but also to interact with
those around us. "...The Lord God said, 'It is not good for the
man to be alone.'" (Gen 2:18 HCSB) Although this verse re-
lates to marriage, the first institution God created, its wisdom
applies to ALL relationships

The Bible is full of relationships. Actually, it's all about
relationships. And, it's *the* Book of God's relationship to us!
God knows us better than anyone, and what He knows is that
WE NEED RELATIONSHIPS. Every human being has a basic
need and desire to love and be loved, to share, to communicate, to socialize. Even the grumpiest, seemingly most unap-
proachable person needs to talk to someone! Perhaps that's
why social media is so popular today. (But social media is no
substitute for face-to face friendships)

Two people working together are better able to achieve
their goals and realize their dreams, because there is power
in two people who are mutually supportive and accountable;
two people who can encourage and assist each other. That's
what the "buddy system" is all about. That's why there are
support groups such as AA, and mentoring groups such as
Big Brothers and Big Sisters. That's why a prayer partner can
help keep us tuned in to God. And why corporations hope
you have a "best friend" at work. Such connections make
work more bearable, and life more enjoyable.

"You are better off to have a friend than to be all alone,
because then you will get more enjoyment out of what you
earn." (Eccl 4:9 CEV)

God knows. In Genesis 2:18, He declares, in regards to
Adam, "It is not good for the man to be alone. I will make a
helper who is just right for him." (NLT) In this case, the helper
is Eve, his wife; and we believe she helped her husband with

his creative pursuits. With this cooperative union between husband and wife, God set the standard for all marriages to come: "A man will leave his father and mother [in the sense of a new primary loyalty] and be united with his wife, and the two will become one body." (Gen 2:24 EXB)

According to the One who created men and women, as well as the institution of marriage, a husband and wife should act as one body: two people mutually supporting one another, sharing their hopes and dreams, and working together to reach their full potential. God knows that a man can accomplish far more if his wife is on his side—and vice-versa. Remember Sylvester Stallone's movie character Rocky Balboa? Rocky felt as though he could take on any opponent in the boxing ring, as long as his beloved Adrian was in his corner.

With her approval and moral support, Rocky eventually realizes (against overwhelming odds) his great dream of becoming the World Heavyweight Champion. Could he have done it alone? Maybe. But that's not how Stallone saw it when he wrote the script. His message (and ours) is that it's important for a married person pursuing a big dream to have the love, support, and cooperation of the spouse. Period. So all you couples out there, get together and get it together. Make God the center of your marriage, because "A rope made from three strands of cord is hard to break." (Eccl 4:12 CEV) Then dream together, work together, and succeed together.

And if you're not married, don't worry. Find a friend, whether online, on the job, at your local faith assembly, or next door. Recruit your parents, grandparents, an uncle, an aunt, or a cousin twice removed, but find someone who can share in and support your dreams. If there's no one around who fits the bill, then tune in to an encouraging television ministry such as TBN's programs or Joel Osteen's weekly message. Or find a website such as ours, to help keep you inspired and motivated.

Above all, don't forget that the Lord also wants to partner with you in every endeavor. He's "... a friend who sticks closer than a brother." (Prov 18:24 NIV)

Please don't face the challenges of life alone. Every successful creator and dreamer had the support and encouragement of a least one person who believed in both them and their dreams, whether it was a spouse, a parent, a friend, a coworker, a teacher, a coach, a spiritual leader....

As the English poet and clergyman John Donne wrote, "No man [or woman] is an Island, entire of itself; every man is a piece of the Continent, a part of the main." We must live and work together. And together we must "share each other's troubles and problems, and so obey our Lord's command." (Gal 6:2 TLB)

"Be devoted to one another with [authentic] brotherly affection [as members of one family], give preference to one another in honor. ...Live in harmony with one another; do not be haughty [conceited, self-important, exclusive], but associate with humble people [those with a realistic self-view]. Do not overestimate yourself." (Rom 12:10,16 AMP)

Or, to quote some of the lyrics of Bill Withers' 1972 song "Lean On Me":

> *Please swallow your pride,*
> *If I have things you need to borrow.*
> *For no one can fill those of your needs*
> *That you don't let show....*
> *Lean on me, when you're not strong,*
> *And I'll be your friend—I'll help you carry on.*
> *For it won't be long ...'till I'm gonna need*
> *Somebody to lean on.*
> *If there is a load you have to bear,*
> *That you can't carry....*
> *I'm right up the road—I'll share your load,*
> *If you just call me.*
> *So just call on me, brother, when you need a hand*
> *—We all need somebody to lean on.*
> *I just might have a problem that you'd understand*
> *—We all need somebody to lean on.*

PRAY FOR A BARNABAS

SOMETIMES TALENT AND ENTHUSIASM AREN'T ENOUGH. Sometimes *what* you know or *what* you can accomplish aren't as important as *who* you know. This is a sad but true fact of life.

Having friends, family, and associates who encourage and support you in the pursuit of your dreams can mean the difference between success and failure; but unfortunately, there are times when even this is not enough. Creators and dreamers often need capable and influential people who can help open doors of opportunity; people who are willing to assist, facilitate, and promote others. As we stated earlier, many of us will find it nearly impossible to succeed without a helping hand. Truth is, practically no one ever makes it ALONE.

Harrison Ford might still be a carpenter, if not for some savvy Hollywood producers who saw his potential and offered him a shot at stardom. Today the veteran actor is famous for portraying three iconic characters: archeologist and lost ark discoverer Indiana Jones; good-hearted space rogue Han Solo; and Tom Clancy's patriotic CIA operative, Jack Ryan.

Popular Christian recording artist Ricardo Sanchez (who cowrote the classic "Moving Forward") might be unknown today, if not for the support and encouragement he received from Pastor Jentezen Franklin. The same can be said of Bishop T. D. Jakes, who struggled for years in obscurity until TBN cofounder Paul Crouch, Sr. chanced upon a local broadcast featuring the minister—and then went out of his way to find and promote the man.

Star Wars creator George Lucas got a helping hand from director Francis Ford Coppola; and Francis Ford Coppola got a hand from director Roger Corman. In fact, Corman, the king of low-budget "B" movies, either discovered, promoted, or facilitated dozens of future creators and dreamers, including director Ron Howard and actor Jack Nicholson.

Author Dr. Phil can thank Oprah Winfrey; and Oprah can thank producer Steven Spielberg. But if you prefer a more exciting example, Captain John Smith can thank the young Native American princess Pocahontas—for saving his red-bearded head from the chopping block! Thank God for understanding people who are willing to help others realize their dreams. Even Jesus Christ had a band of believers who helped Him with the legwork of His ministry on earth.

Could you use a similar boost? Have you ever felt like you were spinning your wheels on the road to success? Well, to achieve tough goals, to fulfill huge dreams, you may need a little help from someone with specialized skills, experience, connections, or capital. A "friend" who's willing to lend a helping hand, give some guidance, introduce you to the right people. You may need an agent, a mentor, a facilitator, a collaborator. You may need a Barnabas—a person who's willing to help another complete their "mission" in life. Someone who can open the right door for you, point you in the right direction, and get you started on your way.

NEED A BARNABAS?

Sooner or later we all need a little help—someone to put in a good word, help us with a project, give us a job, or just be a good friend. No matter how self-sufficient we are, we can accomplish even more with a little help from our friends. But where do we dreamers and creators find such a wonderful and giving person, especially in a society filled with people who only look out for themselves?

Why aren't there more Barnabas people in the world? The reasons range from simple to strange:

People tend to be selfish and self-absorbed. Hence, they're usually more interested in helping themselves than in aiding someone else. These people may insist they're too busy—they may even believe it themselves—but the fact of the matter is, people always find time for what's important ... to them. Helping a dreamer reach a goal is usually very low on their priority list. For this reason, the Apostle Paul writes, "Don't be selfish.... Don't look out only for your own interests, but take an interest in others, too." (Phil 2:3-4 NLT)

Fear, pride, jealousy, insecurity, stubbornness, and self-importance often lead people to willfully ignore and neglect those who could otherwise benefit from their influence and expertise. Sad but true. There are people who have connections, influence, and expertise, as well as the time and opportunity to promote others. However, due to feelings of pride and/or insecurity, they simply will NOT. In fact, depending on how deep these feelings run—and hence, what's buried deep within their hearts—instead of offering you assistance, these hurting people may actually try to throw a monkey wrench into your plans.

Jonathan Swift once wrote, in his *Thoughts on Various Subjects, Moral and Diverting*, "When a true genius appears in the world, you may know him by this sign, that the dunces are all in confederacy against him." Well, in reality, you needn't be a genius to become the target of someone's wrath; you only need an exciting dream, and a sense of real purpose and destiny, like the Apostle Paul had.

That's right. Paul had more than a few "reverse" facilitators, too. He wrote from his prison cell, "I am well aware that some people out there are preaching ... because of jealousies and rivalries. Their motives aren't pure. They're driven by selfish ambitions and personal agendas, hoping somehow to add to my pain...." (Phil 1:15 VOICE) Did he allow it to steal his peace and joy? Not at all, because Paul knew that God was on his side. Not to mention, the Apostle had plenty of others who genuinely aided him, including THE Barnabas.

The world is Barnabas deficient—because WE aren't doing our part! If we want life to be filled with Barnabas people, we all need to start being Barnabas people. In other words, if we want to make our world a better place, we can start by being better.

"Therefore encourage one another and build one another up, just as you are doing." (1 Thess 5:11 ESV) "Share each other's burdens, and in this way obey the law of Christ." (Gal 6:2 NLT)

The cool thing about being someone else's Barnabas is that your good deeds will eventually find their way back to you. That's the way God works. It's called the *Law of Reciprocity*. Remember?

WALK LIKE A BARNABAS

So, how do we act like Barnabas people?

If we have connections or influence that can benefit others, we should by all means use them to help. "Do not withhold good from those who deserve it when it's in your power to help them." (Prov 3:27 NLT)

If you've already attained a degree of success, don't allow your fame, fortune, or prominent position to go to your head. Despite those fanciful tales of self-made men and women, we seriously doubt you got where you are today all by yourself. So show your appreciation to God for sending mentors and facilitators into your life—by being open to any requests for assistance.

If you have a platform (a ministry, a program, an audience, a readership) then consider sharing it with those individuals God sends to you. After all, it's actually God's platform. He's just loaning it to you. Never give Him sufficient reason to consider passing it to someone else.

Pastors and spiritual leaders, please be facilitators both within and outside your faith communities. We realize you have a vision for the future, but the people you serve often have their own God-given dreams. Don't expect these believers to use their gifts and talents exclusively to support your ministries and agenda.

If you can assist another creator or dreamer financially, then do so. Support new businesses by trying their products and services. Support budding actors, singers, and musicians by attending their performances. Support writers by buying their books ... and so forth.

Beyond this, we can offer genuine friendship and encouragement. We can earnestly pray for the endeavors of others and also do our part to spread the word about them, their talents, their works, or their products and services.

Please take the time to see what people "are about." Hear them out. Don't slam the door before you even give them a chance. And then do what you can to encourage, support, and facilitate them. "Seize any opportunity the Lord gives you to do good things and be a blessing to everyone, especially those within our faithful family." (Gal 6:10 VOICE)

IN SEARCH
OF A BARNABAS

H OW DOES ONE GO ABOUT FINDING a Barnabas and obtaining his or her help?

First things first: During the journey from childhood to mature adult, most people lose the confidence or the boldness or the freedom to ask anyone for anything. Adults actually hate asking. Most assume the answer will be a "no" anyway, so why waste the time. There's even an old expression in the workplace, "It's easier to ask for forgiveness than for permission"!

Nobody likes to face rejection, and a "NO" leaves us out in the cold, standing there with our hat in our hand, looking stupid—or so we think. We dreamers and creators need to realize, however, that at worst, a "no" is simply a "no" and often only means "not now" or "not here"; but at best, a "no" is just one of the tiniest words in the English language that means **"keep on knocking, keep on trying"**!

For some people the thought of getting a NO can be paralyzing. Result? They won't ask for anything. Pride may also play into their reluctance, as well as the idea they might be inconveniencing someone. If only we could recapture the freedom and fearlessness of childhood. Kids don't worry about silly stuff, and they don't hesitate to ask for anything. For instance, if a child's friend has an ice cream cone, he'll probably ask his friend, "Can I have a lick or two?" True, most kids have no sense of propriety, but they also aren't limited by the fear of a "NO"!

Sons and daughters know it never hurts to ask mom and dad for a new bike or, a few years later, if they can borrow the car. Why should they? The worst that could happen is they get a NO. But the answer just might be a glorious, filled-with-possibilities YES!!

In a child's mind, the sky's the limit, and our Heavenly Father wants us to have that same childlike faith. He wants us to view life as filled with possibilities. God also wants us to ask Him for the things we need and even some of the things we simply want. After all, He is our Heavenly Father, and it never hurts to ask. Sometimes His answer is "NO"; but when it is a "No" God has His reasons—and they're always good reasons.

If you need a Barnabas yourself, **the first thing you need to do is ASK—and keep on asking.**

Finding the right people who are willing to assist you in the pursuit of your dreams and creative endeavors can take time, patience, tons of effort, and some supernatural intervention. As we stated, people tend to be self-absorbed and generally—depending on their level of spiritual maturity—disinclined to support, serve, and assist others. What can we do?

Pray for a Barnabas. Oftentimes, God has lined up precisely the right people you need, long before you realize you need them. Nevertheless, God expects us to be confident and make our requests known to Him. "Do not be anxious about anything, but in every situation, by prayer and petition, with thanksgiving, present your requests to God." (Phil 4:6 NLT)

Don't be shy: open your mouth and ask!

Hey, nothing ventured, nothing gained! That's why we've asked store managers to honor their sales beyond the deadline—and often received a YES. One of us once asked to be considered for a job that required far more experience—and got both a YES and the job!

So, ASK already! Want a raise, or time off? Want a loan? Want to marry that special person? Want a customer to buy your new product or service? Want a publisher to accept your book? Have you asked? Again, the worst that can happen is you hear a "NO." But imagine a YES, instead. Remember: "You do not have because you do not ask." (James 4:2 NASB)

Don't be limited by the fear of a "NO"! Now, if we can ask the God of the Universe, then why can't we ask each other for support? The worst that can happen is you get a "No!" Big deal. Rejection is part of the process. Simply try someone else.

Keep on knocking. Persistence pays off. "Keep on asking, and you will receive what you ask for. Keep on seeking, and you will find. Keep on knocking, and the door will be opened to you." (Mathew 7:7 NLT)

Remember the young entrepreneur who mailed out hundreds of letters requesting help for a truly great idea he had. That took a lot of stamps and perseverance; because his pleas were almost universally met with silence. But his persistence paid off, after he received a single response from the last person he ever expected to hear from: a wealthy and influential businessman destined to hold the highest office in America—who agreed to facilitate the young man's dream.

And don't expect people to intuitively understand what you need, or how they can help. Sometimes people just don't get it. So tell them. Be specific about what you need. Offer them ideas as to how they may assist you.

Keep on creating, keep on dreaming, and pray for a Barnabas. "...If you keep knocking long enough, [someone] will get up and give you everything you want—just because of your persistence." (Luke 11:8 TLB)

Above all, trust God to bring the right people into your life. And when you finally do find yourself in the spotlight, remember to pull someone else in. This pleases God: "This is what our Scriptures come to teach: in everything, in every circumstance, do to others as you would have them do to you." (Matt 7:12 VOICE)

THE FACTS OF FOCUS & MOTIVATION

No, dear brothers and sisters, I have not achieved it, but I focus on this one thing: Forgetting the past and looking forward to what lies ahead, I press on to reach the end of the race....

—Philippians 3:13-14 NLT

To focus our minds on the human nature leads to death, but to focus our minds on the Spirit leads to life and peace.

—Romans 8:6 NIV

STAY FOCUSED

WE LIVE IN A FAST-PACED, OFTEN HECTIC WORLD—at the height of the Information Age. Vying for our attention, in addition to occupational demands and the needs of friends and family, are countless electronic distractions, such as video games and social media websites. If we want to realize our dreams, or accomplish something worthwhile, we'll need to minimize these distractions and stay focused on our main objectives.

To *focus* is to concentrate one's interest and/or activity on a particular goal or pursuit. **How do you stay focused?** Each morning, after spending quiet time with the Lord, followed by meeting daily responsibilities and fulfilling any outstanding obligations, you then apply your remaining time and energy to the pursuit of your dreams and creative endeavors. Simple. Well, not always.

Distractions are always a mouse-click away, or lurking within the TV or the smart phone. One false move and you can find yourself transported to the near future, looking back and wondering how you managed to waste so much valuable time. However, we can **safeguard against these distractions** (and hence, maximize our free time) **by staying organized and maintaining a "Things-to-Do List."**

We recently heard from a fellow dreamer who lamented the loss of his mornings (a precious and particularly creative time of day). He had the habit of switching on the news each morning, to catch up on important social and political issues. A worthy activity; but he'd always end up getting sucked in— and before he knew it, he'd wasted several precious hours (and was no closer to achieving his goals).

Like many of our fellow dreamers, and most creative people, we have far too many interests. We live in an endlessly fascinating world, and we genuinely love people. In fact, we're into hospitality, and we love having guests over for food and fellowship. (We even wrote a book on the topic of hospitality, *The Heart of an Angel*, available online wherever fine books are sold; and that, dear friends, is our shameless plug for the day.) Nonetheless, we generally remain focused.

If you're multitalented, have tons of interests, and tend to be sociable, staying focused will be a constant challenge. You'll need to evaluate your activities, carefully weigh your choices, and **be on your guard for unnecessary activities** that can eat up your time but give nothing in return.

You'll occasionally need to re-read your "vision" (the goals and dreams you committed to paper), and frequently review your plans.

To stay focused, **you'll also need to stick to ONE project at a time.** If you're called to write, then spend your time writing. If you want to be a concert pianist, then stay away from the tuba. Don't be a "jack-of-all-trades but master of none."

Use one gifting at a time—or at least concentrate on one particular area of your gifts and talents. Some dreams and creative endeavors require a number of gifts and talents; and some of these gifts and talents are interconnected or overlap. But if you try to succeed in more than one of them, chances are, you'll fail in ALL of them. So, narrow your vision. Set your sights on the one thing that most excites you. Have a clear objective: aim for a bullseye, and you'll increase your chances of hitting the target.

The Apostle Paul was both multitalented and extremely sociable—but he never allowed these characteristics to interfere with his main purpose in life. Despite numerous distractions, He made time to spread the Gospel across several provinces, and wrote most of the New Testament. How'd he do it? Paul writes, "...I focus on this one thing: ...looking forward to what lies ahead, I press on to reach the end of the race and receive the heavenly prize for which God, through Christ Jesus, is calling us." (Phil 3:13-14 TLB) By the way, the apostle wrote these words while he was in prison.

What's your "one thing"? Other than following Christ and leading a life that's pleasing to God (these goals should be primary), what's the one thing you feel you're truly good at? What's your great passion in life, your particular niche, your special assignment from the Lord?

Once you've answered these questions and settled on your own unique purpose and destiny in life—your "one thing"— write it down. Then focus upon it and press forward to obtain it. And whenever fear and doubt assail you, read the words you wrote regarding your vision (this one thing)—as well as the numerous promises of God, which support it.

We're reminded that when Jesus Christ walked the earth in human form, He never lost sight of His "one thing": that He was to be crucified for the sins of the world—thereby becoming our Passover lamb—in order to redeem us and to restore our relationship with God the Father.

Jesus (or Yeshua) lived a sinless life, during which He taught and fed the multitudes, healed the sick, raised the dead, and demonstrated God's infinite Love for humanity. Our Lord did all this and more, but His focus always remained on the Cross that lay at the end of His sojourn on earth. Christ said, "...It is for this [very] purpose that I have come to this hour [this time and place]." (John 12:27 AMP)

Follow our Lord's example. Stay focused ... on your dreams and on your faith! "We must get rid of everything that slows us down, especially sin that distracts us. We must run the race that lies ahead of us and never give up. We must focus on Jesus, the source and goal of our faith." (Heb 12:1-2 GW)

And lest we forget, here's one last thought: Three days after His sacrificial death on a Roman cross, God's only Son, Jesus Christ, rose from the grave: "The women [who discovered His empty tomb] were terrified and bowed with their faces to the ground. Then the men [angels in disguise] asked, 'Why are you looking among the dead for someone who is alive? He isn't here! He is risen from the dead! Remember what he told you back in Galilee...?'" (Luke 24:5-6 NLT)

DON'T GET DISTRACTED

WHAT'S YOUR "ONE THING"? Well, when using your special gifts or talents, which one brings you the most joy? And which projects or activities provide the greatest satisfaction? What's the one thing that excites you most and brings a sense of fulfillment to your life?

In the Academy Award-winning movie *Chariots of Fire* (Best Picture, 1981), there's a line of dialogue that beautifully sums up the emotional and spiritual feeling of the "one thing": Eric Liddell (portrayed by Ian Charleson) is training for the 1924 Paris Olympics. Liddell is a devout Christian missionary to China, a role to which he is deeply committed; but he's also convinced God has called him to run: "I believe God made me for a purpose, but He also made me fast. And when I run I feel His pleasure."[1]

Once we streamline our goals and dreams, once we realize what is truly our "one thing" in life, we too should feel God's pleasure. As the Apostle Paul states, "God has made us what we are. He has created us in Christ Jesus to live lives filled with good works that he has prepared for us to do." (Eph 2:10 GW)

Sensing God's approval, as well as His steadfast faithfulness, each of us should focus on our "one thing" and stick with it, no matter what challenges we face; no matter what obstacles we encounter. This is precisely what Liddell did.

---

[1] Eric Liddell (1902-1945) was a sprinter, rugby player, and missionary to China. Often called the "Flying Scotsman," he was favored to win the 100-metres at the 1924 Summer Olympic Games; but Liddell refused to participate in that event because the heats were held on Sunday (the Christian Sabbath). Instead, he competed in, and won, the 400-metres. In 1925 Liddell returned to China to serve as a missionary teacher. He remained there until his death in a Japanese civilian internment camp in 1945.

In one memorable scene, Liddell stumbles and falls while competing in an important, pre-Olympics race. Down—with precious seconds ticking away and the other runners closing in on the finish-line—but not out, Liddell scrambles to his feet and sprints like a wild animal. He soon catches up to the other runners—and then passes them—winning the race, partly through speed, but just as much through sheer determination and a deep sense of conviction.

Watching Eric Liddell from the sidelines is another champion athlete, Harold Abrahams.[2] Abrahams, an equally determined runner (who is destined to compete against Liddell) is astonished by Liddell's prowess: "I've never seen such drive, such commitment.... He unnerves me."

Abrahams was so unnerved, in fact, that he committed the unpardonable sin among runners: in the middle of a race, Abrahams looked around to see how the competition was performing. For a brief moment he took his eyes off the finish line and looked to see where Eric Liddell was—and that cost Abrams the race.

Friends, in the pursuit of our dreams, we cannot afford to allow anyone or anything to unnerve us (or distract us). We have to stay focused, and that means **keeping our eyes on the goal and the prize.** (Phil 3:12-14).

Similarly, we need to keep our eyes on the Lord, the source of our strength, the One who equips us to achieve our goals and reach our destination. Remember, the Apostle Simon Peter was able to walk on water—but only for as long as he kept his eyes on Jesus Christ. The moment Peter's focus shifted away from his Lord, and onto his circumstances (a raging, storm-tossed sea), the apostle began to sink. (Matt 14:25-31)

When we creators and dreamers choose to focus on God the storm-stopper—instead of on the frequent storms of life—we can accomplish the seemingly impossible. If, however, we

---

[2] Harold Abrahams (1899-1978) was a lawyer by profession. He won a Gold Medal (for the 100-metres) at the 1924 Paris Olympics. A year later, a serious leg injury ended his competitive career, but he continued to distinguish himself as a writer and broadcaster, and he remained committed to developing Jewish sports activities in Great Britain.

focus on our problems, challenges, setbacks, delays, and disappointments ... we're sunk!

But if (and when) we do get distracted, or fall, as Eric Liddell did, **we must get back into the race immediately!**

And, like Harold Abrahams, who went on to win Olympic Gold, **we must learn from our past mistakes.** When something doesn't work out, then try something else.

Thomas Edison is reported to have tried more than two thousand different experiments that failed before he finally got the lightbulb to work. He once told a journalist that from his perspective he had never failed at all; inventing the lightbulb was just a two-thousand-step process. Edison kept a clear and positive focus: he concentrated on what he learned from his mistakes, not on the failures themselves—or the delays.

Like Edison, we must realize that staying focused requires patience. Reaching a goal or fulfilling a dream is an involved process, and oftentimes the process can be long. Rome wasn't built in a day, so why should we expect instant success when it comes to our fondest hopes and dreams? Everything worthwhile in life takes time.

Stop watching the clock, stop crossing off the days, months, and years on the calendar. Instead, focus on where you're heading, not how long it's taking to get there.

Keep moving forward, and watch where you're going, not where you've been. This means letting go of past mistakes, hurts, disappointments, and regrets.

Forgive the people who failed you, who didn't encourage or support your dreams. Holding onto the past is like having a ball-and-chain fastened at the ankle. It will only weigh you down and impede your progress. Keep your focus on the Lord and the future He's prepared for you; because He will never let you down. (Jer 29:11)

Follow the advice of the Apostle Paul: "It's not that I've already reached the goal or ... completed the course. But I run to win that which Jesus Christ has already won for me. Brothers and sisters.... This is what I do: I don't look back, I lengthen my stride, and I run straight toward the goal to win the prize that God's heavenly call offers in Christ Jesus." (Phil 3:12-14 GW)

DON'T BE DOUBLE-MINDED

THERE'S YET ANOTHER WAY TO STAY FOCUSED, which involves making decisions and choices—and then sticking to them: Don't be double-minded.

Can creators accomplish anything worthwhile and lasting if they're double-minded? Can dreamers truly reach their goals and see their visions fulfilled if they don't avoid this state of mind? Perhaps Stranger things have happened.

However, the Apostle James writes: "Such a person should not expect to receive anything from the Lord. He is a double-minded man, unstable in all he undertakes." (James 1:7-8 ISV)

Merriam-Webster defines double-minded as **"wavering in mind: undecided, vacillating."** The term first appears in the above quoted verse, and no doubt James, the half-brother of Jesus Christ, derived the word from the Greek *dipsuchos*, which denotes "a person with two minds or souls." Related words include: fickle ("marked by lack of steadfastness, constancy, or stability: given to erratic changeableness"); indecisive; disloyal; wishy-washy (ineffectual); fair-weather (as in "fair-weather friend") and even schizophrenic (in its popular usage)!

It's not a particularly nice way of describing an individual, because people generally disdain this quality. We impatiently ask our friends to "please make up your mind!" We criticize politicians for being wishy-washy regarding key issues. And in the classic Hitchcock thriller Psycho, poor confused Norman Bates—who frequently dresses up and acts like his own mother—is definitely "double-minded" (as in schizoid).

One might say that Dr. Jekyll and Mr. Hyde are double-minded, as well. (Or should we write "is double-minded"—

since the two identities are simply facets of one misguided fool.)

In the context of the Book of James, the quality of double-mindedness has more to do with divided allegiances, and the fear and doubt people experience when they take their eyes off God and start concentrating on their problems and circumstances. Such people, to put it mildly, are distracted—definitely NOT focused. As a result, they may choose a course of action or start a new project only to abandon it at the first sign of trouble.

Double-mindedness is also about being undisciplined in one's way of thinking. It's being unresolved and unsettled. It results in a person second-guessing each and every step taken.

Double-mindedness is being pulled in multiple directions; following all the latest fads, diving into every controversy (whether in the community, at the job, or on social-media platforms). It can result in a "yoyo personality" in which one experiences frequent and sudden emotional ups and downs.

Another symptom of double-mindedness is a heart in constant state of conflict—between what the Lord has called you to do (your "one thing") and what others expect you to do.

The Apostle James warns, "If you don't know what you're doing, pray to the Father. He loves to help. You'll get His help, and won't be condescended to when you ask for it. Ask boldly, believing, without a second thought. People who "worry their prayers" are like wind-whipped waves. Don't think you're going to get anything from the Master that way, adrift at sea, keeping all your options open." (James 1:5-8 MSG)

In other words, **make a decision based on what God has shown you, and then stick with it.** If we don't stay focused, regardless of all the distractions in life, and continually rely on the Lord to help us, we will not accomplish our goals and realize our dreams. Instead of "arriving" on the shores of destiny, we'll continue to be lost at sea, so to speak.

In part, staying focused (not double-minded) requires learning how to say "No," and really meaning it. People will continually make requests, invite you to activities, expect you to meet a variety of needs, many of which may be worthwhile.

But the timing and circumstances, as well as one's priorities, must always be considered.

When confronting a request (or expectation), ask yourself the following questions:

Is this a real need—or a want?
Am I the person best suited to meet this need?
Am I the only person who can meet this need or request?
Does the requester have other untapped resources or
*   relationships?*
Has the requester become a continual drain on my time and
resources? (Is this a one-sided relationship?)
Is the person's need or request the result of his or her reckless
or wasteful lifestyle? (Could God be using this need to teach
accountability and foster positive change?)

Then, regardless of the individual and the circumstances, ask the Lord if the need/request is something He wants you to get involved in.

Sadly, staying focused on your goals and creative pursuits will require you to say "no" more often than "yes." You'll never realize your dreams if you're constantly trying to solve the world's problems. That said, God does expect us to "bear one another's burdens." (Gal 6:2) He doesn't want us to become so self-centered and self-absorbed that we become insensitive to the needs of those around us. After all, God has called each of His followers to serve. (Read Luke 22:27. We'll have more on this later.)

And yet, the Apostle Paul admonishes us, "Don't just think about your own affairs, but be interested in others, too, and in what they are doing." (Phil 2:4 TLB)

What's that? In the midst of giving and serving we can also look out for own hopes, dreams, and needs? Contradiction? No. But maintaining a sensible balance is essential.

SET BOUNDARIES AND PLEASE GOD

Staying focused is saying NO.
—Steve Jobs

DO YOU HAVE TROUBLE SAYING **"NO"?** Then you need to re-evaluate your priorities and learn to set boundaries. Again, we never want to get so focused and bent on our own agendas that we neglect the precious people God puts in our paths. But it's okay to tend to our own needs—and to pursue the dreams God has placed in our hearts. Balance is key. Unfortunately, many of us never mastered the balancing act. Instead we try to juggle too many tasks and requests; and generally end up dropping the ball (or several).

How do we maintain a balance?

Make time for yourself. Don't get greedy—but be kind to YOU. God expects us to give and to serve, but He's certainly NOT a taskmaster! In fact, He reassures us, "...The teaching that I ask you to accept is easy. The load I give you to carry is light." (Matt 11:30 ERV)

Stop feeling guilty. You cannot meet every need or live up to every expectation. This may come as a complete surprise to you, but we have it on good authority that you're only human. Besides, even our Lord Jesus Christ was careful to take time out from His mission on earth. He taught the truth, fed thousands, and healed the sick; but He also scheduled times of rest and recreation: dinner and fellowship with a friend; and retreats with His Heavenly Father. Jesus maintained a balance and never felt guilty about it. Why would He feel guilt? He was without sin. (2 Cor 5:21)

Learn to discern between a genuine need (that only you can meet) and a want (which can often be selfish, unreasonable, unnecessary, and even frivolous).

Regardless, ask yourself: "Is it time for someone else to step up to the plate." By not taking on more than your share, you can silently help your brothers and sisters to be accountable: "Help each other with your troubles. When you do this, you are obeying the law of Christ. If you think you are too important to do this, you are only fooling yourself. ...You must each accept the responsibilities that are yours." (Gal 6:2-5 ERV)

Distinguish between what's urgent versus what's important. President Dwight D. Eisenhower used this principle to guide him through a major war and two terms in the White House. He once stated, "What is important is seldom urgent and what is urgent is seldom important." Confusing?

Phil Libin, CEO of Evernote, explains: "Urgent tasks are tasks that have to be dealt with immediately. ...Things like phone calls, tasks with impending deadlines, and situations where you have to respond quickly. Responding to an email, when you have to do it, is usually an urgent task. Important tasks are tasks that contribute to long-term missions and goals. ...Things like that book you want to write, the presentation you'd like to make for a promotion, and the company you plan on starting."

Got that? No? Well then ... we have a coupon for a free bar of soap, but it expires at midnight. We need to go to the store RIGHT NOW! Please stop what you're doing and drive us—so we can pick up our free soap and save seventy-nine cents!

Recognize that there will always be demands on your time. Meet the ones which are truly important.

Set boundaries. Christian authors Dr. Henry Cloud and Dr. John Townsend explain in their book, *Boundaries: When to Say Yes, How to Say No*, "Just as homeowners set physical property lines around their land, we need to set mental, physical, emotional and spiritual boundaries for our lives to help us distinguish what is our responsibility and what is not."

We always want to be loving, accepting and helpful, but

there are some problems we can't fix, some needs we cannot or should not meet. And even when we can help solve things, we need to remember that we're only human and that our time and resources, as well as our physical and emotional energies, are limited. "If we fail to set some boundaries, people can even keep us from doing the work God wants us to do! So, drawing the line is not being selfish. To the contrary, the "...Goal of learning boundaries is to free us up to protect, nurture and develop the lives God has given us stewardship over."

Sad to say, life is full of needy people (some who are well-meaning, but also some who are just "takers") who will try to hog your time, abuse your willingness to help and serve, invade your privacy, manipulate your emotions, exploit your gifts—basically control your life! If allowed to, these people (especially the takers) can pull you way off course. Whether unintentionally or not, they can keep you from achieving your own everyday goals and, ultimately, fulfilling your dreams.

Realize that every time we say "yes" to something, we're automatically saying NO to something else. And, if you're a true servant and/or giver, don't be surprised when people start lining up at your door. The world desperately needs more Barnabas people who are willing to lend a helping hand. Therefore, once a friend, relative, or coworker discovers one, they'll want to "dip into the well" as many times as possible.

But nobody's well is inexhaustible. So, before yours runs completely dry, start setting limits. If we fail to set boundaries, someone will always have us jumping at their every whim and cry, and we'll end up constantly stressed out and frustrated with life. Eventually, we burn out!

On that note:

STOP TRYING TO BE A PEOPLE-PLEASER! You cannot be all things to all people. Nor can you ever hope to meet all their expectations. You're not here to win a popularity contest. And in regards to your life, dreams, and creative pursuits, you don't need the approval of men—so seek God's approval instead. The Apostle Paul writes, "I'm not trying to win the approval of people, but of God. If pleasing people were my goal, I would not be Christ's servant." (Gal 1:10 NLV)

Don't waste time wondering why someone doesn't want to hang out with you—or support you in the pursuit of your dreams. Obviously that person is not part of your destiny. Not to worry, because Jesus experienced the same thing. Many of the religious leaders of the day snubbed Him, but God supplied our Lord with plenty of genuine friends who fully supported Christ's mission on earth (and with no strings attached). Jesus never had to play politics or buy their devotion. He simply shared His great dream and stayed focused, thus changing the world forever. Let's do likewise!

"...I am single-minded: ...Reaching out
for the things that are ahead, with this goal in mind,
I strive toward the prize...."   (Phil 3:13-14 NET)

STAY MOTIVATED

LET'S PLAY A WORD GAME. What's our motive? Funny you asked.

According to one of our favorite reference works, *Noah Webster's American Dictionary of the English Language*, the 1828 Edition, the word *motive* means: "that which incites to action; that which determines the choice, or moves the will." Hey, times change, but why should the basic definitions of words? Webster's classic original version works just fine for us.

Of course, new words have a knack for finding their way into our lexicon, and for those we must resort to later editions of Webster's. Such is the case with the term motivate, which means "to provide with a motive; or to impel" (to urge or drive forward). Neat, huh?

Motive (and motivation) is the inner drive, impulse, or intention that leads a person to respond or act in a certain manner. It's the goal, stimulus, or incentive (often a reward) that inspires and encourages one to action. Motive is also the inducement that spurs one to increased activity and endurance.

Other words associated with motive and motivate include "drive" (the urge or force that moves people to greater heights of achievement) and "push" (as in "a good kick in the pants"). In the Disney movie *Marvel's The Avengers*, super-spy and fabulous facilitator Nick Fury assembles the world's greatest heroes to defend the earth against an alien attack; however, his would-be team is fragmented by colossal egos and conflicting viewpoints. One of the Avengers comments: "What are we, a team? No. We're a chemical mixture that makes chaos. We're ... we're a time-bomb."

But then something terrible happens: S.H.I.E.L.D. Agent Phil Coulson, the ultimate "nice guy" and everyone's best friend, is killed in action. Saddened and in despair, Nick Fury gathers his Avengers and tells them, "There was an idea ... to bring together a group of remarkable people to see if they could become something more. To see if they could work together when we needed them to, to fight the battles that we never could. Phil Coulson died, still believing in that idea—in heroes. Well, it's an old-fashioned notion."

Fury didn't despair for long, though, because the Avengers found, in the death of their lost friend Phil Coulson, a reason to put aside their differences, and arise to meet the challenges they faced. Agent Maria Hill, Fury's right-hand woman, asks her boss, Why the change? And Fury softly responds, "They needed a push."

We creators and dreamers usually need a similar push to keep us motivated and moving forward. Call it a "great cause" or a "higher purpose," but it's often a reason or an objective that's bigger than ourselves. Perhaps it's a vision so fabulous, so fantastic, that we'll never be able to pull it off without God's help. Perhaps it's the idea that what we're trying to accomplish will bless the people we love, our families, our communities, and our brothers and sisters in the Lord; a divine assignment God has chosen us to complete.

Everyone, in fact, needs a sense of purpose. But where does one turn to discover purpose? The search begins with the Creator of the Universe: God.

"It's not about you." That's how pastor and author Rick Warren begins his best-selling book The Purpose-Driven Life. "The purpose of your life," Warren writes, "is far greater than your own personal fulfillment, your peace of mind, or even your happiness. It's far greater than your family, your career, or even your wildest dreams and ambitions. If you want to know why you were placed on this planet, you must begin with God. You were born by His purpose and for His purpose."

The Apostle Paul writes, "God is always at work in you to make you willing and able to obey His own purpose." (Phil 2:13 GNT)

So how do I find my purpose?

"The search for the purpose of life has puzzled people for thousands of years," Warren states. "That's because we typically begin at the wrong starting point—ourselves. We ask self-centered questions like ... What are my goals, my ambitions, my dreams for my future? But focusing on ourselves will never reveal our life's purpose. The Bible says, "It is God who directs the lives of his creatures; everyone's life is in his power." [Job 12:10 GNT]

Rest assured, however, that a significant part of God's purpose is for each of us to become all we can be. "God has made us what we are [For we are his handiwork/workmanship/work of art]. In Christ Jesus, God made [created] us to do good works, which God planned in advance for us to live our lives doing." (Eph 2:10 EXB) Part of those good works are the creativity, hopes, and dreams we cherish.

But it all starts with God. He's the One who grants us the vision; who puts the dream into our hearts; and He's the One who bestows the gifts and talents necessary to achieve great things. "For in Him we live and move and have our being. As some of your own poets have said, 'We are His offspring.'" (Acts 17:28 MEV) Therefore, "Whatever you do, work heartily, as for the Lord and not for men...." (Col 3:23 ESV)

Got purpose? Pursue God. Then pursue your dreams with the help of God. "But first, be concerned about His kingdom and what has His approval. Then all these things will be provided for you." (Matt 6:33 GW)

Your Heavenly Father will become your personal "dream coach." Knowing He's on your side will keep you motivated ... so you can achieve great things.

"I am convinced and confident of this very thing, that He who has begun a good work in you will [continue to] perfect and complete it until the day of Christ Jesus [the time of His return]." (Phil 1:6 AMP)

"For God's gifts and his call are irrevocable." (Rom 11:29 NIV)

MEANING & MOTIVATION

WHAT MOTIVATES YOU? Ultimately, your worldview—your beliefs and core values, how these affect your view of life, God (the Creator of the Universe), and the part you play in the world—will shape your outlook and define your sense of purpose. These factors in turn will determine your level of motivation.

The first sentence of the Bible, the bestselling book of all time, states, "In the beginning God created heaven and earth." (Gen 1:1 GW) The first sentence of the Gospel of John makes a similar statement: "In the beginning the Word already existed. The Word was with God, and the Word was God." (John 1:1, 14 GW) The gospel then explains, "The Word became human and lived among us. We saw His glory. It was the glory that the Father shares with his only Son, a glory full of kindness and truth." (John 1:1,14 GW)

With these opening sentences, the Word of God is proclaiming (as we stated last session) that everything, including our hopes, goals, and creative pursuits, starts with God (and originates from Him). **He birthed each of us, as well as the dreams we hold**—and the gifts and talents necessary to achieve them.

What's your worldview? Are you here by accident—or by divine choice? What do you truly believe? Are you simply part of the matter forming the Universe—or a unique individual who matters to your Heavenly Father? Remember, you are what you think. According to King Solomon, the wisest man who ever lived, "As [a man] thinks within himself, so is he." (Prov 23:7 KJV)

An individual with a Judeo-Christian (Biblically-based) Worldview will have an awareness of God in every area, situation and circumstance. That person will know that he or she is not alone; that the Lord is with them and for them. Such a person also realizes that God is not some impersonal "force"; but rather a loving Heavenly Father who is personally interested and actively involved in every aspect of their life; who proclaims "I can never forget you! I have written your name on the palms of My hands" (Isa 49:16 GNT) a God who "even knows [numbers; counts] how many hairs are on your head." (Matt 10:30 EXB)

Hence, a person with a Judeo-Christian (Biblically-based) Worldview sees him- or herself, as well as others, as highly valued because **all people are created in the image of God.** (Gen 1:27) In fact, for those who place their trust in the Lord, "He has by his own action given us everything that is necessary for living the truly good life, in allowing us to know the One who has called us to Him, through His own glorious goodness. It is through Him that God's greatest and most precious promises have become available to us ... making it possible ... to share in God's essential nature." (2 Peter 1:4 PHILLIPS)

Whether you realize it or not, you are a one-of-a-kind masterpiece created by God. There's a spark of the divine within you; and you share God's creative DNA. We want you to be aware of these things—not so you can get cocky; but because these are the facts of life. These are the wonderful truths God reveals about you in His Word. Now, why would you (or anyone) want to dispute such things with your maker? Simply put, God doesn't make junk.

King David, the great psalmist, writes "Such knowledge is too wonderful for me; it is high; I cannot attain it. I praise you, for I am fearfully and wonderfully made. Wonderful are Your works; my soul knows it very well." (Ps 139:6,14 ESV) With this statement, David is expressing what he believes, his worldview.

Fellow dreamers and creators, **we're not part of a cosmic accident;** nor are we descendants of primordial slime. The Creature from the Black Lagoon is not your daddy! Again, we were created in the image of God and placed here by divine appointment. We have a destiny to fulfill within God's grand plan for humankind. He wants us to fulfill that destiny; to reach our full potential; to become everything He designed us to be.

WE MATTER! We have purpose and meaning. We're here to glorify God, to be a blessing to others, to touch lives with His love and to make a difference ... within our homes and communities, both now and for eternity. We accomplish this "mission"—at least in part—by seriously pursuing the dreams God's given each of us. How's that for a motivating force?

An individual with a Judeo-Christian Worldview must develop and maintain an orderly, focused, and God-centered life. This is the "one thing" the Apostle Paul spoke of. Make this your "one thing" and everything else will quickly fall into place. Why? Because a life with meaning this deep, with purpose this intense, produces people who are highly motivated; people who pursue their dreams all the way to the end, who create lasting works and achieve great things. People who live by the motto: "With humans, this is impossible. But with God, all things are possible." (Matt 19:26 DLNT)

Got dreams? What do you really believe? Here's what we believe. It's something Jesus Christ promised us: "The person who trusts Me will not only do what I'm doing but even greater things ... You can count on it." (John 14:12-14 MSG)

"We, of course, have plenty of wisdom to pass on to you once you get your feet on firm spiritual ground, but it's not popular wisdom, the fashionable wisdom of high-priced experts that will be out-of-date in a year or so. God's wisdom is something mysterious that goes deep into the interior of his purposes. You don't find it lying around on the surface. It's not the latest message, but more like the oldest—what God determined as the way to bring out His best in us, long before we ever arrived on the scene. The experts of our day haven't a clue about what this eternal plan is. ...That's why we have this Scripture text:

"No one's ever seen or heard anything like this, never so much as imagined anything quite like it—What God has arranged for those who love him." (1 Cor 2:8-10 MSG)

MAXIMUM MOTIVATION

WHERE DOES MAXIMUM MOTIVATION ORIGINATE?
Once you realize you were created by a loving God, who takes a personal interest in every aspect of your life, and an active role in the pursuit of your goals and aspirations, you'll quickly discover the motivation to always do your best; to become all God created you to be. Once you understand the value God places upon you (and all people), and realize that you share your Heavenly Father's creative DNA, you'll begin to see yourself in a positive, can-do light—which has the power to shift your pursuits into maximum gear.

Once you realize God put you here for a reason—to make a difference in your home, workplace, and community; and that your life truly matters, you'll experience a deep sense of purpose which will bring new meaning to everything you do. Once you understand that your God-given hopes and dreams are part of His divine assignment for your life, you'll discover the inner conviction that won't allow you to quit until you cross the finish-line. This is the mindset that generates maximum motivation to invent, innovate, and implement; to create wonderful works of lasting value; to achieve even the most seemingly impossible dreams.

Now, catch your breath. Before we continue, we need to be sure you know HOW to acquire the highly-motivating Judeo-Christian Worldview. (Hint: You can't grab one at a convenience store.)

The Judeo-Christian Worldview is a keen awareness of God, His identity, His position, His power, and His authority on earth; all of which leads to a God-centered life that puts Him (and His priorities) first; and which never excludes Him from any area or facet of life (including our goals, dreams, and aspirations). In a nutshell, the Judeo-Christian Worldview is (doh!) seeing the world from God's point of view.

Some of today's greatest creators and dreamers share this worldview; and history is filled with men and women who changed the world with their art, music, writings, research, accomplishments, discoveries, inventions—and willingness to please God and keep Him first. But ... you can't please God if you don't know what He wants.

HOW can we dreamers and creators acquire God's point of view? How can we gain His divine perspective on life, love, and everything in-between?

Our Heavenly Father shares His perspective in a long "love letter" called the Bible. It's the most influential book of all time. It's God's Instruction Manual for Life on Earth. And it's the greatest source of inspiration and motivation our world will ever know.

The Bible is also one continuous story: His story! It includes the "Old" Testament and the "New" Testament, but don't let these descriptors throw you. The Bible is a supernatural book and every last word of it is still relevant today. It reveals God's principles and practices—the wisdom and guidelines necessary to enjoy healthy relationships with our Heavenly Father, and with other people.

God's standards and guidelines are the absolute and eternal truth; and not up for debate. Every last word of it was issued by God Himself, through the divine agency of the Holy Spirit: "All Scripture is God-breathed [given by divine inspiration] and is profitable for instruction, for conviction [of sin], for correction [of error and restoration to obedience], for training in righteousness [learning to live in conformity to God's will, both publicly and privately—behaving honorably with personal integrity and moral courage]; so that the [people] of God may be complete and proficient, outfitted and thoroughly equipped for every good work." (2 Tim 3:16 AMP)

The phrase "God-breathed" explains the significance of the Holy Scriptures: breath signifies life or essence. Hence, God's Word is Living. And it embodies the very nature of the Creator of the Universe: love, hope, faith, and above all, truth. "The Word that God speaks is alive and full of power [making it active, operative, energizing, and effective]" (Heb 4:12 AMPC)

God's instruction manual is like a spiritual Swiss Army knife; it's useful in so many ways:

It's a moral and spiritual compass, pointing the way to God and eternal salvation;

A roadmap for our journey through life, helping us stay on the right path;

The Guidelines for handling every issue our world faces;

An energizing fountain of encouragement;

A source of comfort in times of trouble;

Daily spiritual food for growth and good "grooming"; as well as ...

The secret to Maximum Motivation (and so much more.)

If you're involved in some creative endeavor or pursuing a dream, you'll definitely need this multipurpose tool. "Don't leave home without it!" (Sorry, American Express card.)

Psalm 119:1-2 begins, "Blessed are those whose lives have integrity, those who follow the teachings of the Lord. Blessed are those who obey his written instructions. They wholeheartedly search for him." (GW) This particular passage of the Holy Scriptures is called a "wisdom psalm." It's main theme can be summarized thus: God's Word contains everything humankind needs to know.

In its entirety, Psalm 119 (depending on which translation you read) uses such terms as the Word; precepts; statutes or decrees; commandments; instruction or revelation; testimonies; and (one of our personal favorites) path to describe the Scriptures. We encourage you to read it—yes, all 176 verses—because it will bless you. It also provides some excellent pointers:

"Your Word I have treasured and stored in my heart,
That I may not sin against You." (Ps 119:11 AMP)

"I will never forget Your precepts, For by them You
have revived me and given me life." (Ps 139:93 AMP)

"Your word is a lamp to my feet
And a light to my path." (Ps 119:105 AMP)

"Establish my footsteps in [the way of] Your Word...."
(Ps 119:133 AMP)

"You are near, O Lord, And all Your
commandments are truth."   (Ps 119:151 AMP)

Fellow creators and dreamers, what are your aspirations in life? Got goals? Need some motivation? How about a little PUSH in the right direction? Then dive into the Bible. Start seeing things from God's perspective. Discover His plan for your life. Follow His guidelines. Claim His promises. Acquire and maintain a Judeo-Christian Worldview.

Embrace the Truth of God's Word—it's an endless, empowering wellspring for MAXIMUM MOTIVATION.

"So let's keep focused on that goal, those of us who want everything God has for us. If any of you have something else in mind, something less than total commitment, God will clear your blurred vision—you'll see it yet! Now that we're on the right track, let's stay on it." (Phil 3:15-16 MSG)

A MIND FOR MOTIVATION

There's vital connection between everything we've discussed thus far. It's the principle of RIGHT THINKING, and it's absolutely essential when it comes to reaching our goals and achieving our dreams. In fact, no one has ever accomplished anything worthwhile and of lasting value without "right thinking."

On the other hand, you may personally know someone with toxic "stinking thinking"—but you'll never hear or read about their achievements, because it's impossible to be a winner if you think you're a failure, or a problem-solver if you dwell on your problems. To paraphrase King Solomon, You are what you think. (Prov 23:7)

"Science is finally catching up with the Bible," according to Dr. Caroline Leaf, author of *Switch on Your Brain.* "Breakthrough neuroscientific research is confirming daily what we instinctively knew all along: What you are thinking every moment of every day becomes a physical reality in your brain and body, which affects your optimal mental and physical health."

Dr. Leaf continues, "These thoughts collectively form your attitude, which is your state of mind, and it's your attitude and not your DNA that determines much of the quality of life. ...If you realized how powerful your thoughts are, you would never think a negative thought."

Food for thought? Frankly, nothing saps your creativity, energy, and motivation more than a negative, faithless, I-can't-do-it mindset; a pessimistic attitude that chooses to see the worst in every person and situation—the "glass half-empty" and never half-full. Such stinking thinking is counterproductive. It's a dream-killer, and it can also lead to hopelessness, deep depression, shortened life-expectancy, and even suicide. (More on this later.)

Everyone has moments during which they lack motivation. But dreamers and creators can't afford to linger in these unproductive times. So, whenever you find yourself feeling unmotivated, evaluate your thoughts, and if necessary, adjust your attitude. Again, ATTITUDE IS EVERYTHING!

Your attitude (your state of mind; your perspective; your personal worldview of God, people and life in general) will determine specifically how you respond to challenges and, in general, your quality of life. You'll either live in victory, despite whatever disappointments, delays, obstacles and setbacks you encounter in the pursuit of your dreams; or you'll live in defeat, eventually giving up on your hopes and aspirations—and abandoning your dreams.

Scary? Yes. But the choice is completely in your hands ... uh, in your head, actually. "...Choose for yourselves this day whom you will serve ... but as for [us] we will serve the Lord." (Josh 24:15 AMPC)

The best way to stay motivated is to **develop a "mind for motivation": a positive, optimistic, faith-filled attitude;** one that truly believes the promises found in God's Word: "I have chosen the way of truth and faithfulness; Your ordinances have I set before me." (Ps 119:30 AMPC) We think the Message translation of Psalm 119:30-32 says it all:

"I'm feeling terrible—I couldn't feel worse! [i.e., NO MOTIVATION!] Get me on my feet again. You promised, remember? ...Train me well in your deep wisdom. Help me understand these things inside and out so I can ponder your miracle-wonders. ...Build me up again by your Word. Barricade the road that goes Nowhere; grace me with your clear revelation. I choose the true road to Somewhere, I post your road signs at every curve and corner. I grasp and cling to whatever you tell me.... I'll run the course you lay out for me if you'll just show me how."

Become positive, optimistic, and faith-filled by following these basic steps to Right Thinking:

Begin with God. As we've pointed out, EVERYTHING starts with God, including our goals and aspirations. Again, God gives meaning to every facet of life; but He also bestows to each of us special dreams and the gifts and talents needed to achieve them. Start with God, stay with God, and finish with God.

Fuel on God's Word. The Bible is the ultimate source of inspiration and motivation. Read it, study it, meditate on it. Accept its truths. Claim its promises. Keep "your tank topped off" with the scriptures and you'll be well fueled for the pursuit of your dreams—no matter how long the journey takes.

We can summarize these two vital steps with this verse: "Don't get off track, either left or right, so as to make sure you get to where you're going. And don't for a minute let this Book of The Revelation be out of mind. Ponder and meditate on it day and night, making sure you practice everything written in it. Then you'll get where you're going; then you'll succeed. Haven't I commanded you? Strength! Courage! Don't be timid; don't get discouraged. God, your God, is with you every step you take." (Josh 1:7-9 MSG)

Remember, you are what you think. Want to live in victory? If so, then think victorious thoughts—you'll find them in the Bible. Want to be motivated? Then devour God's Manual for Maximum Motivation.

"Here is a last piece of advice. If you believe in goodness and if you value the approval of God, fix your minds on the things which are holy and right and pure and beautiful and good. Model your conduct on what you have learned from me, on what I have told you and shown you, and you will find the God of peace will be with you." (Phil 4:8 PHILLIPS)

"...What happens when we live God's way? He brings gifts into our lives, much the same way that fruit appears in an orchard—things like affection for others, exuberance about life, serenity. We develop a willingness to stick with things, a sense of compassion in the heart, and a conviction that a basic holiness permeates things and people. We find ourselves involved in loyal commitments ... able to marshal and direct our energies wisely." (Gal 5:22-24 MSG) Hmm, all this sounds like maximum motivation!

MEET SOME
MORE MOTIVATORS

LET'S MEET SOME MORE MOTIVATORS: inspiration, passion, and enthusiasm.

Ever have a school teacher scold you for having your "head in the clouds"? Sure, daydreaming while you should be paying attention is counterproductive, but on the other hand, we all need dreams to be healthy and happy. Having a dream, a goal to accomplish, a project to complete, adds to our sense of purpose and self-worth—which in turn helps to give us hope. And we NEED hope! Without hope we lose spirit and eventually stop truly living. We lose our enthusiasm for life, and we find ourselves just going through the motions of everyday existence, shuffling along mindlessly like one of those zombies in Night of the Living Dead: no heart, no soul.

A physician once told Dr. Norman Vincent Peale a sobering truth: "I have actually seen people die for a lack of enthusiasm. of course, I can't write that on the death certificate, but the person without enthusiasm can lose the will to live." (*Enthusiasm Makes the Difference!*) This savvy physician had discovered the link between LIFE and ENTHUSIASM.

Forget milk. Got enthusiasm? "Enthusiasm is the electricity of life." (Gordon Parks, American filmmaker and civil rights advocate; 1912-2006)

Dr. Peale, the founder of the inspirational magazine *Guideposts*, wrote several volumes on the subject of this great motivator, but he managed to sum up the main idea in a single book title: Enthusiasm Makes the Difference!

"Enthusiasm is the all-essential human jet propellor," states Dr. Peale. "It is the driving force which elevates men to miracle workers. It begets boldness, courage, kindness, confidence; overcomes doubts. It creates endless energy, the source of all accomplishment."

Interestingly, the word enthusiasm means "full of God." Which shouldn't be too surprising, because after all, it is God who created each of us and then filled us with LIFE. So, to be full of enthusiasm, one must be full of God, the source of abundant life. (John 10:10)

ENTHUSIASM = FULL OF GOD = FULL OF LIFE

The secret to developing enthusiasm is a deep personal faith in the God who Created the Universe. Interestingly, the word enthusiasm is frequently associated with inspiration. Here's why: Enthusiasm is intense and eager interest or zeal in pursuit of a cause or objective; but enthusiasm is also defined as a divine source of supernatural inspiration.

The word inspiration means:

A breathing in, as of air in the lungs; a stimulus to creative thought or action; a prompting of something spoken, written, or accomplished; (in general) an inspiring influence; (specifically) a divine influence; a Theol: a God-sent supernatural source of guidance upon human beings, such as that resulting in the writing of the Scriptures.

To further clarify, enthusiasm is the excitement, energy and renewed interest we experience from a divinely-inspired flow of brilliance, creativity, or timely ideas.

This essential idea underscores just about everything we've covered thus far. We designed this course to inspire and motivate people to accomplish their goals, pursue their dreams, and fulfill their greatest hopes and aspirations. Learning what God has planned for you, and working toward that future, will generate intense enthusiasm, filling each new day with fresh and exciting possibilities. It's an intensely motivating experience.

"How do you go from where you are to where you wanna be? ...I think you have to have an enthusiasm for life. You have to have a dream, a goal. And you have to be willing to work for it." (Jim Valvano, NCSU Basketball coach and broadcaster; 1946-1993)

Enthusiasm comes from a positive, faith-filled, optimistic attitude toward life (the God-centered Judeo-Christian World-view we recently discussed). It is a supernatural byproduct of choosing to embrace God, love life, and always see the best in people and circumstances. Jesus said, "...I came that [My followers] may have and enjoy life, and have it in abundance [to the full, till it overflows]." (John 10:10 AMP)

Being enthusiastic is being fully alive. It's knowing that "the joy of the Lord is your strength and your stronghold." (Neh 8:10 AMP) Being enthusiastic is being grateful for each new day. It's never losing that wide-eyed sense of wonder and excitement for the world God created; or that child-like faith that still believes miracles happen everyday.

We have one more motivator to meet: **PASSION.** Read on.

ENTHUSIASM DEFINITELY MAKES A DIFFERENCE

TO BE ENTHUSIASTIC IS TO BE FULL OF LIFE (AND **GOD**). But where does enthusiasm come from? Well, where does life come from? Answer: the Creator of the Universe.

Everyone is born with enthusiasm. God builds this motivating force into each of us. That's why children are so curious, and seem to be endlessly fascinated by the simplest things in life; the whole world is fresh and new, and kids are excited to explore its many wonders.

Unfortunately, as we age we tend to view life as old and familiar territory. We become too sophisticated and cynical to appreciate the beauty of the world and the joy of life. Our viewpoint narrows, our possibilities become more limited, and worst of all, we lose our God-given enthusiasm.

No wonder people give up on their dreams! Aldous Huxley wrote, "The secret of genius is to carry the spirit of the child into old age, which means never losing your enthusiasm."

The good news is that we can reclaim our enthusiasm—if we're willing to reclaim the positive, appreciative, hopeful, and trusting attitude of childhood. In fact, God wants us to do just that: Jesus said, "...Unless you change your whole outlook and become like little children you will never enter the kingdom of Heaven. It is the man who can be as humble as [a] little child who is greatest in the kingdom of Heaven. (Matt 18:3 PHILLIPS)

How do kids keep such a good attitude? Hint: have you ever noticed how loving and affectionate children can be? That's because kids are brimming over with LOVE. So, if you want to rekindle your enthusiasm, then cultivate love. Love people, love life, love beauty, love the animals of the earth and the birds in the sky under which you move and breathe and have your being. Above all, love God. The person who loves God, life and people cannot help but be full of joy, curiosity and excitement for each new day. Such a man or woman sparkles on the outside because their love (the essence of God) is glowing on the inside; they bubble over with enthusiasm, too!

And to further clarify matters, being enthusiastic is being fully alive. It's knowing that "the joy of the Lord is your strength and your stronghold." (Neh 8:10 AMP) Being enthusiastic is being grateful for each new day. It's never losing that wide-eyed sense of wonder and excitement for the world God created; or that child-like faith that still believes miracles happen everyday.

Another word associated with enthusiasm is passion: *Intense excitement or drive; extreme and compelling emotion; strong love or affection; fervor or ardor; eagerness in the pursuit of an objective; great devotion or commitment (to an activity, a cause or a dream)*

Today passion and enthusiasm are often used interchangeably. If we want to be enthusiastic about something, we need to be passionate about it. Oprah Winfrey once stated, "Passion is energy. Feel the power that comes from focusing on what excites you." So, what are you passionate about?

Are you passionate about your dreams? Passion can keep you on track. Passion keeps you going when the road gets bumpy. Passion helps you make it all the way to the finish. And if you're NOT passionate about something, is it really worth pursuing? For the long haul? If you believe it is, then get passionate about it. Otherwise, discover your passion in life, and start pursuing that instead.

Got dreams? Need motivation? Return to the wonders of childhood. Fill your life with love. (In other words, *BE* loving.) Henry David Thoreau, another great poet, once observed, "None are so old as those who have outlived enthusiasm." In this case, however, "old" has nothing to do with age; it's a state of mind. We've seen twenty-year-olds who are "dying," and sixty-plus people who are full of life—still grateful, still amazed at God's goodness, still dreaming, and still enthusiastic.

By the way, we're never too old (or too young) to dream. In fact, God has promised us, "...I will pour out my Spirit upon all of you! [That's inspiration, folks.] ...Your old men will dream dreams, and your young men see visions." (Joel 2:28 TLB)

And enthusiasm is also ageless. "It's faith in something and enthusiasm for something that makes a life worth living." (Oliver Wendall Holmes, Sr., Physician, author and lecturer; 1809-1894)

And remember these motivators: **Inspiration** (a life directed by God) + **Passion** (a God-given dream) = **Enthusiasm** (full of God, Love, and a zest for life). The American poet and lecturer Ralph Waldo Emerson once wrote, "Nothing great was ever achieved without enthusiasm."

However, Dr. Norman Vincent Peale states it best: "...One of the greatest human needs of our time is a weapon to fight mediocrity, one that will teach us how to make use of zest and vitality and the creative forces buried deep within us. What we so desperately need is the capacity for exercising enthusiasm. ...For I truly believe that enthusiasm makes the difference between success and failure." (*Enthusiasm Makes the Difference*)

THE ELEMENTS OF ENCOURAGEMENT

May our Lord Jesus Christ himself and God our Father, who loved us and by His grace gave us eternal encouragement and good hope, encourage your hearts and strengthen you in every good deed and word.

—Romans 8:6 NIV

STAY ENCOURAGED

WE CAN'T STATE THIS ENOUGH: we creators and dreamers need to stay encouraged. If we fail to do so, the odds of realizing our hopes and aspirations will be stacked against us. Chances are, if we lack encouragement, we'll give up on the bright future God has planned for each of us.

But staying encouraged isn't easy. Actually, it's downright difficult. The long, winding path that leads to our goals and aspirations is often littered with obstacles and pitfalls; life has a way of throwing us a curve when we least expect it; and sometimes, our good intentions and best efforts can end in complete failure and utter disaster. At times like these, it can feel as though your whole world has crumbled around you.

Israel's greatest king, the poet and warrior David, faced just such a crisis, when it felt as though the ground had collapsed beneath his feet. What kept the Psalmist from toppling headlong into the pit of despair?

Close to a thousand years before the Lord Jesus Christ walked the earth in the form of a man, God anointed the Shepard David to be the King of His people Israel. But a big obstacle remained between David and the throne: a pain in David's neck, whose name was Saul.

Saul had been chosen—not by God, but by the Hebrews—to be the first king of the Jews. This might have worked out if Saul hadn't disobeyed God's will in a few key areas (and afterwards made up some really lame excuses for his disobedience).

God ultimately rejected Saul's kingship, and chose David to replace him. Saul, however, wasn't ready to step down, so he devoted all his time and energy to chasing David across the desert, in the hopes of capturing his successor—and executing him! (Life can be complicated.)

David was already an accomplished leader and warrior. He could have easily met Saul in battle and ended all his problems. But David didn't want to kill the people's "King"; so instead, he simply continued to elude Saul.

At one point, though, David grew tired of running. He and his army of 600 men, along with their families, sought refuge in the land of King Saul's enemies, the Philistines. It was a good idea: Saul soon lost interest in David, believing he'd never again see his rival; and David found favor with a Philistine leader named Achish.

Achish gave David and his men the city of Ziklag, where they could live in peace and raise their families. Who knows, they might have remained their, had Achish not given David an ultimatum. For over a year David maintained the appearance that he was serving the interests of the Philistines, by defeating several of the tribes that opposed them. But these warring tribes also opposed the Hebrews—so defeating them was actually in the best interests of God's people.

Again, David was enjoying the best of both worlds, until Achish announced that the Philistines were about to attack King Saul and Israel; and he expected David and his men to join him in the battle—against David's own people.

David probably broke out in a cold sweat. The time had come to "either put up or shut up," and it looked as though hc was going to bc forccd into a battle against his own people. Fortunately for David, Achish's military leaders didn't trust the allegiance of their Hebrew Ally. (Apparently at least some of the Philistines had discernment.)

David was ordered to take his army and go home to Ziklag. They would NOT be fighting in this battle. David was filled with relief, joy, and probably the satisfaction of having pulled a fast one on Achish. And then the bottom fell out of his world.

When David and his men reached Ziklag, they found the city deserted and in ruins. While they were away, the Amalekites (who hated the Philistines, the Hebrews, and just about everybody else) had taken captive all the women and children before burning the city to the ground.

The Bible states that in unison this band of tough, seasoned warriors suffered an emotional meltdown: "David and the people who were with him raised their voices and wept until they had no more strength to weep." (1 Sam 30:4 ESV) They were strangers in a strange land, cut off from the greater part of their people, and now they'd lost everything they had, their wives, their sons and daughters, even their homes.

David's grief was manifold. He, too, was suffering, having lost not one but two wives; and he also realized he'd failed the men who'd trusted him, who'd followed him across the desert into the land of their enemies. David's men were disillusioned and in deep despair. Their future seemed dim, and their great cause lost and buried in the ashes of Ziklag.

As if this were not enough, David then faced yet another devastating blow. The mighty men who had always trusted him, whom he had always relied upon, were ready to turn against him: "the men were thinking of stoning him; each man grieved bitterly over his sons and daughters." (1 Sam 30:6 NET)

Sooner or later we all face situations similar to what happened at Ziklag. Our "Ziklag"s may come in the form of demoralizing disappointments, setbacks, or false starts; unexpected obstacles, opposition, or challenges in life, particularly in the pursuit of our dreams. How do we endure our "Ziklag"s? Well, what did David do?

"David was greatly distressed; for the people spoke of

stoning him, because the soul of all the people was grieved …
but David encouraged himself in the LORD his God. (1 Sam
30:6 AKJV)

**The word *encourage* means to give support, hope,
confidence.** David gave himself these things. He found in
God what was necessary to keep from falling apart, to keep
going and not give up. Other translations correctly render the
word *encouraged* as strengthened: "David was very upset, for
the men were thinking of stoning him; each man grieved bitterly over his sons and daughters. But David drew strength
from the LORD his God." (1 Sam 30:6 NET)

We can learn from David's example. What do we do when
even our closest friends and relatives, our loved ones, abandon us and tell us to give up on our hopes and dreams?

What do we do when we get yet *another* rejection; another
"No!"; another door slammed in our faces? When we think
we've finally found the right person or door of opportunity, or
taken the right steps in the pursuit of a dream—only to learn
later, after expending considerable time, energy, resources,
and prayer, that we've reached just another dead end?

Do we throw in the towel and walk away in disgust? Or,
worse, do we sink into depression?

When we face our "Ziklag," we sincerely hope that instead
of giving up, we can stay encouraged, finding strength and
courage in the Lord—just as David did! And speaking of
David—the giant killer—what ever happened to the poor
fellow? Did his men stone him? Did he flee? Did he find
another wife? Did he get angry at God? Will we ever know? Of
course we will!

DAVID'S DIVINE SOURCE OF ENCOURAGEMENT

HOW MANY OF US CREATORS AND DREAMERS can remember having a "Ziklag" moment, when it seems like all of one's hopes and dreams have gone up in smoke—and that everything is lost? What does one do? The Bible states that, "David encouraged himself in the LORD his God." (1 Sam 30:6 AKJV)

Sounds good. But what exactly does this mean? Simply that David ran into the loving arms of the merciful God of Abraham, Isaac, and Israel—with whom the poet-warrior had developed a deep, personal relationship during the lonely days he'd spent in the fields tending his sheep. David did NOT flee from God in bitterness or blind hysterics, the way some people do when things go wrong. That's what David was trying to explain, when he composed Psalm 23; the most beloved and well-known poem ever written; the Shepherd's Psalm which continues to bring solace to new generations; a genuine source of encouragement for all creators and dreamers. Read it regularly and memorize it.

David also trusted God. He knew that Jehovah is faithful. Indeed, God had enabled David to slay the giant Goliath, to escape the murderous clutches of King Saul, and to survive—and even thrive—in the territory of his enemies, the Philistines.

So, when David faced his greatest challenge of all—his "Ziklag"—he reviewed his history with God and knew his Lord would see him through. God would not abandon him nor forsake him. And David's history lesson is one we need to learn: God is willing and able to see each of us through our own personal "Ziklag"s; He will not abandon us in our time of need. (Ps 94:14)

To the contrary, God is always at the front line in every

battle we face. And He's already planning our victory celebration, which is why we can proclaim with David, "You prepare a feast for me in the presence of my enemies. ...Surely your goodness and unfailing love will pursue me all the days of my life, and I will live in the house of the LORD forever." (Ps 23:5-6 NLT)

God called David "a man after My own heart." Not because David was "perfect" or super-spiritual, and certainly not because he never made mistakes. No, David made plenty of mistakes, but according to God, "he will do everything I want him to do." (Acts 13:22 NLT) And one of the main things God wants us to do, is to rely totally on Him.

That's what faith is all about, "and without faith it is impossible to please God." (Heb 11:6 NIV) David had unwavering faith in the face of overwhelming odds—which made him a "man after God's own heart." David's faith also took him from the lowly position of shepherd to the highest office in the land.

David had discovered the keys to victory and success in this life and the life to come: whenever he "messed up," whenever he was facing fearful obstacles and challenges, or suffered a crushing defeat—the "Ziklag"s of life—David immediately *(1) consulted his Lord, by praying (talking) to God.* And then? David simply *(2) trusted his Lord to see him through.*

Fellow dreamers and creators, when facing a "Ziklag"—an impossible situation, a difficulty, a betrayal, a setback, a closed door, yet another rejection, or any major disappointment that leaves you feeling as though the bottom has dropped out beneath your world—cry out for help to your Heavenly Father. Do it immediately. Do it before you say or do anything else.

Get God's perspective on the situation. Seek God's instruction on how to handle it. Then have faith that He will see you through.

Actually, learn to do these things daily, as a matter of routine practice, no matter how great or small your problems seem. God cares about it all. Remember, relying on Him makes our Lord happy. (Refer back to what we've covered thus far—because these truths are vital to success in life and the pursuit of dreams.)

To "encourage oneself in the Lord" also means: Being willing to stand alone, without human help or encouragement. Face it, sometimes the people closest to us, our immediate family, our best friends, even those who previously stuck by us through thick and thin (the way David's "Mighty Men of Valor" had previously stuck by him) may abandon you when you encounter your "Ziklag"!

There's truth to the old saying, "When the going gets tough, the tough get going"—often leaving us alone on life's battlefields. In regards to our goals and dreams, disappointments, betrayals, and a general lack of support are all part of the territory. Sometimes, for a variety of reasons, people will refuse to help you. Sometimes they're just too busy. Sometimes they get caught up in their own world. And sometimes, they actually want to be there for you, but they can't, due to circumstances beyond their control (such as illness or a family obligation).

Still, whatever the reasons, there will be times when the people you were counting on the most, aren't there for you; when you must face your problems alone; when there's absolutely no one to support you except your Lord. You may cry out for help, but even your loved ones may fail to hear your cries, because they're preoccupied; or, then again, they may simply turn a deaf ear to your needs.

It's possible that these "silent" people won't even have an encouraging word for you. Nothing. Nada. Zilch. Zero. Too bad.

Depressing? Yes, and that's what can make a "Ziklag" so devastating. The good news is, our Heavenly Father always hears our cries. He's never too busy for us, and He promises, "I will never fail you. I will never abandon you." (Heb 13:5 NLT)

Facing a tough situation? Follow David's example: Ask God for help and make the same positive confession he made: "I _____ (insert your name) encourage myself in You, Lord; I find my strength in You, my God." (1 Sam 30:6) You'll soon learn—for those times when your circumstances appear bleak, or when people let you down—that you can stand alone when you must (but always WITH God by your side). You'll have victory over every "Ziklag" you encounter in life, along the road to fulfilling your dreams!

BE A FIRST RESPONDER

THROUGHOUT THIS JOURNEY CALLED LIFE, as we pursue our dreams, we will face many "Ziklag" situations. If we're going to reach our goals and fulfill our visions for the future—if we want to become "giant killers" and history-makers—we'll need to respond to the "Ziklag"s of life the same way King David did.

A "Ziklag" (as previously discussed) is an overwhelming challenge or problem, an extreme obstacle or crisis. It's a daunting set of circumstances, an impossible situation, or any major storm we may face in life. Depending on your emotional resilience (or lack thereof) your Ziklag could range from a life-changing problem to which you can see no possible solution, to something more common to creators and dreamers, such as another rejection, a closed door, a setback, a betrayal, or simply a lack of support and encouragement from the people you were counting on the most.

A "Ziklag" is any life event that leaves you feeling abandoned, at the end of your rope, and possibly a little hopeless—as though your world is crumbling, and the bottom has suddenly dropped out beneath you. You can encounter a "Ziklag" event just around the corner and without any warning. But some "Ziklag" events are slow-burn situations that have been building for months or years—like the proverbial "last straw that breaks the camel's back" (a dream that's taking far too long to fulfill, a creative pursuit with far too many rejections, or a relationship or venture with one too many difficulties).

As discussed in our last session, we can respond to these events the way David did, who "encouraged himself in the Lord" and came through his "Ziklag" victorious (1 Sam 30:6) Or we can accept defeat—and watch our dreams go up in smoke. "Ziklag" events are inevitable, but the outcomes are up to us. Each of us essentially has only two responses to a "Ziklag" event:

Disconnect: Run away from God; get angry at Him (and those closest to us); and perhaps even blame God for our misfortunes. The end result is bitterness, emotional turmoil, and a total disconnect from the divine source of our strength and creativity. This defeatist attitude (and resultant disconnection with God) is the natural (unspiritual and unbiblical) response to adversity. This is how David's warriors responded when their world had seemingly collapsed. Admitting defeat and abandoning all hope and reason, out of ideas and looking for a convenient target (someone at whom they could vent their anger and frustration), they wanted to stone to death their leader, David.

Quick Connect: David was just as distraught as his men. He, too, had suffered a devastating blow. But he chose the supernatural, biblical response to the events at Ziklag—and he wasted no time doing so. He immediately ran to God. And he immediately prayed. In other words, David talked to God, shared his frustrations with his Creator, and got instructions on how to handle the situation, and what to do next.

David didn't disconnect from God the problem-solver, the storm-stopper, the miracle worker, the God of the impossible, "who is able, through His mighty power at work within us, to accomplish infinitely more than we might ask or think." (Eph 3:20 NLT) As a result, God was able to give His servant a plan of action, a strategy that enabled David and his men to rescue their families and recover all they had lost—and then some! (1 Sam 30:18-20)

Like the Psalmist, David, we too must be spiritual "first responders": people whose first (and rapid) response to a "Ziklag" event is to run to the loving, strong and capable arms of our Heavenly Father; who automatically talk to God and utter a quick and simple prayer—Help me, Lord!; who seek His guidance and direction before doing or saying anything else—not just in times of crisis, but each and every day.

King David wrote, "O God, thou art my God; early will I seek thee...." (Ps 63:1 KJV) God wants us to seek His help in every matter, not just the "big stuff." And He wants this action to be our first response to every situation: "Call to me, and I will answer you, and show you great and mighty things, which you know not." (Jer 33:3 AKJV)

We can overcome any "Ziklag" event—and realize our dreams—as long as we stick to this course of action, being first responders to the Lord, because "God ... always causes us to triumph in Christ...." (2 Cor 2:14 AKJV)

Respond to God as David did, and He will respond to you. Here's what He'll tell you: "I am the LORD, the God of all the peoples of the world. Is anything too hard for Me?" (Jer 32:27 NLT) Of course not!

"Nothing is impossible with God." (Luke 1:37 NLT)

"For no word from God will ever fail." (Luke 1:37 NIV)

SOME SECRETS FOR STAYING ENCOURAGED

HERE ARE SOME PRACTICAL, Biblically-based and time-tested tips to help creators and dreamers stay encouraged while they're waiting upon the Lord for the answer to a prayer; for a divine connection; for a door to open; for a "Barnabas"; for their breakthrough; and ultimately, for the realization of their hopes and dreams. Most of these were previously discussed, but because staying encouraged is so important, we want to review them and admonish readers to implement them. Let's review:

Be a "first responder" (like King David), and always run *to* God in the midst of a storm—not *away* from Him. Immediately connect with the source of strength and inspiration. Don't panic and disconnect. Here are the most important spiritual steps:

Train your mind to think like a "giant-killer" and a history-maker. "For as [a person] thinks within himself, so he is [in attitude and behavior]." (Prov 23:7 NASB) In other words, you are what you think. In fact, our thoughts affect everything. They shape our attitude (how we view life) and determine how our day will go—and how we'll handle any challenging situations that arise (including those daunting "Ziklag" events).

Will you be a victor or victim? Well, what do you think? No, literally, what's in your head?

Our thoughts and resultant attitudes will determine our quality of life. They are the deciding factors between success and failure, between reaching our goals and realizing our dreams ... or NOT!

So, make up your mind! (Pun intended.) Decide whether you will live in victory or defeat. This is easier said than done, of course. Living in fear and defeat comes natural to most people, because they never do anything to change their faith-less, hopeless, uninspired, negative, pessimistic, "what-can-go-wrong-will-go-wrong" way of thinking.

On the other hand, having the right mindset—a faith-filled, positive, optimistic, "I-can-do-all-things-through-Christ" attitude (Phil 4:13)—requires training, discipline, and a "proper diet"! Remember the saying, "Garbage in, garbage out"? We must be careful (and mindful) of what we feed our brains, which is why the Apostle Paul states, "Set your mind and keep focused habitually on the things above...." (Col 3:2 AMP)

It's essential for creators and dreamers (that's everyone, really) to **learn to replace any naturally-occurring negative and discouraging thoughts with positive and uplifting ones.** The best way to do this is to get into God's Word, the Handbook for Life, the Instruction Manual for Overcomers, the greatest source of inspiration and encouragement on the entire planet!

Hyperbole? King David, the quintessential giant-killer and history-maker frequently speaks of the inherent power of God's Word. In the longest psalm in the Bible, David describes the miracle-working wonders of God's principles, precepts, and wisdom:

> "Your word is like a lamp that guides my steps,
> a light that shows the path I should take."
> (Ps 119:105 ERV)

> "Establish my footsteps in [the way of] Your Word;
> Do not let any human weakness have power over me...."
> (Ps 119:133 AMP)

> "You are my hiding place and my shield.
> My hope is based on Your Word." (Ps 119:114 NOG)

> "How I love your instruction!
> It is my meditation all day long." (Ps 119:97 CSB)

> "I will never forget Your precepts,
> For by them You have revived me and given me life."
> (Ps 119:93 AMP)

Wow! Precious stuff, right? Which is why the psalmist also declares, "Your word I have treasured and stored in my heart, That I may not sin against You." (Ps 119:11 AMP)

Of course, David didn't have the full resources to which we have access. He had only a large portion of the Old Testament, the writings that foreshadow the coming of the Jewish Messiah, Yeshua (Jesus). We're blessed with an extra helping of God's Word, the New Testament. And for the record, it's all one complete narrative about the nature of God and His creation and ultimate salvation of humankind. "All Scripture is given by inspiration of God and is profitable for doctrine, for reproof, for correction, for instruction in righteousness...." (2 Tim 3:16 KJ21)

In order to stay encouraged, read and study God's Word, the Bible, each and everyday. Meditate on it. Memorize it. Quote it and claim its promises. "Finally, believers, whatever is true, whatever is honorable and worthy of respect, whatever is right and confirmed by God's Word, whatever is pure and wholesome, whatever is lovely and brings peace, whatever is admirable and of good repute; if there is any excellence, if there is anything worthy of praise, think continually on these things [center your mind on them, and implant them in your heart]." (Phil 4:8 AMP)

Doing this is how we flush out the negative, stinking thinking of failure and defeat. It's also the surest way to develop the mind of a winner and be victorious in any "Ziklag" event. It's the key to pursuing and realizing your dreams, and sticking to your creative endeavors—even when the going gets rough!

"This Book of the Law shall not depart out of thy mouth, but thou shalt meditate therein day and night, that thou mayest observe to do according to all that is written therein. For then thou shalt make thy way prosperous, and then thou shalt have good success."   (Josh 1:8 KJ21)

DON'T LOOK DOWN!

IT'S NOT AN EASY TRUTH TO ADMIT, but whenever we get discouraged, it's often because we've wandered into the "realm of stinking thinking." We've allowed ourselves to focus on the problems of life, the challenges, the storms, the "Ziklag" events—instead of on the solutions; and as a result, our thoughts have grown dark, negative and pessimistic.

Problems can be solved, and challenges overcome. The storms of life will eventually pass, and as we previously stated, rainbows of promise tend to follow these periods of "foul weather."

The Bible records one such occasion of foul weather (literal), when the Lord's disciples were crossing the Sea of Galilea. Their "boat ... was a long way from the land, beaten by the waves, for the wind was against them." (Matt 14:24 ESV) We'd like to think these twelve men took the storm in stride, calm, cool and collected. But apparently this temporarily doubting dozen gazed into the blackness of the violent waves and declared, "Oh look, we're all gonna die." In fact, their nerves were so on edge that, when Jesus came to their rescue—walking across the water (a quite natural thing for Him to do)—His disciples were terrified.

Jesus had to encourage them, "Don't be afraid. Take courage. I am here!" (Matt 14:27 NLT) And what followed is both amazing and sobering. The Apostle Peter got out of the boat and started walking toward his Lord ... on the surface of the water ... without sinking ... defying the law of gravity ... so eat your heart out, Sir Isaac Newton!

Alas, Peter's impossible feat was momentary. As long as he kept his eyes on Jesus, and not the heavy waves, the apostle was able to tread water. But when Peter took his focus off God, when he started paying more attention to the storm than the Storm-stopper, the disciple began to sink. (Matt

14:30) Fortunately Jesus was right there with Peter, in the midst of the storm, and He kept the apostle from drowning from a lack of "I-can-do-all-things-through-Christ" faith.

We can't really blame Peter for allowing the foul weather to frighten him. Storms are scary. So are heights. Which is why movie heroes, when rescuing people from high places, always utter the precaution, "Don't look down!" Good advice. If we concentrate on the problems and perils of life, our faith can falter and we can freeze up, unable to think soundly and act correctly.

Besides, as in the case of Peter, God is always with us in the midst of every storm we weather. In every challenge we encounter, in every "Ziklag" event we face, the Lord is there, encouraging us through His Word, so that we won't sink into depression and despair. Question is, are we focusing on Him, or what's going on around us and in our lives?

Creators and dreamers (that would be all of us): staying "encouraged in the Lord"—just as David did in Ziklag (1 Sam 30:6)—is dependent on our perspective in life. But we can choose how we view the world, circumstances, problems, and other people. Again, we have a decision to make, between the natural and the supernatural.

The natural response to any problem is to focus on the difficulties involved, the reasons ("Why me?"), the regrets ("How could I allow myself to get into this mess!"), and the what-ifs ("What if I can't fix this problem?") If we choose the natural response to problems, and hence, adopt a strictly natural perspective, we'll usually get discouraged and *stay* discouraged. And that's a real downer!

So don't look down—and keep your chin up!

"Why are you cast down, O my soul? And why are you disquieted within me? Hope in God; For I shall yet praise Him, The help of my countenance and my God." (Ps 42:11 NKJV)

LOOK UP!

MOSES SENT A SMALL GROUP OF MEN into Canaan, to reconnoiter and get the lay of the land. When the men returned, all but two of the scouts (Joshua and Caleb) were in despair. Why? The country God had promised the Hebrews was just as the Lord had described it, a "land flowing with milk and honey" (Deut 31:20 NIV)—and grapes so big that it took two men to carry a single cluster. However, the men who saw these wondrous blessings with their own eyes, also saw huge obstacles. And unfortunately, it was the obstacles they chose to focus on: "The land we traveled through and explored will devour anyone who goes to live there. All the people we saw were huge. We even saw giants there.... Next to them we felt like grasshoppers...!" (Num 13:23; 32-33 NLT)

Giants? Okay, that *is* an obstacle. But life, as well as the pursuit of every dream and creative endeavor, has its share of obstacles. When we continually focus on these obstacles, we eventually acquire a negative, pessimistic mindset. We get a victim mentality, a fatalistic attitude, and then we really start focusing on—and magnifying—every problem that comes our way. Suddenly every little difficulty, every little challenge seems way too big to cope with.

This is known as a **"grasshopper complex"**—as in, "I'm just a tiny grasshopper, and life is just one big shoe waiting to stomp on me!" This is precisely how Moses' "advance party of spies" viewed the circumstances of their "promised land." These men focused on the perils and problems inherent in claiming their new home—and returned terrified. They were so focused on the *downside* of life that they failed to see the *upside*.

So, fellow creators and dreamers, do we look *down* and dwell on the negative? Do we allow the problems and pitfalls of life to keep us from pursuing and receiving God's blessings?

Or do we look *up*, to our Father in Heaven, who has made us "more than conquerors"? (Rom 8:37 NIV)

"Looking up" is the supernatural response to life's problems and challenges. When we do, we begin to see ourselves as God sees us: as overcomers and achievers, who stay encouraged because we remain full of Love, Hope, and Faith. "...If we have trouble or calamity, or are persecuted, or hungry, or destitute, or in danger, or threatened with death ... despite all these things, overwhelming victory is ours through Christ, who loved us." (Rom 8:35-37 NLT)

When we focus on God's infinite love, mercy, and faithfulness, and His abilities and resources, we get a victor mentality: an optimistic, courageous, "I-can-do-all-things-though-Christ" mindset. In fact, we'll actually begin to look for and welcome challenges, the way Caleb did! Remember Caleb? He was one of the two scouts who returned with a POSITIVE report: "Giants? Yeah, but we can take 'em down!"

Caleb chose to focus on God's power and promises—not on the perils and problems—and as a result, he was still slaying giants well into his eighties! Read his testimony: "I was forty years old when Moses ... sent me ... to explore the land of Canaan. I returned and gave an honest report, but my brothers who went with me frightened the people from entering the Promised Land. For my part, I wholeheartedly followed the LORD my God. ...Today I am eighty-five years old. I am as strong now as I was when Moses sent me ... and I can still ... fight as well as I could then. So give me the hill country that the LORD promised me. You will remember that as scouts we found [giants] living there in great, walled towns. But if the LORD is with me, I will drive them out ... just as the LORD said." (Josh 14:7-12 NLT)

Clearly, Caleb was looking up, to the power and promises of God, and not down at his problems. What's your focus today? Are you magnifying your difficulties? Or are you magnifying the miracle-working God of the impossible? We hope it's the latter: the supernatural choice of giant-slayers and history-makers. He is the solution to every problem, the answer to every challenge, the provider of every need, "the God who is able, through His mighty power at work within us, to accomplish infinitely more than we might ask or think" (Eph 3:20 NLT) —including our most cherished dreams and aspirations!

Fellow creators and dreamers, adjust your focus and get a divine perspective on life. Read, study, and meditate on the Word of God. Quote it and claim its promises. And LOOK UP!

"I look up toward the mountains. Where can I find help? My help comes from the Lord.... He will not let you fall. Your guardian will not fall asleep. Indeed, the Guardian of Israel never rests or sleeps." (Ps 121:1-4 GW)

COUNT YOUR BLESSINGS!

MAINTAIN A CAN-DO, GIANT-SLAYER, history-maker mindset —by keeping a divine perspective and choosing to focus on the solution to the challenges we face (and not the problems): the God of the impossible (Luke 1:37) "who is able to do immeasurably more than all we ask or imagine." (Eph 3:20 NIV) Here are some additional strategies for staying encouraged.

Develop an Attitude of Gratitude.

If you're asking yourself, "What do I have to be thankful for?" then you really need to implement this. No matter what we're facing, no matter what's wrong in our lives, we can at least thank God for life itself. In fact, each new morning is a gift from God. So is the sun on a warm day. And for what it's worth, so is the rain on a chilly day! Unfortunately, people seem to find it easier to keep track of the bad stuff: what we can't be, what we can't do, what we don't have. In fact, some people lie awake at night taking inventory of every deficiency, failure, slight, and unfulfilled need.

In the 1954 musical *White Christmas*, Bing Crosby offers some sound advice when he croons a wonderful Irving Berlin song:

When I'm worried and I can't sleep,
I count my blessings instead of sheep;
And I fall asleep … Counting my blessings.
When my bankroll is getting small,
I think of when I had none at all;
And I fall asleep … Counting my blessings.

Count your blessings. Like most of the strategies we've discussed, counting one's blessings—and not one's "curses"

—is a matter of choice ... fueled by one's perspective in life. But it's a choice God wants each of us to make. The Apostle Paul writes, "...In every situation [no matter what the circumstances] be thankful and continually give thanks to God; for this is the will of God for you in Christ Jesus." (1 Thess 5:18 AMP) Please note the first word of Paul's advice: *IN*. The apostle is not asking us to thank God *FOR* adverse circumstances; however, he is, in essence, asking us to remember God's faithfulness when we find ourselves in the midst of such circumstances.

Be thankful for the "little things" in life. Truly appreciating, and being thankful for, the simplest pleasures of life is a practical way to develop a grateful heart. The little things (which, in truth, are actually pretty tremendous) can include: a gorgeous sunset on a quiet beach ... and the eyes to see it; a bird cheerfully chirping in the backyard ... and the ears to hear it; finding a good parking spot, right in front of the store ... and strong legs to hoof it, when we don't!; the cordial conversation and comforting companionship of family and good friends; not to mention food on the table, clothes on our backs, and a roof over our heads.

King David writes, "Praise the Lord, my soul, and never forget all the good He has done: He is the One who forgives all your sins, the One who heals all your diseases, the One who rescues your life from the pit, the One who crowns you with mercy and compassion...." (Ps 103:2-4 GW) David was a giant-slayer and history-maker, a man after God's own heart. (Acts 13:22) The Psalmist was also a creator and a dreamer, who knew adversity. But he stayed encouraged because he remained grateful for all his Lord had done—and would do in the days and years to come.

David's advice to us for staying encouraged: Don't forget all the wondrous things wrought by the hand of God. Besides, no one—including God—wants to be taken for granted. We should appreciate and always remember to thank Him, not just when He meets a need or blesses us with the answer to a prayer, but also for the privilege of knowing the Creator of the Universe and being able to serve Him.

And speaking of developing a grateful heart, being appreciative and thankful should extend into our earthly relationships, as well—especially in marriage. We should be mindful of the "little things" our friends and family do, which make life more enjoyable. Did mom make breakfast for you—the way she has for years? Did you thank her and tell her how much you appreciate her? Did dad fix your bike or give you money to buy candy? Did you tell him he's the greatest?

On the flip side: Hello, men. Nothing encourages a hard-working gal like a thoughtful card or an inexpensive "fun bunch" of flowers—for no special reason! Hello, ladies! Lovingly preparing a meal featuring his favorites can help lift his spirits. Any kind of "just because" deed or blessing goes a long way toward helping others stay encouraged. And we are called to "encourage one another daily." (Hebrew 3:13 NIV)

Still feeling a bit overwhelmed? Here's an additional strategy that goes hand-in-hand with counting your blessings and being grateful:

HIT THE PAUSE BUTTON. Whenever you find yourself getting down and mopey, especially regarding your dreams and creative pursuits, it's time to shift gears, take a break, catch your breath—and pause to reflect.

Our goals and dreams are important, but don't overdo it. **Stop once in awhile to smell the roses!** (We mean this both literally and figuratively!) Continue to pursue your dreams but make frequent stops to take in all the wonderful sights, sounds, and people you encounter along the journey! Don't let life pass you by as one big blur!

Change your routine! When you find yourself constantly in "fight mode"—then you're ready for some much needed R&R. Take a break from whatever it is that you're constantly doing or pursuing. Get out and do something fun. Give your goals a rest and go shopping. Have an ice cream cone—with sprinkles! Curl up with a good book or watch a fun movie ... and even take a nap!

Get outdoors and enjoy God's creation. Go for a walk in the park or on the beach. Find a nature trail. Take in a sunset (or a sunrise)! Norman Vincent Peale once stated, "A walk a day keeps the gloomies away!"

Consider how far you've come, not how far you've still to go; what you've accomplished, not what you've yet to achieve; and the fact that you're still in the game! Yes, despite all the odds, despite all you've been through—*you're still standing!*

Above all, start focusing on what you have, not what you want. Again, count your blessings: if you enjoy good health, have running hot water, a roof that doesn't leak, and something good to eat, then you are indeed successful and blessed.

And *please* don't forget to thank God for all He's done and yet to do. After all, He's given you the gift of eternal life! Develop a genuine attitude of gratitude. To quote Houston Pastor Joel Osteen, one of the greatest encouragers of our time, "The seeds of discouragement cannot take root in the soil of a grateful heart."

So count your blessings!

"I said to the Lord, 'You are my Lord.
All the good things I have come from You.'"   (Ps 16:2 NLV)

AVOID EYE POLLUTION!

STAYING ENCOURAGED IS A MATTER of keeping a divine perspective, having an attitude of gratitude, and focusing on the good and not the bad: the solution and not the problem; the storm-stopper (God) and not the storm. We especially don't want to focus on anything that will lead us to "stinking thinking." This includes "eye pollution."

In today's world we are constantly bombarded with unsettling and unwholesome imagery. More and more, movies and television shows tend to focus on gory violence and carnality: what we like to call "severed heads and unmade beds." Even at the grocery checkout we're assaulted by the unsavory covers of the tabloids, boasting outrageous headlines and highlighting the latest gossip, rumors, and scandals.

This eye pollution actually appeals to the baser side of human nature, which is why carnival sideshows featuring snake-charmers and bearded ladies were once popular attractions. But such things are not uplifting, edifying, or encouraging. In fact, these lurid and debased offerings can easily lead people into the realm of stinking thinking. Besides, this stuff fails the "Philippians 4:8 Test"[3]—big time!

On the other hand, focusing on positive, uplifting, and wholesome fare helps to raise our spirits and keep us encouraged.

You've probably realized by now that we love movies! We can't count the number of times the Lord has used these modern-day parables to encourage and motivate us. And

---

[3] Philippians 4:8 admonishes us: "Finally, brothers and sisters, whatever is true, whatever is noble, whatever is right, whatever is pure, whatever is lovely, whatever is admirable—if anything is excellent or praiseworthy—think about such things." (NIV)

we're not just talking about faith-based films, either. We've already mentioned *Rocky*, *Chariots of Fire*, and *The Avengers*; but we also enjoy all the superhero movies in which the heroes overcome overwhelming odds, defeat the bad guys, and save the day.

The Lord of the Rings trilogy is another favorite: it's a wonderful allegory of spiritual warfare, in which good triumphs over evil. And how about all those old WWII movies? The Allied forces prevail, John Wayne gets to swagger, and Hitler and the Nazis get their just desserts. And lest we forget, the numerous inspiring movies and documentaries focusing on the struggle and miraculous survival of the Jewish people, and the glorious rebirth of the nation of Israel.

Yes, movies comprise a powerful medium that can lift us up and inspire us to reach higher and never give up. Something we all need, but especially important to dreamers and creators. This power comes in part from the strong impression and sheer impact such vivid imagery can make. Which leads us to another truth: the eyes are the windows to the soul.

This oft-spoken truth is a paraphrasing of the Words of Christ: "The eye is the lamp of the body. You draw light into your body through your eyes, and light shines out to the world through your eyes. So if your eye is well and shows you what is true, then your whole body will be filled with light. But if your eye is clouded or evil, then your body will be filled with evil and dark clouds." (Matt 6:22-24 VOICE) What the Lord is communicating here is that what we take in—through our eyes—affects our thoughts, attitudes, and wellbeing. In essence, we are what we constantly view; or, *garbage in, garbage out!*

The long-suffering Job also has some good eye-advice. Job is the poster child for adversity, and yet, the Lord signified him as a righteous man. Although Job lost everything, he kept his faith and trust in God, even though he didn't understand the "why" of his trials. For those unfamiliar with Job's adventures, we'll share the end of his story. It's really quite simple: God restored everything Job had lost—and more. (Job 42:10,12)

Job said: "I have made a covenant (agreement) with my

eyes...." (Job 31:1 AMP) In other words, he made a commitment to God and to himself, that he would not view worthless and unwholesome things. It was a decision that served Job well.

We're certainly grateful for Christian television and programming designed to inspire and educate us. But there are many other shows which ultimately point us to God, including a host of animal and nature programs. Like Isaiah said, "The whole earth is filled with his glory." (Isa 6:3 GW)

If you want to stay encouraged during the sometimes long and winding pursuit of your goals and dreams, be careful what you watch, or stare at while you're in the checkout line. Whether it's on TV, at the movies, on the Internet, or along the street, use some discretion. Take stock of what's illuminating (or darkening) your thoughts through the windows of your eyes. Follow Job's example, and remember these additional promises:

"...The eyes of the Lord move to and fro throughout the earth that He may strongly support those whose heart is completely His." (2 Chr 16:9 NASB)

"...The eyes of the Lord are on the righteous and his ears are attentive to their prayer...." (1 Peter 3:12 NIV)

"And God will wipe away every tear from their eyes...."
(Rev 21:4 NKJV)

FACE THE MUSIC!

IN THE MEDICAL PROFESSION there are Eye, Ear, Nose and Throat specialists. This affiliation with all four facial features may at first seem unusual, but these body parts are actually linked. Previously we discussed the important role our eyes—the windows to the soul—play in staying encouraged. We warned our fellow creators and dreamers to avoid "eye pollution," which can affect our thoughts and attitudes, and if unchecked, can kill our creativity and derail our dreams.

The ears also play a vital role in our ability to stay encouraged. Through them we hear sounds, music, and receive information that allows us to verbally communicate and fully enjoy the world around us. Question is, what are we listening to? What are we "tuning" our ears to?

What type of music is pouring into our brains? Is it positive, wholesome, and uplifting? Again, would it pass the "Philippians 4:8 Test"? Relax, we're not suggesting that people should only listen to "spiritual" music. (Christian, gospel, praise & worship, etc.) We do, however, recommend that it comprise a large portion of the music you routinely listen to—for some very good reasons we'll discuss in our next session.

Just as with mainstream movies, our Lord can and does use all types of music to minister to people. In fact, if we're in tune with God and His purposes, we can see His hand and "hear" His voice in just about everything, from the rustle of leaves in an autumn breeze, to a baby's cries when it's feeding time. Jesus says, "My sheep recognize my voice. I know them, and they follow me. I give them real and eternal life." (John 10:27 MSG)

Like movies, music is a powerful medium. It's the universal language, transcending all cultures, religions, ethnicity, and geographic and political boundaries. Music is also the language of the soul. It can energize and motivate us; inspire us and even move us to tears—because music impacts us on an emotional level.

When music fills the air, it creates an aural atmosphere that can either lift us up or drag us down, put us in a peaceful and mellow mood—or a sour state of anger and agitation. Ultimately, what we're listening to has the power to encourage us or drag us down to despair and depression. Music is therefore NOT neutral; nor has it ever been so. To the contrary, music of all types, is either beneficial or detrimental, spiritual or profane.

Years ago, we heard of a carefully controlled experiment in which plants were exposed to various forms of music. The plants grew and thrived in an atmosphere of Classical music, but when subjected to Acid Rock, they eventually withered and died. Conclusive? People and plants respond to light in similar ways, so why not sound also?

As it happens, people respond positively to rousing anthems and moving film scores. Indeed, movie scores help audiences connect to the characters on a deeper emotional level. An inspired score can make an otherwise mediocre movie shine, just as a poor musical score can drag down an otherwise excellent movie. Face it, in addition to great acting and dazzling special effects, to truly succeed at the box office, a movie absolutely must have a worthy and excellent score.

If you're a movie buff you can probably rattle off a few of your favorites. Ponder for a moment: how many of them have beautiful and hauntingly memorable music? One of our all-time favorites is *Rocky*, with Sylvester Stallone. But for us, what truly makes the movie is the rousing, "Gonna Fly Now" theme with it's "getting stronger" lyrics. We actually can't watch it without wanting to get outdoors and exercise—or leap into a new creative project and pursue our dreams with renewed vigor! We listen to this theme music whenever we need some encouragement and motivation.

Other memorable movie music includes composer John Williams' scores for *Star Wars*, *Indiana Jones*, and *Jurassic Park*. And how about those classic Hollywood musicals? *The Sound of Music* summed up the power of music in it's theme:

The hills are alive with the sound of music...
With songs they have sung for a thousand years.
The hills fill my heart with the sound of music.
My heart wants to sing every song it hears!

Most musicals tend to have at least one incredibly encouraging and inspiring song. Disney's *Frozen* has "Let it Go." *Annie* has "Tomorrow"; *Man of La Mancha* has "To Dream the Impossible Dream; and *Singing in the Rain* has ... er, "Singing in the Rain"!

So, are you taking full advantage of the power of music to stay encouraged? And are you being selective about what enters your brain through your ears? Truth is, what you listen to regularly becomes the musical backdrop to your dreams and creative endeavors. It can be an atmosphere that drags you down—or an inspiring score that elevates your spirit and facilitates your efforts, by keeping you encouraged and motivated; a score that ensures your dreams will be a smash at the "box office" of life.

The success of your "movie" (the story of your life) is linked to the music you choose to accompany it. So ask yourself, what's your "score"? What's the musical backdrop of my life? Does it really fit my story? Is it inspiring, uplifting and memorable? And most importantly, does it help to move my story forward?

Dear friends, make your musical selections wisely and intentionally. Be sure your ears are filled with God's kind of music so your spirit and dreams can grow and thrive. If you don't ... well, someday you may have to face the music of your poor choices.

"He who has ears to hear, let him be listening and let him consider and perceive and comprehend by hearing."
(Matt 11:15 NKJV)

"...Blessed are your eyes, because they see; and your ears, because they hear."
(Matt 13:16 NLT)

PLEASE LISTEN UP!

If we creators and dreamers want to reach our goals and realize our dreams, then staying encouraged is an absolute must. But it requires avoiding eye pollution and, as we discussed last session, "facing the music" for our choices. As with film, music is a powerful medium that can affect our emotions, thoughts, and attitudes. So, regardless of the type of music, it's vital that we be selective and choose what's uplifting.

Decisions, decisions. There is, however, a type of music that's always uplifting. Inspirational music, which includes Gospel, praise and worship, and contemporary Christian (music written for and about God), elevates and encourages the human spirit—and that's exactly what's needed for the sometimes long and winding pursuit of dreams.

"Secular music," no matter how positive and uplifting, only reaches us on an emotional level. There's nothing wrong with that, except that we're far more than just a bundle of emotions wrapped in a physical body. Each of us has a spirit, which enables us to connect to God the Creator. And we need to feed our spirits. Unfortunately, secular music is neither created nor equipped to the minister to the spirit. It may stir the emotions—it may even get our feet tapping—but it does nothing for our spirits.

That's the purview of inspirational music, but not just any inspirational music. It must be "anointed" (or supernaturally endowed) by God's Holy Spirit. Jesus Christ stated, "…The helper, the Holy Spirit, whom the Father will send in My name, will teach you everything. He will remind you of everything that I have ever told you." (John 14:26 GW) Michael W. Smith illustrates this ministry of "reminding" in his song "I See You":

Well, the eagle flies, And the rivers run.
I look through the night, And I can see the rising sun—
And everywhere I go, I see You...!

Anointed music—or sacred music—impacts our whole being; spirit, soul and body. It brings clarity to our minds, peace to our emotions, and hope to our spirits. Truly anointed (sacred) music draws us closer to God.

And being in His presence is extremely beneficial: "...In Your presence there is fullness of joy; at Your right hand are pleasures forevermore." (Ps 16:11 ESV) Joy is essential to staying encouraged. "...For the joy of the LORD is your strength." (Neh 8:10 ESV)

And speaking of strength: "Seek the LORD and His strength, seek His face continually. ...Glory and beauty are in His presence; strength and gladness are in His place." (1 Chr 16:11, 27 JUB) The Messianic Psalmist and worship leader Paul Wilbur sums the benefits in his moving praise song, "In Your presence":

In Your presence, that's where I am strong
In Your presence, O Lord, my God
In Your presence, that's where I belong
Seeking Your face, touching Your grace
In the cleft of the rock—In Your presence, O God....

Fellow creators and dreamers, one sure way to stay encouraged—in addition to daily "renewing our minds with God's Word" (Rom 12:1-3)—is to "seek" His presence throughout the day. It's not difficult, thanks to the wonderful resources that are now available: CDs, DVDs, iTunes, etc.

Sacred music also helps to build our faith. It points us to our all-knowing, all-powerful, supernatural God and reminds us how awesome He is. Just listen to Chris Tomlin's "How Great is Our God," Paul Wilbur's "Worthy," or Michael W. Smith's classic "Awesome God."

Sacred music imparts truth from the Bible and often uses scriptures in the lyrics: Handel's Messiah covers the entire book of Isaiah and includes the quotes such as "Wonderful Counselor, Mighty God, Everlasting Father, Prince of Peace."

(Isa 9:6) By the way, although Messiah has become a Christmas tradition, Handel wrote it (and intended it) for our year-round listening pleasure and inspiration.

Sacred music reminds us of who we are in relation to our awesome Heavenly Father, who loves us so much that He sent His only Son to earth, to redeem us and reconcile us to God through Christ's death on the cross. Israel Houghton's "I Am a Friend of God" is a good example.

We're just as passionate about sacred music as we are about inspiring movies. God has reached us and inspired us with His music throughout our long journey with the Lord. So we can truly proclaim with Andre Crouch, "Through it all, I've learned to trust in Jesus; Through it all, I've learned to depend upon His Word"!

And sacred music has been a real source of encouragement in the pursuit of our dreams. Which is why we routinely share some of our favorite Christian songs on our website, in our Hump Day Hope & Humor series published each Wednesday. (Regarding the long and winding pursuit of our dreams, we daily sing along with Ricardo Sanchez, "It's Not Over" and "Moving Forward.")

The Lord is always "speaking" to us through books, movies, music, nature and people. Question is, are we listening? Let's take a cue from the great judge and prophet Samuel. When the Lord called him, he quickly responded "Here I am! ...Speak, I'm listening." (1 Sam 3:4,10)

Want to stay encouraged and motivated? Then listen to what God is speaking—through His anointed music.

POWER UP WITH PRAISE AND WORSHIP!

Can you hear it? Thunder in the distance.
When we worship, the Lion of Judah roars;
Strongholds crumble ... all around us ...
In the presence of our Lord!
There'll be vic'try in the camp at the shout of El Shaddai;
Every enemy will flee from the fire in His eyes;
Every captive will be freed in this year of Jubilee,
When we hear the shout of El Shaddai!

THESE LYRICS ARE FROM Paul Wilbur's "The Shout of El Shaddai," exalting God and citing one of His many Hebrew names. *El Shaddai* means "God Almighty." (Exod 6:3; Gen 28:20-21; 48:3-4)

If you allow these words to penetrate your mind, heart, and spirit, and take stock of the message, we guarantee you'll be encouraged—because there's power in praise and worship!

Participating in praise and worship involves our eyes, ears, and mouths: we read the lyrics, hear the music, and sing along; exalting the Creator of the Universe. (Anything involving the hands and feet are encouraged but totally optional.) Remember that we stated there's a connection between the eyes, ears, and mouth? Well, it's not enough to see and hear the goodness of God. We need to voice our admiration: "Death and life are in the power of the tongue...." (Prov 18:21 ESV)

Praise and worship is the act of honoring and glorifying God by expressing our love, gratitude, reverence, and sheer awe of Him. It impacts the mind (thoughts and attitude), the emotions and the spirit. This and other forms of sacred music minister to our whole being.

Praising and worshipping the Creator of the Universe enables us to shift our focus from ourselves (our problems, our challenges, our limited knowledge and resources), to God, (His power to solve problems, His sufficiency and, especially, His faithfulness to help us realize our dreams and purpose in life.)

David, the poet, warrior, and king, was also a worshipper—a characteristic he learned while spending countless nights alone in the fields, when he was nothing more than a young shepherd pondering his future. David was isolated, underestimated, and generally ignored by both his family and society at large, which viewed shepherds as "nobody"s. But during this lonely time, David worshipped God with all his heart. In so doing, he learned to encourage himself in the Lord, tapping into the power to "slay" giant obstacles and to ultimately overcome his greatest challenge, at Ziklag. (1 Sam 30:6)

Like David, we creators and dreamers will have to face giants and weather our own Ziklag moments. And, we can stay encouraged—during the tough times—by following the example of "a man after God's own heart" (Acts 13:22) and tapping into the power of praise and worship. But this means we must honor and exalt God—during the tough times—in spite of less than favorable circumstances, and in spite of how we feel.

> "Why am I discouraged? Why is my heart so sad?
> I will put my hope in God! I will praise Him again
>   —my Savior and my God!" (Ps 42:5-6 NLT)

DO THE RIGHT THING!

By observing the life of David, the legendary dreamer and creator, we can learn several valuable lessons about praise and worship. Remember, before David was a giant-killer, before he became a warrior and a military leader, before he was the greatest king Israel ever had—long before he was a history-maker—he was a worshipper!

David is renowned as the great psalmist, a poet and musician, and a "man after God's own heart" (Acts 13:27) He penned some of the most encouraging and inspiring verses in the Bible; but long before his beautiful psalms were published, to be read and enjoyed by millions of people throughout the ages, David personally sang them to an audience of One: his loving Heavenly Father, the Good Shepherd of Psalm 23 and John 10:11.

David learned to praise God while he was still an unknown—a "nobody" in the eyes of society—during countless lonely nights spent guarding his sheep. So, when he finally faced his greatest challenge at Ziklag, he knew exactly how to encourage himself in the Lord. Here are the lessons David learned firsthand about praise and worship:

Do the right thing! When all hell seems to be breaking loose, when we're still waiting for God to answer our prayers, when we feel like crying and throwing in the towel, even if we feel God has let us down, we need to do the right thing and praise the Lord anyway. In fact, it's during these Ziklag moments, when nothing seems to make sense, that we should (in the words of John Gray) "give Him a crazy praise!" That's faith in action!

Take time to worship God when you're all alone. Corporate praise and worship are important, but private praise parties—when it's just you and the Lord—help to build your faith and strengthen your relationship with God. Praise Him in the midst of pain and disappointment; when your heart is broken and your eyes filled with tears.

Praise and worship God when you feel "stuck": when your best efforts fail and your plans fall apart; when you still haven't achieved your goals or fulfilled your dreams—and you just don't get it!

Praise Him when you're prayed out. Although we personally continue to pray in faith and expectancy, claiming God's promises and waiting for our own breakthrough, we've had days when we felt "prayed out" and more than a little tired of asking. Perhaps you've been there. Like Elijah, in 1 Kings 19, we dreamers and creators can grow tired of "fighting the good fight of faith." (1 Tim 6:12) We can grow "weary in well doing." (Gal 6:9)

No matter how optimistic, energetic, faith-filled and steadfast we are, there will be times when we get just plain tuckered out! It's during times such as these that we can still tap into the power of praise and worship, when we stop asking and just keep on exalting. It's easy: we simply...

Praise God for who He is—NOT for whichever prayers He's answered lately. Vicki Yohe's song "Because of Who You Are" captures this truth perfectly. Check it out.

The next time you feel the blues coming on, slide a praise and worship CD into your car or home stereo system, and have a private praise party. Listen to songs of faith that minister to you—and sing along. Get out and participate in a corporate praise and worship service with a local faith congregation. Come back home and watch a DVD featuring praise music.

Or pull out an old hymnal and sing a few of those wonderful latter-day "psalms" such as "Great is Thy Faithfulness" or "A Mighty Fortress is Our God" or "It is Well with My Soul." And for even more encouragement, Google the backstories of the creators who composed these classics—you'll be amazed and blessed when you read of their trials and ultimate triumphs!

Something supernatural happens when we praise and worship the Lord:

God shows up and makes Himself at home! Because He inhabits the praises of His people. (Ps 22:3)

And when God shows up, sadness, discouragement, and depression must leave! To quote a few more lines of Paul Wilbur's "The Shout of El Shaddai":

> *In your name powers of darkness tremble; Jericho tumbles to the ground! In your name chains of death are broken; Lord of Hosts, pour your power out!*

So praise and worship the Creator of the Universe, who gives us every good thing from above, including our gifts and talents, dreams and creativity—not to mention life itself! (James 1:17) No matter how you feel, no matter how your plans are going, it's always the right thing to do.

STEP UP AND SERVE!

OUR LAST TIP FOR STAYING ENCOURAGED is one which is often neglected, not only by creators and dreamers (who have a tendency to get caught up in their own pursuits to the exclusion of everything and everyone else), but also by the majority of people in our society—including many followers of Jesus Christ. Hence, we call this "step" the Missing Ingredient. The Bible simply calls it serving.

Dr. Martin Luther King, Jr. often stated, "Everyone can be great; Everyone can serve." But although most dreamers and creators want to be great in their field of interest, few care to be servants. Surprising? Not really. What's truly surprising is that even people who long to do great things for God, rarely get involved with serving.

Serving is not easy. Nor is it viewed as particularly glamorous. And yet, when He came to earth in human form, the Son of God set an example for all of us to follow, by assuming the role of a servant. Jesus never viewed the act of serving as beneath Him—despite being the King of Kings. "Although He was in the form of God and equal with God, He did not take advantage of this equality. Instead, He emptied himself by taking on the form of a servant." (Phil 2:6-7 GW)

In following his Lord, the Apostle Paul continually identified himself—first and foremost—as a servant. (Rom 1:1; Phil 1:1; and Titus 1:1) Furthermore, the Apostle admonishes us to do likewise: "In your relationships with one another, have the same mindset as Christ Jesus: ...by taking the very nature of a servant...." (Phil 2:5-7 NIV)

As you may know, the New Testament was originally written in Greek, and the word for rendering service is doulos, which implies a totally selfless commitment to another. This idea is the antithesis of the "me, myself and I" mindset so prevalent today. It's also the complete opposite of the self-serving "Look out for #1" philosophy that drives our society.

But God did not put us here just to look out for #1. He never intended for us to lead selfish lives, in which we care only for our own needs and desires. The Apostle Paul writes, "Don't act out of selfish ambition or be conceited. ...Don't be concerned only about your own interests, but also be concerned about the interests of others." (Phil 2:3-4 GW)

We truly believe that if more people followed this divine advice, there would be fewer heartaches in this world. If we had more servants, we'd have fewer problems and a much lower divorce rate. We would also see more creators and dreamers achieving their goals and fulfilling their aspirations—because there would be far more facilitators to guide and help them on the journey.

Alas, our natural tendency is to be selfish. This is part of the human sin nature depicted throughout the Bible and described in Romans 3:23 and Isaiah 64:6. It's how we start out—just watch children at play and observe their constant "It's mine!" bickering—but it's not how we should continue! True, when we dreamers feel discouraged we want people to be there for us, to give us a word of encouragement, to lift us up, to meet our needs. Oftentimes the furthest thing from our minds is to serve someone else.

We are called, however, to serve—not when we feel like it, not after we solve our own problems, not when it's convenient. Serving is never the natural thing to do. But it is the supernatural thing. It's also the spiritually mature thing to do. When we need encouragement, we should encourage others. When we need a blessing, we should do our best to bless others. If we're waiting for a door to open, for a "Barnabas" who will help us rise to the next level, we should be like Barnabas: facilitating and opening doors for someone else. "For we are God's handiwork, created in Christ Jesus to do good works [including service!]...." (Eph 2:10 NIV)

Interestingly, serving is actually an antidote to discouragement, depression, hopelessness and a general lack of joy. Serving leads us to take our eyes off ourselves and our own problems and challenges, and to focus instead on the Lord and the needs and concerns of other people. So, if you're feeling disappointed and discouraged because you still have not achieved your goals or realized your dreams, then get out and serve!

Find someone at home, work, or in your neighborhood, who's going through tough times, and probably facing even bigger challenges than you are. Visit someone in the hospital, or drop in on a sick and shut-in person. Send a card, or better still, pick up the phone and give someone a cheer-up call. Offer to run an errand or do the shopping for a busy mom. And if you can afford it, treat someone to lunch (or even coffee) and allow them to discuss their problems.

By all means, be sure to serve in your local faith congregation; but don't neglect to volunteer in your community, as well. Serve at a local soup kitchen. Hook up with the Salvation Army or Samaritan's Purse or Operation Blessing. The possibilities for serving are endless. You can even make a difference at your local animal shelter. "Each of you should use whatever gift you have received to serve others, as faithful stewards of God's grace in its various forms." (1 Peter 4:10 NIV)

Ask the Lord to give you ideas and direct your steps We promise, God will delight in your willingness to serve, and bless you in the process. So step out and serve! Then, at the end of each day, and at the end of life's journey, you can imagine your loving Heavenly Father smiling at you and saying, "Well done, good and faithful servant!" (Matt 25:21 NIV)

GO NOW AND GIVE!

IN HIS BOOK, *IMPROVING YOUR SERVE,* Charles Swindoll writes, "You are most godlike when you give." We totally agree. But please note, "giving" encompasses far more than sharing one's financial and material resources. We should by all means do that whenever the opportunity arises. And we certainly should give on a regular basis within our local faith communities, as well as to worthy causes and charitable institutions. But "giving" also includes sharing one's time and talents. It includes the giving of one's self, by making oneself available—and then being there for others.

Generosity is not a natural tendency, however. Therefore, "giving" is a supernatural act with supernatural repercussions. "…The Lord Jesus himself said: 'It is more blessed to give than to receive.'" (Acts 20:35 NIV) Again, "giving" is about more than money. Remember, Christ gave His life for us! So precisely what kind of "giving" makes us more godlike?

The kind of giving characterized by Jesus Christ, falls under the broader heading of HOSPITALITY.

Now, before we go any further, **hospitality (in the true, Biblical sense) is NOT the same as modern entertaining!** To understand the huge difference, we direct you to our most recent book, *The Heart of an Angel.*

Biblical Hospitality expresses the full nature of our Lord: loving, accepting, welcoming, giving, and self-sacrificing. These traits are summed up in a single verse: "For God so loved the world, that he gave His only begotten Son, that whosoever believeth in Him should not perish, but have everlasting life." (John 3:16 KJV)

Clearly, God welcomes everyone—all of us "whosoever"s! Indeed, the whole message of the Gospel is about a Hospitable Heavenly Father who lays out the welcome mat to Heaven (through His Son Jesus Christ). He invites us in, to become a part of His spiritual family, and welcomes us back to a right relationship with Himself. In fact, the greatest act of hospitality ever demonstrated, was at the Cross, where Christ the promised Messiah and Savior of the world, Yeshua, served Himself as the Passover Lamb! (1 Cor 5:7)

Serving goes hand in hand with giving, but both are part of Hospitality. Here's a definition that ties together these divine attributes:

Biblical Hospitality is an attitude of the heart (love) expressed through a lifestyle of giving and serving. It's the giving of one's time, talents, and resources. It's the giving of oneself!

Both giving and serving involve sacrifice. Face it, serving is almost never convenient, and it's often not easy. For instance: it's rarely convenient to visit a coworker in the hospital when the medical facility is several miles out of your way; it's not easy to purchase a gift for someone's special occasion when you'd rather spend the money on yourself; and it's neither easy nor convenient to help out a struggling neighbor with household chores. Such acts of giving and serving generally involve some type of sacrifice. And that's another reason why being hospitable is also being like Christ.

Being hospitable can be as simple as inviting someone over for coffee or tea—but who among us creators and dreamers has the time for that?!?

Well, if you're too busy to reach out to others, particularly to those closest to you, or to establish and strengthen relationships (the true aim of hospitality), then you're really too busy! So make some time for giving to (and serving) others. And here's a sobering thought: Thank God our Heavenly Father is never too busy for us!

HUSH UP AND
BE HOSPITABLE!

GIVING AND SERVING FALL UNDER the broader heading of Biblical Hospitality: an attitude of the heart (love) expressed through a lifestyle of giving and serving. It's the giving of one's time, talents, and resources. It's the giving of oneself. We're never more like God than when we're extending hospitality, but hospitable acts of giving and serving are usually not easy and almost never convenient, so why bother?

Hospitality literally defines Our Lord; and our Hospitable God wants each of His followers to be like Him—um, hospitable![4] Unfortunately, acts of Biblical Hospitality generally require a degree of personal sacrifice regarding our time, talents, and resources. And who in the world likes to make sacrifices? Before we creators and dreamers start whining, we need to hush up and face the truth about hospitality:

If we wait until we feel like extending hospitality; or until we have more time; or get some extra cash—if we wait until everything is just right—we will NEVER be hospitable!

We are commanded to be hospitable.

"Offer hospitality to one another without grumbling. Each of you should use whatever gift you have received to serve others, as faithful stewards of God's grace...." (1 Peter 4:9-10 NIV)

Hospitality is the supernatural expression of God's love.

Love is the essence of God. "God is love, and all who live in love live in God, and God lives in them." (1 John 4:16 NLT) And acts of hospitality are how we express God's love in a

---

[4] For further reading on the benefits and significance of practicing hospitality, grab our book *The Heart of an Angel: Becoming God's Messengers of Love and Hospitality to a World in Need,* published by Ravens' Reads.

practical way. In essence, the practice of Biblical Hospitality gives hands and feet to God's love; meeting needs, whatever they may be, with whatever we have to offer.

Interestingly, we get the word hospitality from the Latin hospitalis. We also take our idea of "hospital" from this Latin word, which is wholly appropriate: a hospital is a place of healing and restoration, and that's the true focus of hospitality. Hence ...

When we practice Biblical Hospitality, opening up our hearts and homes to others, we become God's conduits of healing and restoration. Through us, God is able to pour on "the oil and wine" for weary and hurting people. (Just as the Good Samaritan did, in Luke 10:34.) We become His hands extended, and our homes become mini-hospitals, each an oasis of rest and refreshing in a "parched and dry" world.

Being hospitable is therapeutic and beneficial. Leading a God-centered life with a focus on others leaves no room for discouragement—which plagues most of us creators and dreamers. Plus, when we serve and meet the needs of others, a most unusual, supernatural phenomenon occurs: God meets our needs and blesses us. It's a win-win scenario.

Want to stay encouraged? Want to live a joyful life, even if you're still struggling to reach your goals, and have yet to realize your dreams? Then practice Biblical Hospitality. When you meet someone's needs, you'll have the satisfaction of knowing you were God's divine instrument of blessing others. You'll know the personal fulfillment that comes from following the example of Christ—touching people and making a real difference in the world, one life at a time.

Will it be convenient? Probably not. But don't complain. Instead, hush up and be hospitable! "Always be eager to practice hospitality." (Rom 12:13 NLT)

SECTION IV:
BATTLE BRIEFING

Indeed, the battle is the LORD's....
—1 Samuel 17:47 GNT

*But thanks be to God who gives us the victory
through our Lord Jesus Christ!*
—1 Corinthians 15:57 ISV

FIGHT THE GOOD FIGHT!

FELLOW CREATORS AND DREAMERS, no matter what the circumstances, no matter how "impossible" things may seem, keep fighting the good fight! When it comes to realizing your goals and aspirations, *don't throw in the towel.*

Instead, follow the example of Sir Winston Churchill, who was a history-maker! He PERSEVERED—and stirred an entire nation to rally behind him during England's darkest hour—to oppose the greatest evil of modern times.[5] How? He stood as a lone voice warning the world of the evils of Nazism before the start of WWII.

To quote Churchill, in a speech he made on June 4, 1940: "I have, myself, full confidence that if all do their duty, if nothing is neglected, and if the best arrangements are made ... <u>we</u>

---

[5] This pivotal moment in history is depicted in the well-made 2017 movie *Darkest Hour.*

shall prove ourselves once again able....

"...We shall not flag or fail. We shall go on to the end, ...we shall fight on the seas and oceans, we shall fight with growing confidence and growing strength ... whatever the cost may be, we shall fight on the beaches, we shall fight on the landing grounds, we shall fight in the fields and in the streets, we shall fight in the hills; we shall never surrender...."

Never give up on your dreams! Persevere! Have the same unwavering determination as Sir Churchill, a man of letters known for his eloquence and powerful rhetoric; a great leader who became the Prime Minister of England, replacing Chamberlain, a weak official who was deceived by Adolf Hitler, and who sought to appease him.

Fight the good fight!

Churchill's words represent the kind of resolve he had in the face of the diabolical schemes of Hitler and his Nazi henchmen. And this is the same kind of resolve we must have in the face of the demonic forces facing us today.

Demonic forces? Really? Don't scoff. Read on.

As we stated previously, we love movies! We view many of them as modern parables and have used *Chariots of Fire* and other examples to illustrate important spiritual truths in our inspirational books. We're also WWII buffs. History truly is the best teacher—or should be, if we're willing to learn from it. So allow us to draw a few analogies between the Second World War, divine purpose, the pursuit of goals and dreams, and the fulfillment of God-given destiny.

Before the Free World could triumph in WWII, England and her allies first needed to face some very uncomfortable and frequently-ignored Biblical truths. Jesus said, "...Remain faithful to My teachings. And you will know the truth, and the truth will set you free." (John 8:31-32 NLT)

Hitler was unequivocally the enemy of freedom and all that is good, honest, and decent in the world. Without provocation, he declared war on the Jewish people, the "apple of God's eye." (Zechariah 2:8) In fact, Hitler's "Final Solution" was engineered to wipe every last Jew from the face of the earth. That is the most concentrated form hatred ever known; evil in its purest form—swaggering and delivering speeches, all the while plotting the ruin of the world.

Can anything so vile and hideous have a presence in the physical realm without **a counterpart in the unseen super-natural world?** Powers of Darkness? Spiritual forces of Evil?

"...We do not wrestle against flesh and blood, but against principalities, against powers, against the rulers of the darkness of this age, against spiritual hosts of wickedness in the heavenly places." (Eph 6:12 NKJV)

We, too, must contend with a formidable enemy, who seeks the "final solution" of both the Jews of today as well the Gentile followers of Jesus Christ (the Son of God who walked the earth two millennia ago, in the form of a Jewish Rabbi.) Call this foe Lucifer, or the Devil, or the Dragon, or Beelzebub, or Old Scratch; he is known by many names, and in every corner and culture of the world. Jesus described him as "The thief [who] comes only to steal and kill and destroy." (John 10:10 NIV) Bad News?

Yes and no. **Satan's power is limited.** He's not equal to God in any way, shape or form. Satan is just a rebellious and, hence, fallen angel, whose mantra is "Misery loves company." Please don't keep company with him, though, because....

Friends, if you allow Satan to steal your joy, he definitely will. He knows that the joy of the Lord is your strength (Neh 8:10) and that, by robbing you of it, he can weaken your spirit, your motivation, and your resolve. Once he's done this, he'll take the next step in his plan....

If Satan can steal your hope, by discouraging you, he can also kill your dream! Matter of fact, he'd love to destroy your entire future. Now why would he want to do that? Well, why did Hitler want to murder 6 million innocent (and highly creative) Jewish men, women, and children—plus millions of others?

Discouragement is the destroyer of enthusiasm and motivation; the killer of creativity and dreams. And it's Satan's first explosive volley in an emotional and spiritual war we all wage daily. So, now you know why we spent so much time emphasizing the need to stay encouraged. And why we want to be sure you have the proper "weapons" to fight this battle.

Satan, like Hitler and the Nazi Party, is a formidable force of evil who never takes a day off. He's ready to assail us 24/7.

But we have a far more powerful ally who assures us the victory in every single skirmish: Jesus Christ (or Yeshua), "whose purpose [unlike that of our enemy] is to give [us] a rich and satisfying life," (John 10:10 NLT) has defeated both Satan and death. He is the Savior of the world in *every* way, and when we rely on Him, our Lord will foil every scheme of our spiritual enemy.

Furthermore, Jesus said, "Behold! I have given you <u>authority and power</u> to trample upon serpents and scorpions, and [physical and mental strength and ability] over all the power that the enemy [possesses]; and nothing shall in any way harm you." (Luke 10:19 AMPC)

The word *authority* means the power or right to command or rule, to act or to influence. Another, related definition speaks of responsibility, respectability, and weight of character. Authority and power are often used synonymously.

Fellow creators and dreamers, whether you realize it, **you have already won the victory** ... "because the Spirit who lives in you is greater than the spirit who lives in the world." (1 John 4:4 NLT) God, the Spirit in us—the All-Powerful, Sovereign Creator of the Universe who breathed life into each of us—loves you and wants the best for your life. He's the One who blesses us with the dreams we pursue, and grants us the gifts, talents, and strength to achieve them.

So continue to be determined in the pursuit of your goals and dreams. Persevere and—following in the footsteps of Sir Winston Churchill— "Fight the good fight of the faith [in the conflict with evil]; take hold of the eternal life...." (1 Tim 6:12 AMP)

KNOW YOUR ENEMY

POWERS OF DARKNESS? Spiritual forces of Evil? The fallen angel Lucifer marshals his demonic forces daily—to steal, kill and destroy. (John 10:10 NIV) He knows that the joy of the Lord is your strength (Neh 8:10) and that, by robbing you of it, he can weaken your spirit, your motivation, and your resolve. Once he's done this, he can destroy your hopes and kill your dreams. Call him the "Hitler" from Hell.

In his Chinese military treatise, *The Art of War*, Sun Tzu states, "If you know both yourself and your enemy, you can win a hundred battles without jeopardy." One of the reasons Great Britain, the United States, and their allies prevailed in WWII is that the leaders of these nations knew their enemies. They were able to recognize and understand the forces of evil threatening human life and freedom. Thus, the Allies succeeded in defeating the most powerful military force ever assembled, the combined might of the Axis Powers—Hitler's murderous Third Reich; Italy's fascist dictator, Benito Mussolini; and Japan's opportunistic Emperor Hirohito—all because a few great men such as Winston Churchill and U.S. President Franklin D. Roosevelt were able to discern the evil of their times.

We, too, must be able to **recognize and understand the enemy of our souls** ... and our hopes and dreams. Satan is that enemy. He is the epitome of evil, and like the crazed leaders of the Axis Powers, he has a definite agenda. In fact, he has an ax to grind with each and every one of us. Which is why the Apostle Peter admonishes us to watch our step: "Stay alert! Watch out for your great enemy, the devil. He prowls around like a roaring lion, looking for someone to devour." (1 Peter 5:8 NLT)

Sounds incredible, right? After all, what did we do to get on Satan's bad side? Well, first off, Satan doesn't have a good side—it's all bad: left, right, top, bottom, and in-between. Second, Satan doesn't need a reason. And yet, many will scoff at the idea, or discount the danger.

Folks, we can make the same mistake the European Jews made right before WWII—a mistake which cost millions of Jewish men and women their very lives. Upon hearing the news of massive roundups and increased persecutions, and later of the horrors of the death camps and the mass shootings, many people of Hebrew heritage gathered their families, packed their belongings, and slipped away quietly. But unfortunately, far too many remained in the path of danger. Why? Many of them simply refused to believe that such evil could exist in our world.

In particular, the German Jews, many of whom were secular, highly educated, and well established in German society, mistakenly believed they would be exempt from this latest wave of antiSemitism. In appearance, custom, and mannerisms, they were completely indistinguishable from their Teutonic neighbors. Furthermore, viewing themselves as solid, successful, law-abiding and truly patriotic German citizens, they felt sure they would escape Hitler's wrath. Nothing could have been further from the truth.

Hitler clearly took his cues from the devil himself: he hated without provocation, and lived to steal, kill, and destroy. And he needed no excuse to indiscriminately murder any and all Jews. It was in his nature.

Many German Jews were in denial—until it was too late. They knew Hitler was a lunatic but failed to recognize him for the evil maniac he truly was. We creators and dreamers can't afford to live in similar denial. **We can't afford to pretend that Satan doesn't exist,** or that we're not on his radar. Don't think he's merely a product of "the Dark Ages," with no place in the enlightened 21st Century. And don't fancy yourself too sophisticated to believe in such an evil entity.

Satan does exist! He's not a character from a fairy tale; nor is he the figment of an overworked and ignorant imagination. The Hebrew word for Satan literally means "adversary"—or one who opposes God. And, as the title of Hal Lindsey's best-selling book proclaims, *Satan is Alive and Well on Planet Earth.*

And you can expect Satan, sooner or later, to be "dropping in" to see how you're doing.

"...When the angels came to report to God, Satan, who was the Designated Accuser, came along with them. God singled out Satan and said, 'What have you been up to?' Satan answered God, 'Going here and there, checking things out on earth.'" (Job 1:6 MSG)

After the bombing of Pearl Harbor, on December 6, 1941, which President Roosevelt described as "a day that will live in infamy," the Allied Forces realized they had met yet another formidable enemy: clearly, the Japanese Imperial Army would use any means necessary to win; and they would destroy any people that stood in their way.

We must also realize that the enemy of our soul is far more formidable than his human instruments; and he, too, will use any means to win his battle—destroy anything good and worthwhile in his path, be it people, principles, relationships, hopes, dreams ... the list is endless. Remember the verse we quoted earlier? "Satan ... is ... seeking whom he may devour." (1 Peter 5:8 Aramaic) The word devour means to eat quickly and eagerly; or to consume completely and destructively.

When you devour something—a huge slice of apple pie, for instance—you pretty much leave behind only a few crumbs on an empty plate, often bemoaning "I can't believe I ate the whole thing!" That's how Satan operates: he consumes ALL, leaving nothing behind but crumbs, emptiness, and regrets. He is committed to "finishing us off"—right down to the last morsel.

So we can't let down our guards. We must understand that the enemy of our souls (like the Fascists) will do whatever it takes to derail our future. Satan will use any means possible—or anyone, including even those closest to you—to keep you from fulfilling your dreams and realizing your purpose and destiny. He'll place obstacles in your path and throw a monkey wrench into your plans, all to sabotage your progress.

In his teaching series "Promise, Problem, Provision," San Antonio, Texas pastor and author John Hagee writes, "The bigger the vision [or dream] the bigger the challenges." Hagee uses the Biblical patriarch Joseph as an example, who had a monumental dream and endured astonishing tribulations to ultimately realize it. But when you have a huge God-given dream, especially one that will bless people and bring glory to God, you can expect to face some opposition from His and your enemy, Satan!

But we need not fear nor falter: "If God is for us, who can be [successful] against us?" (Rom 8:31 AMP)

Like Joseph, we can say with confidence, "...You planned evil against me but God used those same plans for my good, as you see all around you right now—life for many people [through the fulfillment of the dream]." (Gen 50:20 MSG) Proof that "...God [who is deeply concerned about us] causes all things to work together [as a plan] for good for those who love God, to those who are called according to His plan and purpose." (Rom 8:28 AMP)

Fellow creators and dreamers, take heart! Anyone who has ever achieved great things has also faced great obstacles and opposition. Anyone who's worked to build a God-centered marriage, or raise a God-fearing child, or live a productive life that honors God, has faced their share of struggles. So, again, NEVER GIVE UP!

> "...Thanks be to God, who always leads us in triumph
> in Christ...."   (2 Cor 2:14 NASB)

AVOID ENEMY STRONGHOLDS

WHEN **GREAT BRITAIN AND HER ALLIES** entered World War II, these countries were ill-prepared for a conflict with the German juggernaut that had already carved up most of Western Europe. Adolf Hitler had been marshalling his forces since 1935, assembling and training the mightiest military war machine of the twentieth century. By 1943, the German Army peaked at six and half million soldiers. By the end of WWII, over 13 million, mostly conscripted, German men had served. And worldwide, close to 85 million men, women and children had perished in the deadliest conflict in human history.

The U.S., in particular, needed time to build up its invasion forces. And in war, time is of the essence. Furthermore, having to transport men and equipment overseas, to fight a battle "over there"—to quote the lyrics of George M. Cohan's popular song—involved great expense and elaborate planning, not to mention still more time. Having been caught "snoozing," the Good Guys were clearly at a disadvantage.

In contrast, God "never rests or sleeps" (Ps 121:4 GW); and His spiritual army is always ready and well-equipped to triumph in every situation, and under any circumstances. But the Creator of the Universe does not wage war with our enemy in convential ways. The Apostle Paul wrote about such spiritual battles, stating "The weapons we fight with are not the weapons of the world. On the contrary, they have divine power to demolish strongholds." (2 Cor 10:4 NIV)

Friends, we have **a mighty spiritual arsenal at our disposal,** which no demonic forces can withstand. Don't worry about army requisitioning forms filled out in triplicate; and forget about faulty equipment that won't fire or operate properly! Our divine arms are manufactured by God Himself, and to quote Broadway singer and actress Ethel Waters, "God don't make no junk!"

But here's the catch: we can't use these weapons until we appropriate them. We also need to learn how to use them. All the spiritual weapons in God's arsenal are at our disposal, including prayer, praise, worship, Bible study, and others—all of which we've discussed.

Unlike the U.S. Forces which had to fight "over there," our spiritual war is waged right here where we live. In fact, the main battlefield of our conflict is our minds! And before we go any further, let's get one thing straight: No, Satan CAN-NOT read our thoughts. Neither can he control them, because God created each of us with a free will. Satan, however, can influence our thinking.

Remember, we are what we think: "As a man thinks in his heart, so he is." (Prov 23:7) So what occupies your thoughts? Be careful: "Garbage in—garbage out."

Wrong thinking can lead to strongholds in our lives. In a war, a formidable stronghold is a fortress or tower, a military installation or any fortified position. In WWII, both the Nazi and Japanese forces were masters at fortifying their positions: they would dig into the high ground and set up bunkers. When Allied troops had to storm these enemy bunkers, they were met with a barrage of fire power that slowed their progress and decimated their numbers.

Director Stephen Spielberg captures the horror of confronting these strongholds. In *Saving Private Ryan*, he depicts the Allies storming Normandy Beach, where the enemy has "dug in" on the higher ground. The slaughter that takes place is horrific and truly hard to watch.

In the spiritual realm, the enemy of our souls also likes to dig in. He sets up strongholds in our lives in an attempt to defeat us. His tactics are intended to slow us down, decimate our faith, family and fortunes, and ultimately destroy our lives. Where does he build these strongholds? The "high ground" of our thoughts.

Friends, if Satan can blast you into the realm of "stinking thinking": a defeatist attitude; a victim mentality; a self-absorbed mindset that focuses on your problems and challenges, instead of on God, the answer to your every need ... then he can wreak havoc in your life and ultimately defeat you. He'll steal your joy, your enthusiasm and your motivation—leaving you on the battlefield of the mind with a wounded spirit bleeding with fear and doubt, hopelessness and despair.

Next comes deep depression and the death of your dreams and aspirations. So please, don't make yourself a target! Don't open the door to anything that is contrary to God's perfect plan for your life—"to prosper you and not to harm you, ...to give you hope and a future." (Jer 29:11 NIV)

The Apostle Paul writes, "...the weapons of our warfare are not carnal but mighty in God for pulling down strongholds, casting down arguments and every high thing that exalts itself against the knowledge of God, bringing every thought into captivity to the obedience of Christ." (2 Cor 10:4-5 NKJV)

Casting down arguments? If a thought, belief, position, or attitude doesn't line up with the Word of God/the Bible, then dismiss it! **Replace any negative and destructive thinking with a Scriptural principle or a promise from God.** This is exactly how Jesus defeated Satan in the wilderness, when our Lord firmly stated: "It is written, 'Man shall not live by bread alone, but by every word of God.' ...Get behind Me, Satan! For it is written, 'You shall worship the Lord your God, and Him only you shall serve.'" (Luke 4:4,8 NKJV) And folks, wielding (and relying on) the Word of God is a battle strategy that still works today.

Fellow creators and dreamers, we who battle Satan and his schemes belong to the Spiritual Army of the Lion of the the Tribe of Judah, the Creator of the Universe, the Great "I AM"! We are never ill-equipped or disadvantaged. To the contrary, we are "joint heirs" with Christ Jesus (Rom 8:17); "seated in Heavenly places." (Eph 1:20; Col 2:12)

"If you listen to these commands of the LORD your God ... and if you carefully obey them, the LORD will make you the head and not the tail, and you will always be on top and never at the bottom." (Deut 28:13)

Here's a prayer written by the Biblical King David, perhaps the greatest warrior of all time. Let it be your prayer, too: "I love you, LORD; you are my strength. The LORD is my rock, my fortress, and my savior; my God is my rock, in whom I find protection. He is my shield, the power that saves me, and my place of safety. I called on the LORD, who is worthy of praise, and He saved me from my enemies." (Ps 18:1-3 NLT)

THE BIG LIE

WHEN HE DICTATED HIS 1925 BOOK *Mein Kampf,* Adolf Hitler coined the phrase "The Big Lie." The future leader of Nazi Germany was describing a propaganda trick: the spreading of a lie so "colossal" that everyone will believe it—because no one would ever imagine that a civilized human being could "have the impudence to distort the truth so infamously." Hitler was banking, of course, that people hadn't yet realized what an impudent and foul fiend *he* was.

Hitler wrote, "If you tell a big enough lie and tell it frequently enough, it will be believed." Ironically, he was ascribing the technique to "the Jews": He claimed they were trying to convince the masses that German Jews were blaming the prominent nationalist and anti-Semitic political leader Erich Ludendorff for their country's defeat in WWI. This was yet another "Big Lie" of Hitler, designed to fuel resentment toward the Jewish people who were leading quiet lives and essentially minding their own business.

Such is the power of *propaganda*, a major tool employed throughout history by every oppressive totalitarian group or regime—be it the Communists, the Nazi fascists, or the Islamic Jihadists of today. Propaganda is **the intentional spread of information that is not objective, to influence a people group and further an agenda.** It is a selective presentation of facts designed to shape perception, or the use of "loaded language to produce an emotional rather than a rational response to the information that is presented."

Propaganda can be just as destructive as open warfare; it can result in the internal decay and eventual collapse of countries, companies, and communities. It allows special interest groups to gain control and stay in power by distorting the truth or the perception of the truth. And although most of us associate propaganda with materials and reports prepared by governments, activist groups and even entertainment and news media can produce propaganda designed to manipulate the masses. Are we vulnerable to such manipulation?

Today's "Fake News" and "Urban Legends" actually fit the description of propaganda, in which the actions or statements of a person, group or organization are taken out of context, the facts distorted—and in some instances totally fabricated—in order to bias the public and advance an agenda. And, as was the case with Nazi propaganda targeting German Jews, the aim of this fake news is to cast someone in such an unfavorable light as to bring about their destruction either socially, economically or politically.

Speaking of fake news, under Hitler's regime Joseph Goebbels was in charge of Germany's "Reich Ministry of Public Enlightenment and Propaganda"—a powerful (and greatly feared) government agency created for a single purpose: to promote the evil ideology and murderous (and anti-Semitic) agenda of Hitler's regime through the intentional, methodical, and continual dissemination of outright lies.

Founded in March 1933, Hitler's propaganda machine had a single purpose: to ensure complete Nazi control of information—in every aspect of German cultural and intellectual life, including news media, broadcasting, filmmaking, literature, and the performing arts. Through Goebbel's careful censorship and manipulation of the truth, Hitler hoped to control every aspect of an individual's life. Goebbels once stated, "Propaganda works best when those who are being manipulated are confident they are acting on their own free will."

Goebbel's Ministry of Public Enlightenment worked overtime to shape public opinion in Germany. Among it's favorite topics (and targets): the spread of anti-Semitism and attacks on Christian churches. And after the start of WWII, it attempted to keep up civilian morale in the face of impending defeat. Parroting the words of his Führer, Goebbel's wrote, "If you tell a lie big enough and keep repeating it, people will eventually come to believe it. The lie can be maintained only for such time as the State can shield the people from the political, economic and/or military consequences of the lie. It thus becomes vitally important for the State to use all of its powers to repress dissent, for <u>the truth is the mortal enemy of the lie, and thus by extension, the truth is the greatest enemy of the State.</u>"

What a contrast to our free society which is founded upon Judeo-Christian principles. And what a contrast to what Jesus Christ proclaimed, in John 8:31-32: "You are truly my disciples if you remain faithful to my teachings. And you will know the truth, and the truth will set you free." (NLT) Jesus *was* and *is* all about the truth. And for full disclosure, Christ revealed that He is the *embodiment* of truth: "I am the way, the truth, and the life." (John 14:6 NLT)

Satan, by the way, actually invented propaganda, way back in the Garden of Eden, when he pitched to Eve the idea that God was being unfair, unreasonable and untruthful. (Read Genesis 3:1-6) He is the quintessential master of deceit and deception, the prime purveyor of falsehood, forgery and fraud, and he's had centuries to perfect his craft (and craftiness). And yet, "Satan disguises himself as an angel of light" (2 Cor 11:14 NLT)—and thus he is able to fool many people.

The Bible warns about this wolf in sheep's clothing. (Matt 7:15) Fortunately for us, this trickster has nothing new up his sleeve. He's not at all original, so he resorts to the same old tactics time and again—all of which have been exposed in the Word of God.

Jesus aptly describes Satan: "...He was a murderer from the beginning. He has always hated the truth, because there is no truth in him. When he lies, it is consistent with his character; for he is a liar and the father of lies." (John 8:44 NLT) Jesus also points out that, owing to Satan's propaganda trail (fake news about our Lord and Savior) "...When I tell the truth, you just naturally don't believe me!" (John 8:45 NLT)

Thanks to Satan's Big Lie, many people miss out on the "abundant life" Christ promises us in John 10:10. Face it, Satan is the enemy of our souls, and he doesn't want us to find peace and contentment. This means he certainly doesn't want us to reach our goals or realize our dreams. He doesn't want us to enjoy success in our creative endeavors using the gifts and talents God has bestowed; or to fulfill our divine purpose in life, being a positive influence in the lives of others while bringing glory to the Lord of Heaven and Earth.

Not to worry, we don't have to swallow the lies of Satan's

propaganda. Nor do we have to be constantly watching over our shoulder. The devil is NOT all-powerful or all-knowing. He doesn't know what our futures hold, although he suspects that God has destined each of us for great things and this bothers him to no end. Remember, Satan is not equal to God in anything. He's only a fallen angel with very limited powers. He had *his* chance and failed—and misery loves company! Don't give it to him! Live your life *God-centered*—NOT Satan-conscious!

Our focus should always be on the Creator of the Universe, the all-powerful One who formed each of us in His own image. We need to take confidence in the truth that "...You have already won a victory ... because the Spirit who lives in you is greater than the spirit who lives in the world." (1 john 4:4 NLT)

"What shall we say about such wonderful things as these? If God is for us, who can ever be against us?" (Rom 8:31 NLT)

Nevertheless, we must know our enemy and be wary of his tactics, to avoid falling for his old tricks or swallowing his big lies. If you recall, at the start of our discussion on spiritual warfare, we mentioned that most of our struggles with the enemy (including disappointment, depression and despair) are fought on the battlefield of the mind. That's why it's vital that we continually "renew our minds" with the truth of God's Word—as described in Romans 12:1-3.

The face of our enemy is Satan, the "father of lies." (John 8:44) As the "accuser of the brethren" (Rev 12:10), Satan is constantly bombarding our thoughts with lies about God, lies about our self-worth and our place in God's Kingdom, as well as lies about the "hopelessness" of our circumstances and situation, and the "futility" of our goals and dreams. It's easy to get swept away by the pounding waves of Satan's propaganda—*unless* we stay anchored in the truth of God's Word.

Truth is the best defense against Satan's propaganda. Jesus said, "...Know the truth, and the truth will set you free." (John 8:32 NIV) Free from fear, doubt, anxiety, hopelessness ... and all the other lies of Satan.

The truth of the Bible is a safeguard against *all* the schemes of Satan. And the best *defense* to His tactics is a good *offense.* Which is why the Apostle Paul writes, "...Put on every piece of God's armor so you will be able to resist the enemy in the time of evil. Then after the battle you will still be standing firm. Stand your ground, ...and take the sword of the Spirit, which is the Word of God...." (Eph 6:13-17 NLT) "The sword of the Spirit" is God's Holy Word. Interestingly, it's the only offensive weapon the Apostle mentions when describing our spiritual battle gear.

Paul again admonishes us, in Hebrews 4:12, "...The Word of God is alive and powerful. It is sharper than the sharpest two-edged sword...." (NLT) We get a demonstration of this power, in the Book of Matthew. While fasting and praying in the wilderness, Jesus is tempted three times by Satan. He overcomes His enemy by wielding the sword of the Spirit: three times Satan thrusts at our Lord with lies, and three times Jesus triumphantly counters with the truth of God's Word—declaring *"It is written"!* (Matt 4:4-10)

We must learn to do likewise in each and every skirmish. We must learn to "wield the sword"— "a worker who does not need to be ashamed and who correctly handles the Word of Truth." (2 Tim 2:15 NIV)

10 OF SATAN'S BIGGEST LIES TO CREATORS & DREAMERS

SATAN'S PROPAGANDA, like Hitler's and Goebbel's, is systematic and endless. He capitalizes on emotions, targeting our fears, doubts, and insecurities, focusing on the *natural* (our circumstances and present situation). He does his best to distract us from our faith in God and trust in His *supernatural* promises. But rest assured that the devil and all his demons—regardless of your circumstances and regardless of what people might do or say—*cannot* keep you from your destiny! The Prophet Isaiah writes, "No weapon forged against you will prevail, and you will refute every tongue that accuses you." (Isa 54:17 NIV)

Friends, the only power the enemy has over the followers of Yeshua is the power we willingly give him, by believing his lies and responding to the trials of life with a defeatist attitude. But we can overcome him through our faith in God and a strong reliance on the truth of His word. "Submit yourselves, then, to God. Resist the devil, and he will flee from you." (James 4:7 NIV)

Resist the enemy of your soul and *win* the spiritual war by "renewing your mind" (Rom 12:1-3) and avoiding "stinking thinking": replace negative, faithless thoughts (Satan's lies) with God's Word (Truth).

Here are 10 of Satan's Biggest Lies to Creators & Dreamers—AND GOD'S TRUTH TO COMBAT THEM!

Whenever Satan, "the Father of Lies" (John 8:44) and "the accuser of the brethren" (Rev 12:10), spews his venomous propaganda, follow the example of Jesus (in Matt 4:1-10) and declare: "It is written...."

Lie #1: *Your hopes and dreams are not in the cards. Just who do you think you are?*

God's Truth: It is written...
I am a child of the Most High God; the Creator of the Universe, who made me in His very own image. (Read Genesis 1:26)

"I am fearfully and wonderfully made." (Ps 139:14 NIV)

I am a joint heir with Christ Jesus: "Since we are His children, we will share His treasures—for all God gives to his Son Jesus is now ours too." (Rom 8:17 TLB)

"I can do all things through Christ who strengthens me." (Phil 4:13 NKJV)

Lie #2: *You don't have what it takes!* *You have no title, no connections, no platform and no financial resources. Face it, YOU are a nobody!*

God's Truth: It is written...
My Heavenly Father is the God of the whosoevers: the "4Fs" and the "Nobodies"! (Read John 3:16)

"The Lord does not look at the things people look at. People look at the outward appearance, but the Lord looks at the heart." (1 Sam 16:7 NIV)

"God does not show favoritism." (Acts 10:34 NIV) "[He] does not consider some people to be better than others." (ERV)

"Instead, God chose things the world considers foolish in order to shame those who think they are wise. And he chose things that are powerless to shame those who are powerful." (1 Cor 1:27)

"Remember the LORD your God, because He is the one who gives you the ability to produce wealth." (Deut 8:18 ISV)

"And my God shall supply all your need according to His riches in glory by Christ Jesus." (Phil 4:19 NKJV)

*Lie #3: **You're too old!*** *Your best years are behind you. You've missed your opportunity!*

God's Truth: It is written...
Abraham was 100 years old and his wife Sarah was 90, when the couple conceived and gave birth to Isaac, the Son of Promise! (Read Genesis 17:17; 21:5)

Moses was already on the "downhill" side of forty when God called him to be the deliverer of His people the Hebrews. He then spent the next 40 years in the wilderness before returning to Egypt and beginning this monumental work. So the guy God used to part the Red Sea and bring down the Ten Commandments was indeed a well-seasoned saint! (Exod 2:11; 3; Acts 7:23)

And Joshua and Caleb were slaying giants at 85! (Josh 14:10-11; Num 13:30)

"...The people who know their God shall be strong, and carry out *great exploits.*" (Dan 11:32 NKJV)

"The Lord blessed the <u>latter</u> part of Job's life (insert your name) <u>more</u> than the former part." (Job 42:12 NIV)

*Lie #4: **You're too young!*** *Nobody will take you seriously. Wait until you're older and wiser and more experienced.*

God's Truth: It is written...
David was just a shepherd boy—the lowest social status in his time and culture—with no military training (or any other experience) when he defeated Goliath! (1 Sam 17:14,50,58)

The Virgin Mary was a teenager when God chose her to become the Mother of Jesus Christ; Yeshua, the Messiah of Israel and the Savior of the World! (Luke 1:26-38)

Saint Paul said to Timothy, the young leader he mentored, "Don't let anyone look down on you because you are young, but set an example ... in speech, in conduct, in love, in faith and in purity. (1 Tim 4:12 NIV)

Now picture the Lord saying to you: "Before I formed you in the womb I knew you, before you were born I set you apart." (Jer 1:5 NIV)

Lie #5: You're not worthy! *You've made too many mistakes. You've sinned too much so God can't use you.*

God's Truth: It is written...
"Come now, let us settle the matter," says the Lord. **"Though your sins are like scarlet, they shall be as white as snow."** (Isa 1:18 NIV)

"If we confess our sins, He is faithful and just and will forgive us our sins and purify us from all unrighteousness." (1 John 1:9 NIV)

"Therefore, if anyone *is* in Christ, *he is* a new creation; old things have passed away; behold, all things have become new." (2 Cor 5:17 NKJV)

"For by grace you have been saved through faith, and that not of yourselves; *it is* the gift of God, not of works, lest anyone should boast. For we are His workmanship, created in Christ Jesus for good works...." (Eph 2:8 NKJV)

Lie #6: God doesn't love you! *He doesn't care about you—or your stupid goals and dreams!*

God's Truth: It is written...
"For God so loved the world (<u>insert your name here</u>), that He gave His only begotten Son, that whosoever believeth in Him should not perish, but have everlasting life." (John 3:16 KJV)
Welcome to God's prestigious club of whosoevers!

"...God is love." (1 John 4:8 KJV) (1 Cor 13:4-8 describes God's amazing kind of love.)

"In this is love, not that we loved God, but that He loved us and sent His Son *to be* the propitiation for our sins. (1 John 4:10 KJV)

"'I have loved you with an everlasting love; ...with lovingkindness I have drawn you *and* continued My faithfulness to you.'" (Jer 31:3 AMP) "'I've never quit loving you and never will. Expect love, love, and more love! And so now I'll start over with you and build you up again....'" (MSG)

Lie #7: God has forgotten you *and your hopes and dreams!*

God's Truth: It is written...
"I have inscribed you on the palms *of My hands*." (Isa 49:6 NASB)

"'For I know the plans *and* thoughts that I have for you,' says the Lord, 'plans for peace *and* well-being and not for disaster, to give you a future and a hope.'" (Jer 29:11 AMP)

"God even knows [numbers; counts] how many hairs are on your head." (Matt 10:29-31 EXB)

"You keep track of all my sorrows. You have collected all my tears in your bottle. You have recorded each one in your book." (Ps 56:8 NLT)

"He who has begun a good work in you will complete *it*...." (Phil 1:6 NKJV)

"For the gifts and the calling of God *are* irrevocable." (Rom 11:29 NKJV)

Lie #8: God has abandoned you! *Just look at all the bad things that have happened in your life—and where you are now!*

God's Truth: It is written...
"I will never leave you nor forsake you." (Heb 13:5 NKJV)

"...I am with you always, *even* to the end of the age." (Matt 28:20 NKJV)

"And we know [with great confidence] that God [who is deeply concerned about us] causes all things to work together [as a plan] for good for those who love God...." (Rom 8:28 AMP)

He turns every curse into a blessing! (Deut 32:5)

"Ye thought to do evil to me, but God turned it into good, and he used what you did to me to <u>advance</u> me...." (Gen 50:20 WYC)

The Lord promises: "And I will restore *or* replace for you the years that the locust has eaten...." (Joel 2:16 AMP)

"For the Lord *is* a God of justice; Blessed *are* all those who wait for Him." (Isa 30:18 NKJV)

"He is the Rock; His deeds are perfect. Everything he does is just and fair. He is a faithful God who does no wrong; how just and upright he is!" (Deut 32:4 NLT)

Lie #9: *Face it,* **it's NEVER going to happen!** *It's taken too long!*

God's Truth: It is written...
"At just the right time, I will respond to you." (Isa 49:8 NLT)

"There is a time for everything.... He has made everything beautiful in its time." (Eccl 3:1-7,11 NIV)

"Wait for the LORD; be strong and take heart and wait for the LORD." (Ps 27:14 NIV)

"For the vision is yet for the appointed time; It hastens toward the goal and it will not fail. Though it tarries, wait for it; For it will certainly come, it will not delay." (Hab 2:3 NASB)

"Let us not become weary in doing good, for at the proper time we will reap a harvest if we do not give up." (Gal 6:9 NIV)

"...Weeping may stay for the night, but rejoicing comes in the morning." (Ps 30:5 NIV)

"For lo, the winter is past, the rain is over *and* gone. The flowers appear on the earth; The time of singing has come...." (Song of Solomon 3:12 NKJV)

Lie #10: *Be realistic,* **your dream is IMPOSSIBLE!** *It's over! Just give up!*

God's Truth: It is written...
"...Nothing is impossible with God." (Luke 1:37 NLT)

"I am the LORD, the God of all the peoples of the world. Is anything too hard for me?" (Jer 32:27 NLT)

"...The just shall live by his faith." (Hab 2:4 KJV)

"Abraham [Insert your name here] never wavered in believing God's promise. In fact, his faith grew stronger.... He was fully convinced that God is able to do whatever he promises. (Rom 4:21 NLT) (See also Hebrews 11:11)

"Call to Me, and I will answer you, and show you great and mighty things, which you do not know." (Jer 33:3 NKJV)

"Now to Him who is able to do exceedingly abundantly above all that we ask or think, according to the power that works in us, to Him *be* glory ... forever and ever. Amen. (Eph 3:20-21 NKJV)

SECTION VI:
NEVER GIVE UP!

Jesus told His disciples a story about how they should keep on praying and never give up....
—Luke 18:1 CEV

...Because of his persistence ... he will give him as much as he needs.
—Luke 11:8 BLB

THE TRIUMPH OF A 4F NOBODY

WHO KNEW A MOVIE BASED on a comic book could teach us so much about spiritual warfare, while inspiring us to keep pursuing our hopes and dreams? *Captain America, the First Avenger*, starring Chris Evans as the red, white and blue super soldier, is not only entertaining, it's also an object lesson in some important Biblical truths.

The Marvel Comics superhero Captain America leaped into action in early 1941, when the first issue of his adventures hit the newsstands. That pioneering premiere issue immediately grabbed the attention of readers both young and old, because on its brightly colored cover, "Cap" was socking Adolf Hitler on the jaw. Today this only seems like the obvious thing to do: knock out one of the vilest villains of all time. But when *Captain America Comics* hit the streets, America was NOT at war with the Nazis.

The United States government didn't enter WWII until after the December 6, 1941 bombing of Pearl Harbor. In the meantime, news was arriving daily of Hitler's conquest across Europe, along with rumors of the atrocities being committed against the Jewish people—which, as many American Jews correctly suspected, were not rumors at all. But the big New York magazines were carefully sidestepping these issues. In fact, in 1938 *Time Magazine* named Adolf Hitler "Man of the Year" and had earlier plastered his puss on the cover of their April 13, 1936 issue.

Time again featured Hitler on a cover dated April 14, 1941, shortly after *Captain America* debuted, further demonstrating a general desire within the United States to continue looking the other way. But as previously stated, ignoring a problem doesn't make it go away—and it can end in disaster.

America's hesitancy to enter the war against Hitler was deeply disturbing to many, but especially to American Jews—in particular, two young men working for Timely Comics, the legendary creative team of Joe Simon and Jack Kirby. When their boss, Martin Goodman, another Jew, asked them to create a patriotic superhero who could compete with DC Comics' Superman, Joe and Jack introduced the world to Steve Rogers, better known as Captain America. And, in answer to those issues of *Time* and other news magazines, they decided to feature Hitler on the first cover of their own publication—getting knock on his backside by the world's newest righter of wrongs!

So now, fellow creators and dreamers, you know the backstory—all except for this part: after the U.S. finally entered WWII, Joe and Jack quickly enlisted to do their part. When they did, they left their Captain America character in the capable hands of a twenty-year-old creator named Stan Lee, another ... um ... Jewish comic book legend. But that's a story for another time.

Fast forward. In the movie, *Captain America, the First Avenger*, young Steve Rogers is a short, skinny kid—the classic ninety-eight-pound weakling—with a medical history of numerous and assorted ailments. Steve wants to do his patriotic duty by enlisting, but after he's examined at the local recruiting office, he's told to "go home." Almost pleading, Steve, says "Look, just give me a chance."

The Recruiting officer responds, "You'd be ineligible on your asthma alone," and then stamps a big **4F** on Steve's file.

Being labeled a 4F is a death sentence to Steve Roger's dream of becoming a U.S. soldier to fight against evil and oppression. But it's a fact, he's just too weak and scrawny for any branch of the Armed Forces.

However, **when you have a big dream,** even a seemingly impossible one, **you can expect to encounter big obstacles.** Undeterred, Steve tries over and over again to enlist. He applies in different cities, under different pretenses, each time falsifying his application. And each time he hears the same verdict: 4F!

And yet, despite all the rejections he's received, Steve keeps hoping. Despite the reality of his health and physical limitations; despite the disadvantages of coming from a lower-middle class family, of losing his parents when he was a teen; despite having no connections; despite being, in the eyes of society, a big 4F—a "nobody"—Steve Rogers never gives up. He continues to pursue his dream.

Fellow creators and dreamers (everyone), this is the kind of tenacity we must have in order to accomplish our goals and realize our hopes and dreams. Dreams demand determination! Because along the path to victory we'll face rejection, obstacles, and lots of closed doors. People will try to label us. They may even stamp us 4F, as not having what it takes to succeed.

Often, if you don't have a nice title, an impressive résumé, a sizable ministry, a solid platform, or the right connections, people will dismiss you and may even label you a "nobody." But our identity and self-worth are not determined by the negative opinions of others—whose values and attitudes are often influenced by the enemy of our soul, Satan.

Our loving Heavenly Father defines who we are: sons and daughters of the Most-High God: "...To all who believed Him and accepted Him, He gave the right to become children of

God." (John 1:12 NLT) In God's eyes NONE of us are 4F no-bodies!

"The LORD will make you the head, not the tail. If you pay attention to the commands of the LORD your God ... and carefully follow them, you will always be at the top, never at the bottom." (Deut 28:13 NIV)

"Thank you for making me so wonderfully complex! Your workmanship is marvelous—how well I know it." (Ps 139:13 NLT; See also Eph 1:6)

Once we become followers of Christ, we have access to all He has and all He's done for us. After all, we are "joint heirs with Jesus Christ" (Rom 8:17); seated with Him in Heavenly places. (Eph 2:6)

Nevertheless, as we previously discussed, if we continue in our stinking thinking we tend to focus on our weaknesses and deficiencies, and on what other people say. On what we lack instead of what we possess in Christ. The Apostle Paul writes, "God said to me, 'My grace is sufficient for you, for My power is made perfect in weakness.' ...That is why, for Christ's sake, I delight in weaknesses, in insults, in hard-ships, in persecutions, in difficulties.... For when I am weak, then I am strong." (2 Cor 12:9-10 NIV)

Counterintuitive? No, because we should always rely on His strength. When we do, He gives us the victory. We don't need to have it all together. As we encounter the challenges of life—and engage in spiritual warfare—we need to depend on His grace in order to enjoy a triumphant life. By the way, GRACE means unmerited favor, manifested through super-natural strength and power. It's what enables us to live a faith-filled life.

Your present circumstances might be less than advanta-geous. The facts may not be in your favor. **But we don't de-pend on facts and circumstances alone.** "For we live by faith, not by sight." (2 Cor 5:7; Hab 2:4) We don't deny the facts, but we rely on God to determine the outcome in every situation, trusting that He can and will change our present reality by "working all things together for our good." (Roman 8:28)

God always has the final say, not people—and certainly not the "father of lies": Satan. (John 8:44) In the natural state of affairs, we may be disadvantaged. The odds may be stacked against us, as they were with Steve Rogers. But in the spiritual realm, we have a definite advantage that carries far more weight than our present circumstances.

Like Steve, we may have a seemingly impossible dream, but as stated earlier, throughout our journey we can remain confident that we serve a God who makes a way where there seems to be no way. (Isa 43:16-17) A God who "opens doors that no one can shut." (Rev 3:8 NIV)

Got impossible dreams? "Humanly speaking, it is impossible. But not with God. Everything is possible with God." (Mark 10:27 NLT) So stay in faith and never give up! A day will come—as it did for Steve Rogers—when you'll get your chance and experience a breakthrough!

IT HAPPENED AT
THE WORLD'S FAIR

REFUSING TO GIVE UP, Steve decides to try yet again, when he and his long-time friend Sgt. Bucky Barnes attend the 1943 World Exposition in New York. Bucky, who's more like a brother to Steve, gets a little irritated. Instead of having fun at the fair, Steve's still focused on his seemingly impossible dream of joining the army.

"What is it?" Bucky asks, in exasperation. "You got something to prove?"

Steve calmly responds, "What do you want me to do, collect scrap metal with my little wagon?" He then points out that there are countless guys overseas risking their lives in the fight against Nazi oppression, and he feels he can do no less. "It's not about me!"

Bucky realizes his friend is right. He hugs Steve and they part company in peace. But unknown to these two men, an elderly gentleman has been listening to their conversation. His name is Dr. Abraham Erskine, an unassuming scientist who's destined to play a big part in Steve's life.

In the next scene, Steve is sitting on a cot in a makeshift examination room inside the Expedition's Army Recruiting booth. He's waiting for the doctor to return, when in walks an M.P. followed shortly afterward by Dr. Erskine.

Erskine has a file documenting Steve's numerous failed attempts to enlist in various cities. As he flips through it, he asks, "Where are you from, Mr. Rogers? Is it New Haven? Or Paramus? Five exams in five different cities." During this exchange, Steve is hastily dressing. He knows that falsification of an enlistment application is a serious offense.

But Erskine's not at all interested in legalities. "It's not the exams I'm interested in," he says. "It's the five tries." He also remarks, "So, you want to go overseas. Kill some Nazis."

Steve, who's always been picked on because of his scrawny size, responds honestly: "I don't want to kill anyone. I don't like bullies. I don't care where they're from"

"Well," says Erskine, "there are already so many big men fighting this war. Maybe what we need now is a little guy. I can offer you a chance. Only a chance. ...So where is the little guy from? Actually?"

"Brooklyn," Steve answers.

Dr. Abraham Erskine is true to his word; in the next scene, Steve Rogers is once again standing before an Army recruiter's desk, with his file open before him. Within that file is a history of failure: five separate attempts, four previous verdicts of 4F—unfit to serve. But the response to his fifth try, to Steve's delight, is success. He watches with relief—knowing that at last he's realized his long-held dream of becoming a U.S. soldier, of getting an opportunity to do his part in the fight against evil tyranny—as his application is stamped **1A!**

Spiritual lessons? Yes indeed, including a couple of points we'll share in our next article. For now, we'll examine four truths that apply to all us creators and dreamers—to everyone actually.

Again, **NEVER GIVE UP! When one door closes, try another.** Jesus said, "...keep on asking, and you will receive what you ask for. Keep on seeking, and you will find. Keep on knocking, and the door will be opened to you." (Luke 11:9 NLT)

Because, one day, when you least expect it, **you will have a "divine appointment"** with someone who's God-sent to help you realize your hopes and dreams; a facilitator, a collaborator, a connection; a true "Barnabas" (as Acts 9:26-31) who, like Dr. Erskine, will look beyond the surface to see your potential—and "offer you a chance"! Rest assured the time will come, because God "blesses the righteous man ... [and] surrounds him with favor as with a shield." (Ps 5:12 NASB)

In God's estimation we are all 1A! There are no 4F washouts in His eyes. God created each of us "in His own image" (Gen 1:26); and within each of us He sees tremendous potential. It's God who put the dreams in our hearts, and it's

God who grants us the gifts and talents—the creativity—to pursue and realize those dreams. "A person's gift makes room for him, and leads him before important people." (Prov 18:16 NET)

Our loving Heavenly Father has great plans for us! (Jer 29:11) In fact, God is committed to our success. He will help us realize our hopes and dreams, by sending a Barnabas, by opening doors, by making a way where there seems to be no way. (Isa 43:19) With God's help, we WILL be victorious! We are fully "convinced and confident of this very thing, that He who has begun a good work in you will [continue to] perfect and complete it...." (Phil 1:6 AMP)

When the Lord gives you a dream, a goal, an aspiration—it's a "keeper"; God does NOT change His mind. To quote Romans 11:29, "For the gifts and the calling of God are irrevocable" (ESV) and "can never be withdrawn." (NLT) It doesn't matter if we make poor choices, if we fail, if we have to take a detour, or get delayed, or even grow weary and disillusioned along the way. God always has a plan to get us back on track, back on course, and back in the fight. We just need to trust Him and follow His leading, because He is "Faithful and True"! (Rev 19:11)

"God is not like people. He tells no lies. He is not like humans. He doesn't change his mind. When He says something, he does it. When He makes a promise, He keeps it."

(Num 23:19 GW)

CHOSEN FOR GREATNESS

STEVE ROGERS GETS SHIPPED OFF to Boot Camp, at a special installation under the command of Colonel Chester Phillips, a tough leader played by Tommy Lee Jones. There, under the watchful eye of Dr. Erskine, Steve begins his basic military training—which is far from easy for him.

Steve is part of a hand-picked group of men, one of whom will be chosen for a very special assignment. All around him are vigorous specimens of manhood, and poor Steve's the scrawniest guy in the bunch. Physically, he can barely keep up with his musclebound peers.

Colonel Phillips observes the weakling Rogers as the young man struggles to do a pushup, and then says to Dr. Erskine, "You're not really thinking about picking Rogers, are you? Look at [him]. He's makin' me cry."

Erskine calmly responds, "I am looking for qualities beyond the physical."

Phillips picks up a dummy hand grenade, pulls the pin, and snarls, "You don't win wars with niceness, doctor. You win wars with guts." He tosses it into the midst of the soldiers doing calisthenics, and yells "GRENADE!"

In a heartbeat, all the specimens of superior manhood move with decisiveness and perfect unity—away from the grenade. Steve, on the other hand, dives on the dummy explosive, ready to sacrifice himself, in an effort to save his fellow recruits. When the grenade doesn't go off, he looks around and asks, "Is this a test?" It's the same question Steve asked Dr. Erskine upon their first meeting, at the 1943 World Exposition in New York.

Steve had passed that "test" and he passed this one, too, with flying colors: whatever the young man lacked in muscle mass, he more than made up for—in strength of character.

Colonel Phillips is surprised, and yet, he's still not convinced that this "ninety-pound asthmatic" brought onto his Army base will ever amount to anything. The colonel just grunts, "He's still skinny," and walks away.

Weeks later, at the end of Steve Rogers' basic training, and against the advice of experts and the continued protests of Colonel Phillips, Dr. Erskine chooses Steve for his great experiment: to create the first super-soldier in U.S. Military history, by injecting him with a top-secret serum.

Steve, the weakest and least likely to succeed at anything; the skinny kid from Brooklyn with a long list of physical ailments and personal failures; who previously had no connections or prospects; is about to make headlines. The odds were stacked against him, but this disadvantaged soul has been chosen for bigger things!

He wasn't the smartest, or the most qualified. And he certainly wasn't the strongest. Nor was he favored among other men. He didn't come from a prestigious family, and he wasn't the product of a fine military academy. His "training" was in the school of hard knocks, on the streets of Brooklyn. So, of all people, why in the world had Steve Rogers been chosen to receive Dr. Erskine's secret formula?

The night before the big procedure, Erskine explains to Steve, "This is why you were chosen. Because the strong man who has known power all his life, may lose respect for that power, but a weak man knows the value of strength, and knows ... compassion."

Don't miss this, friends: Steve was chosen because he is weak! Furthermore, his weakness will ultimately result in Steve becoming strong—strong enough to accomplish extraordinary things.

This idea reminds us of an incredible spiritual principle. God chooses the weak to do great things. The "weak" include those who lack credentials and connections, talents and abilities, and anyone who does not rely on his own strength to do the will of God. These "4F nobodies" rely instead on God's strength and abilities and connections—and come out on top. With God's help, they become 1A!

The Apostle Paul writes, "God has chosen the foolish

things of the world, to confound the wise. And God has chosen the weak things of the world, to confound things which are strong." (1 Cor 1:27 NMB)

Here's how the Message Bible states this truth: "Take a good look, friends, at who you were when you got called.... I don't see many of "the brightest and the best" among you, not many influential, not many from high-society families. Isn't it obvious that God deliberately chose men and women that the culture overlooks..., chose these "nobodies" to expose the hollow pretensions of the "somebodies"? That makes it quite clear that none of you can get by with blowing your own horn before God. Everything that we have ... comes from God by way of Jesus Christ...."

Like Steve Rogers, we can be "weak" in body, "weak" in our circumstances, "weak" by worldly standards—and still prevail with God's help, guidance and resources. Again, Paul writes, "...When I am weak [in human strength], then I am strong [truly able, truly powerful, truly drawing from God's strength]." (2 Cor 12:10 AMP)

Fellow creators and dreamers, are you feeling a bit less than super these days? Then stop it! (We say this in love, of course!) Remind yourself of what God's Word says about who you are—and whose you are.

Remember, we already have everything we need to be "super"—because we have a God who "withholds no good thing." (Ps 84:11)

Just as Dr. Erskine chose Steve Rogers, God has chosen YOU ... for great and wonderful things. He has chosen you to:

Use your dreams, talents and creativity to make a positive contribution in your particular field, area of interest, sphere of influence, etc.: 1) **Be a blessing** to your family and those around you; 2) **Make a difference** in the lives of people you encounter along life's journey; 3) **Perhaps, even touch the world!**

Tough assignment? Not when God's in the picture. Because "...You are the ones chosen by God, chosen for the high calling ... God's instruments to do His work and speak out for Him, to tell others of the night-and-day difference He made for you—from nothing to something, from rejected to accepted." (1 Peter 2:9 MSG) From 4F to 1A!

IS THIS A TEST?

TWICE IN *CAPTAIN AMERICA, THE FIRST AVENGER,* Steve Rogers innocently asks, "Is this a test?" In both instances, the reality is YES! In fact, throughout his whole life Steve has continually been put to the test ... by tough times, sad circumstances, and big bullies.

Steve lost both parents at a young age. He grew up handicapped by poor health. And, despite his small stature and physical weakness, he's had to stand up to a succession of street bullies. But win or lose, when things get tough, Steve stands his ground. "You start running," he says, "they'll never let you stop. You stand up, you push back."

Steve is also put to the test in his hopes and aspirations, because despite repeated attempts to enlist, he is continually rejected as unfit to serve. And yet, he never gives up.

At the recruiting booth ... when Dr. Erskine asks him why he wants to enlist so badly: "Do you want to kill Nazis?" Steve's reasons are noble. He's not motivated by pride, hatred or bigotry. Nor does he have a killer instinct: "I don't wanna kill anyone," Steve replies. "I don't like bullies."

On the training field during boot camp ... when he throws his scrawny body atop a grenade thrown into the midst of his fellow recruits. Steve didn't know the grenade was a dummy, intended to test the reactions of the trainees.

And eventually, as a super soldier defending the cause ... the first of many tests on the "frontlines" comes far sooner than Steve expected.

Shortly before Dr. Erskine endows him with great power, the scientist tells Steve, "Whatever happens tomorrow, you must promise me one thing. That you will stay who you are, not a perfect soldier, but a good man." Erskine's desire for Steve to remain true to himself—a good man—is similar to God's desire for each of us: He wants us to remain true to

Him; to become more and more like Christ. As Paul writes, "God chose [us] to be like His Son [conformed to His image]." (Rom 8:29 ICB)

Like Steve Rogers, **we must be willing to make sacrifices.** God probably won't require us to jump on grenades, but we will face challenges in life, many of which will provide us ample opportunity to put the wellbeing and interests of others above our own. Such spiritual sacrifices will require some of the compassion that marked Steve for greatness.

However, like Steve Rogers, **we must go through basic training.** We need to learn how to wage spiritual warfare. But we don't get our training at a military base under the watchful eye of a kind and wise facilitator named Dr. Erskine. Our spiritual boot camp is right here, wherever we happen to be, in whatever circumstances we find ourselves—under the watchful eye of a wise and kind facilitator whom we call Jesus Christ, or Yeshua. The Lord God who promised He'd always stay with us, through thick and thin.

Jesus said, "...Be sure of this: I am with you always, even to the end of the age." (Matt 28:20 NLT)

What's more, we have EVERYTHING we need to realize our hopes and dreams—and to live a victorious (and productive life). As the psalmist David writes, "You go before me and follow me. You place your hand of blessing on my head. ...I can never get away from your presence! If I go up to heaven, you are there; if I go down to the grave, you are there. If I ride the wings of the morning, if I dwell by the farthest oceans, even there your hand will guide me, and your strength will support me." (Ps 139:5-10 NLT)

Steve's days at Boot Camp were relatively brief, but our spiritual training is a lifelong process of learning, growing, maturing, becoming all that God created us to be. And getting stronger in the Lord

"Blessed and greatly favored is the man whose strength is in You.... They go from strength to strength [increasing in victorious power]." (Ps 84:5 AMP)

Like Steve Rogers, **we too need to stand up to bullies,** and one in particular. Just as Hitler was, Satan is nothing more than a big bully. Sure, he's the ultimate Big Bully—one who influences all other bullies. But like all bullies, his bark is more intimidating than his potential bite. Satan makes a lot of noise, but he's just a fallen angel whose power is limited. He may parade around like "a roaring lion, seeking whom he may devour" (1 Peter 5:8) but never forget this:

"...You are of God and you belong to Him and have [already] overcome them ... because He who is in you is greater than he (Satan) who is in the world." Actually, the only real power Satan has over a follower of Yeshua (Christ) is the power we inadvertently give him!

Remember our warnings about "stinking thinking"? Paul warns, "And do not give the devil an opportunity [to lead you into sin by holding a grudge, or nurturing anger, or harboring resentment, or cultivating bitterness]. (Eph 4:27 AMP) Instead, follow the advice of the Apostle, who writes, "So prepare your minds for action, be completely sober [in spirit— steadfast, self-disciplined, spiritually and morally alert], fix your hope completely on the grace [of God] that is coming to you when Jesus Christ is revealed." (1 peter 1:13 AMP)

In other words, be disciplined in your thinking. Don't dwell on negative, fearful, faithless, hurtful experiences or notions. Replace such thoughts with the truth of God's Word. (See Rom 12:1-3) Don't allow the enemy to build strongholds (a negative mindset or a destructive habit) in your life.

God wants each of us to become a heavenly super soldier, able to wage spiritual warfare, capable of overcoming every obstacle, prevailing in every situation, triumphing over every circumstance—and in the words of Colonel Chester Phillips, ready to "escort Adolf Hitler to the gates of Hell." (Uh, that would be Satan, the enemy of our souls.)

Like Steve Rogers, **we, too, will be tested in the never-ending spiritual Boot Camp of life.** We'll face trials in order to reveal what we're made of, and to help develop strong character and total trust in the Lord. We'll be tested to determine if—despite our "weaknesses"—we'll stay in faith and remain true to God. Let's take our cue from the Patriarch Abraham, who is known, among other things, as "the Father of Faith" (Heb 11:8-19) and the "Friend of God." (James 2:23)

Abraham's seemingly impossible dream was to have a son. But just as Steve Rogers was considered too puny to pass the enlistment physical, the patriarch was considered too old. (He was 100.) To further stack the odds against them, Abraham's wife, Sarah, was 90 and barren! Together the couple waited 25 years for the answer to their prayers—the miraculous birth of their son Isaac! Throughout the long wait, the patriarch kept his faith and stayed the course. (You can read his inspiring story in Genesis 11:27 to Gen 25.)

"Abraham never wavered in believing God's promise. In fact, his faith grew stronger, and in this he brought glory to God. He was fully convinced that God is able to do whatever He promises." (Rom 4:20-21 NLT)

We can do the same. We start by confessing it. Got a big, seemingly impossible dream? Substitute your name for the patriarch's: "_____ did not waver in believing God's promise...."

Fellow creators and dreamers, when we face obstacles and disadvantages, rejections and delays; when we're tested along the way to realizing our hopes and dreams, just as Steve Rogers was tested, let's make sure we pass with flying colors ... by staying the course set before us.

We can do it! After all, we've been chosen for great and wonderful things by God Himself. He's equipped us with everything we need to be victorious in all circumstances.

"Have you not known? Have you not heard? The everlasting God, the Lord, The Creator of the ends of the earth, Neither faints nor is weary. His understanding is unsearchable. He gives power to the weak, And to those who have no might He increases strength." (Isa 40:28-29 NKJV)

THE BITTERSWEET TRUTH OF CAPTAIN AMERICA

O N THE DAY OF THE GREAT EXPERIMENT, when Steve Rogers begins to see his once seemingly impossible dream start to come true—to be able to serve the cause of freedom by fighting the Nazi forces of tyranny—he also learns one of the cold hard facts of life.

As several military officers and government officials look on, Steve is placed into a chamber specially designed by the wealthy industrialist Howard Stark, enabling Dr. Abraham Erskine to inject his puny subject with a top-secret super soldier formula. Stark then turns a dial, flooding the chamber with "delta waves"—and an amazing (and for Steve, somewhat painful) transformation takes place.

In mere minutes, through rapid cellular regeneration, Steve grows from a scrawny 90-pound weakling, into the epitome of male perfection; from well below average to far above average; from a scrawny kid no one took notice of—who couldn't buy his way into the army—to the man of the hour who's destined to become the subject of military enlistment posters. Steve goes from runt to hunk!

Erskine's process to transform Steve into a super soldier is a complete success, to the great relief of Special Agent Peggy Carter, who'd been tasked with helping Steve with his training. During those first weeks, and well before his transformation into a superman, Peggy had developed a romantic attachment to Steve. Like Dr. Erskine, she was willing to look beyond the surface, and saw something special in the young man.

The military and government observers are also relieved. One senator quips, "I can think of some folks in Berlin who are about to get very nervous."

And of course, Steve is elated! The results of Erskine's serum are far beyond his highest hopes and wildest imaginings. Finally, he can do his patriotic duty, in the war against German oppression. Finally, he has an open door to fulfill his destiny. "How do you feel?" Peggy asks. Steve responds in awe: "Taller!"

Unfortunately, while everyone is celebrating, and before Steve has a chance to enjoy the sweetness of the moment—of the first huge step on the path to realizing his hopes and dreams—or to mentally process how it will forever change his life for the better, tragedy strikes!

Also present at this highly classified experiment, taking place in a secret facility beneath the streets of Brooklyn, is a Nazi saboteur. Access to this well-guarded underground facility is granted only to those with the proper security clearance and knowledge of a confidential pass code. And yet, in this seemingly safe and secure environment where only friends and allies should be gathered, the enemy has infiltrated.

This evil spy shoots Dr. Erskine, detonates a bomb, and flees with a vial of the precious super serum, leaving behind him death, destruction and mass mayhem.

Steve immediately runs to the side of Dr. Erskine. As he kneels over his dying mentor, Erskine weakly points to Steve's heart, to remind him of who he is; to remind him to please remain a good man, even in the face of evil. Something the doctor asked Steve to promise him, as they sat in an army barracks the night before.

As his friend and mentor dies, Steve realizes that what should have been the happiest day in his life, when his dreams are just beginning to come true, has instead turned out to be one of the saddest. Erskine's death is wrong, cruel, and ill-timed. It's a bitter disappointment that steals most of the sweetness of Steve's first victory on the road to fulfilling his destiny.

How does all this relate to spiritual warfare and the pursuit of our dreams and creative endeavors? In a few ways, one of which we'll discuss now. The rest we'll address in later sessions. (Please bare with us, there's a lot to unpack here.)

First and foremost: **LIFE is often bittersweet!**

Most creators and dreamers should be able to relate to Steve Rogers. Just when we're well along our way to realizing our greatest hopes and dreams, just when we think we've finally got a break, found an open door, met a major goal ... LIFE throws us an unexpected curve. Just when we think we've "arrived"—something totally wrong, seemingly cruel, and incredibly ill-timed happens to steal away the sweetness of our little victory and dim the brightness of an otherwise glorious achievement.

The poet Maya Angelou writes, "You may not control all the events that happen to you, but you can decide not to be reduced by them." Indeed, it's a sad truth, but there are plenty bumps along the road of life, plenty of brambles on the path to your destiny. We may stumble and fall, but what's important is what we do after we get back on our feet—how we FEEL and what we THINK once we recover from a temporary disappointment or defeat.

Jesus said, "In the world you have tribulation and distress and suffering, but be courageous [be confident, be undaunted, be filled with joy]; I have overcome the world." (John 16:33 AMP) In other words, regardless of what life dishes out, never lose heart in the pursuit of your goals and dreams. Stay faithful and you will get there.

By the way, **one of Satan's tactics of warfare is to try to steal your peace when "life happens."** But we have the perfect defense: God's peace is not based on circumstances or feelings; it's based on: **who He is**— "the Prince of Peace" (Isa 9:6); **who we are, and whose we are.** As part of the family of God, we are heirs to His peace.

Interestingly, the Hebrew word for peace is *Shalom*. It means: complete; nothing missing, nothing lacking. The peace of God is knowing that no matter what circumstances or situation you find yourself in, you have everything you need to meet the challenge. No wonder it's a standard form of greeting: Peace be with you!

God's concept of peace is also a part of the Aaronic blessing which Rabbis still declare over their congregants at the end of Jewish Sabbath services (Shabbat). Read it, in Numbers 6:24-26, and claim it's truth.

Have you hit a bump in the road? Is something or someone raining on your parade? If so, run to the loving arms of the Prince of Peace. Trust God even when life throws you an unexpected curve. Stay in peace (Shalom) even in the midst of negative circumstances. Life is often bittersweet, but we can choose not to allow it to sour our disposition or dim our outlook. Focus instead on God's love, His goodness and His faithfulness. When you do, you'll experience the complete triumph of which the prophet Isaiah writes:

"You will keep in perfect and constant peace the one whose mind is steadfast [that is, committed and focused on You—in both inclination and character], Because he trusts and takes refuge in You [with hope and confident expectation]."

(Isa 26:3 AMP)

THE ELEMENT
OF SURPRISE

T HE MILITARY FACILITY CHOSEN for Steve's transformation
into a super soldier was fortified and heavily guarded. It
was supposed to be a safe and secure environment for Dr.
Erskine to work ... among friends and allies only. So the presence of a Nazi spy took everyone by surprise. Even the MPs
were caught off guard by the actions of this saboteur, and the
consequences were horrible: death, destruction, and great
personal loss.

In any wartime situation, the element of surprise always
gives one the advantage. It allows one to attack their enemy
at its weakest and most vulnerable moment—when it's least
expected and they're totally unprepared. For instance, the
unprovoked attack on Pearl Harbor on December 6, 1941 was
a total surprise, and it resulted in chaos and mass destruction for the U.S. Forces stationed there.

Understanding this strategy, the time and precise location
for the Invasion of Normandy on D-Day was one of the most
heavily guarded secrets of WWII. As was the Manhattan Project, which resulted in the creation of the world's first atomic
bomb. Maintaining secrecy is vital to having the upper hand
in military strategy. And uncovering the secrets of one's enemy is just as important—which explains the presence of
spies (often where they are least expected).

Counterintelligence is vital to the war effort. In spiritual
warfare, **we believers have our own Department of Counterintelligence.** Thanks to God's spiritual training manual
(the Bible) for Boot Camp and Life in general, we can know
exactly how Satan operates and what his evil plans are. It's
like having an army of super spies! Hence, we don't have to

ever get caught off guard. To the contrary, we have the element of surprise to our advantage.

In *Captain America, The First Avenger*, the enemy was able to sneak in and wreak havoc: Dr. Erskine is killed, a Nazi spy manages to swipe a vial of the doctor's secret formula, and part of the facility is blown up. Sound familiar? Satan, too, likes to sneak in. And he also "comes to steal, kill and destroy." (John 10:10) But since we know his tactics, since we know the enemy of our soul is relentless, Satan has lost the element of surprise!

The Apostle Peter writes, "Be sober, be vigilant; because your adversary the devil walks about like a roaring lion, seeking whom he may devour." (1Peter 5:8 NKJV) And we particularly like the directness of the Message translation of Peter's warning: "...Stay alert. The Devil is poised to pounce, and would like nothing better than to catch you napping. Keep your guard up."

Let's be clear. Satan doesn't fight fair. Like the bully he truly is, he'll wait for the right opportunity to strike: when everything's going just great and your guard is down; or when you're already struggling through tough times and feeling a little spiritually weak; when you're on a roll and you least expect it; and sadly, when your back is turned. Yes, the enemy of your soul loves to hit you where it hurts most: he'll target the areas of your life where you're most vulnerable— and he'll even use those closest to you when he attacks!

Satan loves to hit below the belt. And he loves to steal our peace, as we previously discussed. And yet, we still have the advantage. First, we have everything we need to defeat him. Second, as the Apostle Paul writes, "...We are not ignorant of his devices." (2 Cor 2:11 NKJV) "The point is that we shouldn't be outsmarted by ... satan. We know what he's up to!" (NTE) Thanks to the truth of God's Word, we have a complete Intelligence Report on all of Satan's tactics and activities: The who, what, when, where and why of all his foul schemes.

Steve Rogers' first triumph on the road to realizing his hopes and dreams was bittersweet. What should have one of the happiest days in his life instead became an occasion for sorrow. With the tragic murder of his friend and mentor Dr. Abraham Erskine, Steve's victory quickly turned to disappointment and sadness.

Fellow creators and dreamers (that's all of us), another of Satan's tactics is to use life's disappointments to halt us in our tracks. Our enemy wants to discourage us to the point that we'll give in and give up ... on people, on God, on our hopes and dreams. Satan wants to derail us long before we reach our destination: the complete fulfillment of the unique plan and divine purpose God's chosen for each and every one of us.

So, to paraphrase an Army recruiting poster, we can be all God intended us to be ... or we can wind up being a train wreck. Don't let Satan win!

Like Steve Rogers, who stood up to bullies, on both the streets of Brooklyn and the German front lines, we also must stand up to Satan, the ultimate bully. "Therefore," the Apostle James writes, "submit to God. Resist the devil and he will flee from you. Draw near to God and He will draw near to you." (James 4:7-8 NKJV)

What's more, if we're going to realize our hopes and dreams, and live a victorious life, we must learn to overcome disappointment—because like wild onions growing amongst the honeysuckle, disappointments are a bittersweet fact of life! After all, we live in a fallen, imperfect world. It's inhabited by imperfect people (that's us) who have a knack (albeit an unintentional one) for letting us down. Then, too, there will always be a few who actually get their kicks by intentionally trying to hurt and disappoint us. Such people, whether or not they realize it, are rendering aid to the enemy; like that Nazi spy who struck down Dr. Erskine in the "Cap" movie, these "aggravating agents of antagonism" allow themselves to perpetrate evil.

It's okay, though. We can foil the enemy and have victory over disappointments in life by putting our trust in God and our expectations on the Lord. HE is the only ONE who is PERFECT. And He will always see us through!

The Great Psalmist, King David, who suffered his fair share of disappointments, left these words of comfort and reassurance: "My soul, wait silently for God alone, For my expectation is from Him. He only is my rock and my salvation; He is my defense; I shall not be moved. In God is my salvation and my glory; The rock of my strength, And my refuge, is in God." (Ps 62:5-7 NKJV)

WHEN TRAGEDY STRIKES CAPTAIN AMERICA

L ESSONS LEARNED THUS FAR: *Life is often bittersweet.* We must choose to focus on the good, not the bad, and stay in peace regardless of the circumstances. (John 7:33; Isa 26:3)

We can't afford to let our guard down, because we, too, have an enemy in Satan, and he wants to destroy us. (John 10:10) *But Satan is essentially the ultimate big bully.* We can and must stand up to him! (James 4:7-8; 1 John 4:4)

We have the element of surprise to our advantage: thanks to the Bible (our spiritual boot camp training manual) we know exactly how Satan operates. (2 Cor 2:11) And if we're ever going to achieve our goals, realize our dreams, and lead victorious and abundant lives, *we must learn to overcome disappointments*—because life is filled with them. (John 16:33)

Captain America, the First Avenger teaches another lesson. The movie illustrates one of Satan's favorite and most effective battle tactics. **He attacks at times of loss and tragedy,** particularly the death of a loved one. But loss can encompass the death of a vision or dream; the destruction of a relationship; a painful betrayal; or some other major disappointment. Tragedy strikes in many forms, and Satan will use each and every one, in an attempt to make us give up on God, people, our hopes, and our dreams. We'll address this more fully in our next article. Meanwhile....

If you'll recall, Dr. Abraham Erskine was the brilliant scientist who invented a super-soldier serum. He chose Steve Rogers to be the recipient of this serum, because he saw something special in the scrawny "kid from Brooklyn" who wouldn't give up. Thus, Erskine gave Steve the chance to realize his seemingly impossible dream.

For Steve Rogers, Dr. Erskine was a friend and a facilitator—a "Barnabas" (as in Acts 9:26-31). He was also a father figure (remember, Steve had lost his dad at an early age), and the young man had learned to admire, respect and even love the good doctor.

Dr. Erskine is truly "a good man" ... who left his beloved home in Augsburg, Germany; turned his back on a chance at power and prestige; all because he refused to support Hitler and his mad schemes to conquer the world and destroy the Jewish people. Instead, Dr. Erskine fled to America, to use his genius, his gifts and talents to help make the world a better, safer place, free from fascist oppression.

This great man, on the verge of blessing millions of people, is brutally shot down by a Nazi traitor—who himself contributed absolutely nothing positive to humanity and the free world. Steve Rogers was there. He saw it. He witnessed the death of his mentor. He experienced the greatest loss in his life since the death of his parents. It was a tragedy, a disappointment, an injustice. And how could he ever hope to make sense of such a senseless act?

We don't pretend to have all the answers. Or understand why things turn out the way they do. Life is filled with such tragedy and loss, **and often there are no "answers"**—at least, not on this side of heaven. The Book of Job explores this mystery of life. We hope you'll read it soon. For now, however, allow us to share some truths and insights from God's timeless Book of Answers.

First, when it comes to spiritual warfare and the pursuit of dreams—and life in general—**ignorance is not bliss!** It's actually detrimental. In fact, the prophet Hosea writes, "My people are destroyed for lack of knowledge." (Hosea 4:6 KJV)

Knowledge is power. But not just any knowledge. Information about God, His commandments (call them the Rules of Engagement), His principles (counter maneuvers against the enemy) and His promises (the Field Guide of Faith)—that is true power!

Don't forget, **we are not ignorant of Satan's schemes.** (2 Cor 2:11) We know exactly how he operates. So we should never be caught off guard or unprepared.

If you're anchored in God's Truths, when tragedy strikes,

when loss, disappointments, or injustice come your way, you can be like "the man who built his house on the Rock"! "...When the rain descended and the floods came, and the winds blew and beat the house; it did not fall, for it was founded on the Rock." (Matt 7:25 NKJV)

Fellow creators and dreamers, here's a great Bible promise you can count on: "God, who gives all grace, will make everything right. He will make you strong ... support you and keep you from falling." (1 Peter 5:10 NCV)

ANOTHER SUPER-SOLDIER SERUM

ONE OF SATAN'S FAVORITE BATTLE TACTICS is to use personal tragedy (loss, betrayal, disappointment, injustice, etc.) to discourage us to the point that we lose faith in God and give up on our hopes and dreams. To combat Satan, we must run to God and stay anchored in the truth and promises of His Word; each of us must build our "house" (our life and our hopes and dreams) upon the Rock of Ages—the God of Abraham, Isaac and Israel! (Matt 7:25)

Now, let's pose the hard questions: **How do we respond to tragedy?** How do we recover from grief, betrayal, or disappointments? How do we stay "good" when things turn out bad? How do we continue to be Godly in a world filled with injustice and … well, evil?

Short answer: We do it supernaturally!

No, we're not talking X-Files stuff here. But we do worship a supernatural God, who inhabits a supernatural world, and who moves and works in supernatural ways. Which is a good thing, because face it, in the natural—in our own strength—we're pretty feeble when it comes to weathering the storms of life. Otherwise, tragedy could strike and utterly destroy us! In fact, our world is filled with spiritual and emotional casualties, people who are so broken that they never fully recover; individuals so shattered that not only do they give up on God, and on their hopes and dreams, they also give up on life itself. In many ways, these people are like the walking dead.

Like zombies in real life, these unfortunate souls do little more than exist, going through the motions of their daily routines, with no hope, no joy, no enthusiasm, no sense of purpose—completely missing out on the abundant life Jesus Christ promises in John 10:10. No doubt, they were once like us. Now they exist as human wreckage. But we shouldn't deal with these emotional zombies in typical television fashion. We're not out to finish them off. To the contrary, we should reach out to them, and attempt to restore them to the land of the abundant living. This is why it's critical to engage in the sacred practice of hospitality.

We certainly don't want to suffer a similar fate. But then, we don't have to! In the supernatural we can weather the storms and endure the tragedies of life. How do we tap into the supernatural? Nothing Arcane. We do it by simply relying on God's strength, and banking on the truth and promises of His Word. As the prophet Zechariah writes, we overcome "Not by might, nor by power, but by My Spirit, says the Lord Almighty—you will succeed because of My Spirit, though you are ... weak.'" (Zechariah 4:6 TLB)

Just as Dr. Erskine injected Steve Rogers with a super-soldier serum, God imbues us with a special spiritual power that can transform us into super men and women. The big difference, however, is that what God injects into our lives is not concocted by human hands in a lab. It's actually ALIEN technology! Like the Tesseract cube so coveted by Captain America's arch enemy, the Red Skull—and later, by the villainous Loki, in the movie *Marvel's The Avengers*, this supernatural power supply is literally out of this world!

The Holy Spirit, the third person of the Trinity, is our super-soldier serum. He is the ONE who comes to dwell within us, at the exact moment we ask Christ to forgive us for our sins, to redeem us, and to come into hearts. After Jesus takes up residence, the door to our souls is "sealed with the Holy Spirit of Promise" (Eph 1:13)—sort of like hanging up a sign that states "Satan Keep Out!"

After His death and resurrection, Jesus said, "...You will receive power when the Holy Spirit comes upon you. And you will be My witnesses, telling people about Me everywhere—in Jerusalem, throughout Judea, in Samaria, and to the ends of the earth." (Acts 1:8 NLT)

The word power means the ability to do something or act (respond) in a particular way; the capacity to direct or influence the behavior of others, or to effect change. Power is the force, energy, strength, influence, momentum ... to build, to create, to accomplish, to achieve—or to withstand any enemy attack!

The Greek word for power is *dunamus*, which roughly translates "Miraculous might." From this word we get the name for dynamite, one of the most powerful explosives used in WWII to destroy bridges, blowup damns, and thereby thwart the advance of the enemy. By the way, are you beginning to see all the parallels to spiritual warfare?

Fellow creators and dreamers empowered by God's Holy Spirit (our super-soldier serum), **our Heavenly Father has given us power and authority** over the dark forces of the enemy. We have what it takes to defeat the schemes of Satan and win the spiritual war for the freedom of our souls. Hence, we can confidently declare: "We have overcome them ... because He who is in [us] is greater than he who is in the world." (1 John 4:4 NKJV)

When we respond supernaturally to the trials of life, those trials can actually make us stronger, not weaker. We come through the battlefield of disappointments, betrayals, loss and heartache BETTER, NOT BITTER. In the end, like Colonel Chester Phillips, the battle-hardened, tough old soldier in *Captain America, the First Avenger*, we'll eventually be able to overcome anything life throws at us.

We'll be victorious in any situation, because after all, we are "heirs of God and joint heirs with Christ" (Rom 8:17 NKJV) ... seated in Heavenly places with the Father. (Eph 1:20)

We'll be *above* our circumstances, not *below* them, because: "The Lord is the strength of my life; Of whom shall I be afraid? When the wicked came against me... My enemies and foes, They stumbled and fell." (Ps 27:1-2 NKJV)

THE CAPTAIN AMERICA LEGACY

With the death of Dr. Erskine, the enemy strikes a real blow to the cause of freedom, but interestingly, it's this tragedy that actually propels Steve Rogers along the road to his destiny—as the first Avenger. On the heels of his tragic loss, and without giving it a second thought, Steve hotly pursues and captures the Nazi spy who shot down his friend and facilitator in cold blood. In the process Steve discoveries his amazing new strength and abilities and uses them for the first time.

The lesson here is that in life, it's often during difficult times—in the midst of loss and tragedy—that we discover our true strength and abilities in God alone; and have an opportunity to see our spiritual super soldier serum (the Holy Spirit) in action. The Apostle Peter writes, "...Greatly rejoice, even though ... you have been distressed by various trials, so that the proof of your faith, being more precious than gold which is perishable, even though tested by fire, may be found to result in praise and glory and honor at the revelation of Jesus Christ." (1 Peter 1:6-7 NASB)

Steve Rogers could have gotten caught up in the moment. And afterwards, he could have spent months mourning the loss of his mentor; losing his focus and getting stuck in the past. Instead, Steve kept his eye on the mission, and the reason Dr. Erskine blessed him with super soldier abilities: to defeat the enemy and have total victory over evil.

We must follow Steve's example, as well as that of the Apostle Paul, who declared, "One thing I do: forgetting what lies behind and straining forward to what lies ahead, I press on toward the goal for the prize of the upward call of God in Christ Jesus." (Phil 3:13-14 NLT)

While pursuing Erskine's murderer, Steve begins to see how fast he can run, how much endurance he can muster, how much inner strength he can summon. The next day all the newspapers recount his exploits, making Steve an overnight sensation. But he doesn't let his newfound abilities or instant celebrity status go to his head. In fact, he handles the limelight with grace and humility.

Let us ponder at this point: with each and every personal triumph, will we handle the spotlight of success just as gracefully? We hope so, because "God opposes the proud but favors the humble." (1 Peter 5:5 NLT)

And thus is born a legend. Steve Rogers, the 4F ninety-pound weakling from Brooklyn, who refused to lose hope and give up on his seemingly impossible dream, begins a new chapter—as Captain America. In both the original Marvel Comics magazines and the big-budget movies based on them, "Cap" is the symbol of all that is good and right and noble in the free world. He embodies the ideal that any one of us, no matter what our circumstances or social status, and regardless of any disability or disadvantage, can still achieve the great American Dream!

Cap is the personification of courage, determination, integrity, goodness and humility. He reflects the Judeo-Christian values upon which our nation was founded; the values of freedom, equality, family and faith which Cap's creators, Joe Simon and Jack Kirby, held dear. These values may not always be practiced, but we should always aspire to them. We must remember that "Godliness makes a nation great, but sin is a disgrace to any people." (Prov 14:34 NLT)

Captain America's optimism, "can do" attitude, patriotism, and sense of duty reflect the strong moral standards that defined what has been called "The Greatest Generation"—the people who endured the Great Depression of the 1930s and stepped up to serve during WWII; the kind of heroes depicted in Cap's handpicked special strike force the Howling Commandos.

Fighting alongside Captain America, the Howling Commandos storm the strongholds of the enemy, confronting any threat to our freedoms, and ultimately preserving our way of "life, liberty and the pursuit of happiness." Cap and the Commandos remind us of the bravery of today's heroes, our military (both our veterans and active-duty personnel), our law enforcement officers, and our emergency first responders, who continue to make great personal sacrifices on our behalf. Jesus said, "Greater love has no one than this: to lay down one's life for one's friends." (John 15:13 NIV)

This is the ideal that prompted Steve Rogers' repeated attempts to join the U.S. Army, and which motivated him to do his patriotic duty throughout the movie. He expresses this profound philosophy when he tells his friend Bucky, at the New York World's Fair, "It's not about me."

Just as Steve came to this sobering realization, WE need to similarly realize that LIFE itself is not about us!

Fellow creators and dreamers, we have a Higher Calling, to do God's Will in all things. We acknowledge this calling in The Lord's Prayer, with the declaration "Thy Kingdom come, thy will be done, on Earth as it is in Heaven." (Matt 6:10)

It's a hard truth, but our main purpose in life is NOT to realize our hopes and dreams. These matters and pursuits certainly are, however, a significant part of God's plan for us. But think of your big dreams and creative pursuits as just "the icing on the cake" the Lord has cooked up for you. Indeed, He's prepared a great future for each of us, but the foundation of this future is that we mature spiritually and become more like Yeshua, the Son of God.

First and foremost, our Heavenly Father wants each of us to be "conformed into His image." (Rom 8:29) He also wants us to bring Glory to His name by reflecting, in our lives, His divine character (love, generosity, service, and sacrifice—the essence of hospitality) through our gifts, talents, and resources ... and through our creativity and dreams.

Like Captain America, who represented the best of the U.S.A., we are to represent the best of ... well, the BEST: the Kingdom of God. As the Apostle Paul writes, "...We are ambassadors for Christ, as though God were making His appeal through us...." (2 Cor 5:20 AMP)

SUIT UP!

AFTER STEVE ROGERS RECEIVES great strength and abilities, thanks to a super soldier serum administered by his friend and mentor Dr. Abraham Erskine, he becomes Captain America, freedom-fighter extraordinaire. As Cap, Steve dons a special suit and takes up a shield emblazoned with a star, all courtesy of Uncle Sam. This distinctive red, white, and blue uniform makes Steve instantly recognizable as America's "first Avenger"—the "Star-spangled man with a plan" and definitely *not* someone you want to tangle with.

At first Steve feels the uniform is a bit much, but halfway through the movie, he changes his mind. His friend Bucky asks, "You're keeping the outfit, right?" And Steve responds, "You know what? It's kinda grown on me." But the truth of the matter is that Steve would *never* go into battle without being properly outfitted. Nor would he allow his team to. In his next cinematic adventure, *Marvel's The Avengers,* he actually tells his associates, prior to facing an alien invasion, to "Suit up!"

Sound advice. **Our God, the Captain of the Lord of Hosts, also asks *His* followers to "suit up!"** And although our "outfit" isn't as colorful as those worn by Cap and the other Avengers, it is nonetheless functional. Like the Black Widow's fighting garb which comes with wristbands capable of sending out a stinging electrical shock; or Agent Barton's uniform which is equipped with a quiver full of deadly trick arrows, our divinely designed suits are also POWERFUL. In fact, they're like Tony Stark's Iron Man armor.

This armor covers us head to toe, protecting the body, mind, and soul! It's supernaturally powered by the Holy Spirit—the super soldier formula flowing through our veins—and, our hearts be still, it comes with a shield that would make even Cap proud! (More on the shield in a moment.)

The Apostle Paul, who was both a Jewish rabbi and a citizen of Rome, uses the uniform and armor of the Roman Legions as a visual aid, to help us understand the purpose and workings of this super suit. Roman soldiers, after all, were a familiar (but unwelcome) sight throughout Jerusalem and the rest of the Empire at the time. Hence, the apostle writes, "…Put on every piece of God's armor so you will be able to resist the enemy in the time of evil. Then after the battle you will still be standing firm." (Eph 6:13 NLT)

Paul is telling us, *you guys are facing an alien invasion (satanic forces from the pit of Hell), so SUIT UP!* He further states, "receive your power from the Lord and from His mighty strength." (Eph 6:10 GW) The apostle knows that the key to victory is to fight the battle in God's supernatural strength, not in our own *natural* efforts and abilities.

When the young shepherd David slew the "unbeatable" giant Goliath, he announced, "You come to me with sword, spear, and javelin, but I come to you in the name of the LORD of Heaven's Armies—the God of the armies of Israel…. Today the LORD will conquer you…. And everyone assembled here will know that the LORD rescues His people, but not with sword and spear. This is the LORD's battle, and he will give you to us!" (1 Sam 17:45-47 NLT)

God assures us we will triumph, but not by conventional means or in our own *human* strength. Which is where the supernatural armor of God comes in. Paul describes the various pieces of this armor, in Ephesians 6:10-18. (Take a moment to read the verses.) We've discussed many of the components here, but we'll review one in particular: PRAYER, which is key to our Heavenly Arsenal. Think about it, even a super soldier like Cap needs to keep in contact with HQ Command!

In *Captain America, The First Avenger,* Steve's uniform came with a shield emblazoned with a star, to represent the United States. This shield was manufactured by the industrialist Howard Stark using the hardest metal known to man, a substance *not of this earth!* And, as we stated earlier, in addition to the supernatural suit God provides each member of His team, **the Lord has also given *us* a shield!**

The "stark" reality is that our shield also has a star, symbolizing its divine maker, "the bright Morning Star" (Rev 22:16); and, likewise, *it's not of this earth!*

"...Put on the full armor of God.... In addition to all this, take up the shield of faith, with which you can extinguish all the flaming arrows of the evil one." (Eph 6:13,16 NIV)

Incidentally, those "fiery arrows" or "darts" of the enemy come primarily from our own thoughts. But we can further protect our minds from "stinking thinking" by donning the head-piece of our spiritual armor, **"the Helmet of Salvation."** (Eph 6:17) How does the helmet function? *Just like Iron Man's!*

There's a computer voice inside Tony Stark's Iron Man helmet, correlating data, keeping him informed, telling him what he needs to know to defeat the bad guy. It's not unlike the voice of the Holy Spirit, who reminds each of us of the things we need to know to defeat Satan: you have received God's unconditional love (John 3:16; Jer 31:3); He has a wonderful plan for your life (Jer 29:11); and your identity and self-worth are based on Him (Ps 139:13-14) and NOT on your circumstances or the opinions of others.

When you wrap your head around these truths from God's Word, NOTHING can defeat you!

If you recall, the main battlefield for spiritual warfare is the mind. It's there that we must conquer thoughts of fear and doubt, and any feelings of inferiority or failure. To quote 2 Corinthians 10:4-5, "The weapons of our warfare are not the weapons of the world. Instead, they have divine power to demolish strongholds. We tear down arguments, and every presumption...; and we take captive every thought to make it obedient to Christ." (BSB)

To take captive any stinking thinking or negative emotion requires FAITH. Faith is accepting God's promises as a matter of fact; and the fulfillment of our hopes and dreams as a "done deal." Not what we see. No matter what we're going through. Instead of focusing on our circumstances, we are "keeping our eyes on Jesus, the champion who initiates and perfects our faith." (Heb 12:2 NLT)

Friends, life can be tough, and the challenges we face daunting. So suit up! Be sure to put on the full armor of God and learn to wield all the other spiritual weapons in our divine arsenal, such as prayer. Above all, take up the shield of faith. At the end of your journey you'll be able to declare with the Apostle Paul, "I have fought the good fight, I have finished the course, I have kept the faith." (2 Tim 4:7 NASB)

NEVER GIVE UP!

THE END? HARDLY! Keep reaching for your goals! Keep aiming higher! Never stop dreaming. Never stop believing. And never stop growing—personally, spiritually, and creatively! Above all ...

NEVER GIVE UP!

After all is said and done, you must determine in your heart and mind that no matter what obstacles you encounter, no matter what suffering and heartaches you endure, no matter how many false starts, closed doors, and disappointments challenge your faith—that you WILL NOT give up!

No matter how difficult your circumstances are, no matter how bleak the outcome seems—even when you're forced to stand alone against incredible odds and the giants of adversity, weathering the darkest storms of life, or suddenly confronted with a Ziklag situation, you must not throw in the towel. When your journey seems like it's taking too long, and you'll never reach your destination; when nothing is working out and things are just looking impossible, don't give up on your hopes and dreams!

Remember the history-maker Sir Winston Churchill? Heed his advice and follow his example!

What is his final message for us?

On October 29, 1941, when Churchill was asked to speak on Britain's progress in the war, in a venue packed with people eager with anticipation, the Prime Minister delivered one of the shortest yet most inspiring addresses ever recorded. He said, in essence, "Never, never, never, never, never give up!"

Fellow creators and dreamers, we doubt we'll ever encounter better advice than this, or a better solution to solving the problems of life, or a more reliable way to realize our goals.

So continue to press forward in the pursuit of your dreams, despite the odds and obstacles! You'll be in good company when you do. Afterwards, in the spirit of Captain America; in the footsteps of Winston Churchill and the Greatest Generation, who helped to defeat Hitler and the Nazi Axis powers; along with the Biblical heroes Abraham and Sarah, King David and his Mighty Men of Valor, the Apostles and *all* the other overcomers we've "met" during this boot camp training—you'll be able to declare, "I have fought a good fight, I have finished *my* course, I have kept the faith." (2 Tim 4:7 KJV)

Keep the faith, be kind and supportive to all, and use your gifts and talents wisely. At the end of your journey through life, you'll hear your Lord proclaim, "Well *done,* good and faithful servant.... Enter into the joy of your lord." (Matt 25:21 NKJV)

After all, "Who shall separate us from the love of Christ? Shall trouble or hardship or persecution or famine or nakedness or danger or sword? ...No, in all these things we are more than conquerors through Him who loved us. For I am convinced that neither death nor life, neither angels nor demons, neither the present nor the future, nor any powers ... will be able to separate us from the love of God that is in Christ Jesus our Lord." (Rom 8:35-39 NIV)

Do your part and cooperate with the Lord. But remember also, "Be not afraid nor dismayed ... for the battle is not yours, but God's." (2 Chr 20:15 KJV) Furthermore, you don't have to be a "Captain America" to triumph in life, because our Lord has empowered you with His own unique "super-soldier serum": "But thanks be to God, who always causes us to triumph in Christ...." (2 Cor 2:14 EHV)

America and her Allies defeated the greatest military arsenal ever assembled. They were outnumbered, outgunned, and initially unprepared. And yet, against all odds, *good* prevailed over evil. Take this lesson to heart when you face your own battles in life. As you pursue your goals and dreams, take confidence in the knowledge that "The eyes of the Lord watch over those who do right, and his ears are open to their prayers." (1 Peter 3:12 NLT)

> "Oh, sing to the Lord a new song! For He has done marvelous things; His right hand and His holy arm have gained Him the victory." (Psalm 98:1 NKJV)

LIST OF BIBLE TRANSLATIONS CITED

AKJV - *Authorized King James Version* (Cambridge University Press)

AMP - *The Amplified Bible*, The Lockman Foundation (2015).

AMPC - *The Amplified Bible: Classic Edition*, Lockman Foundation (1987)

BLB – *Berean Literal Bible*, Bible Hub (2016)

BSB – *Berean Study Bible*, Bible Hub (2016)

CEB - *Common English Bible*, Common English Bible (2011)

CEV - *Contemporary English Version*, American Bible Society (1995)

CJB - David Stern, *Complete Jewish Bible* (1998)

CSB - *Christian Standard Bible*, Holman Bible Publishers (2017)

EHV - *Evangelical Heritage Version*, The Wartburg Project (2017)

ERV - *Easy-to-Read Version*, World Bible Translation Center (2006)

ESV - *The English Standard Version*, Crossway Bibles (2001)

EXB - *The Expanded Bible*, Thomas Nelson Inc. (2011)

GNT - *Good News Translation,* American Bible Society (1992)

GW - *God's Word*, God's Word to the Nations (1995)

HCSB - *Holman Christian Standard Bible*, Holman Bible Publishers (2003)

ICB - *International Children's Bible*, Thomas Nelson (2015)

ISV - *International Standard Version*, ISV Foundation (1996-2012)

JUB - *Jubilee Bible*, Life Sentence Publishing (2000, 2001, 2010)

KJV - *King James Version* (1611; revised 1769)

KJ21 - *21st Century King James Version,* Deuel Enterprises, Inc. (1994)

MSG - *The Message,* E. H. Peterson (2002)

NASB - *New American Standard Bible*, Lockman Foundation (1995)

NCV - *New Century Version*, Thomas Nelson, Inc. (2005)

NET - *The NET Bible*/New English Trans., Biblical Studies Press (2005)

NIV - *The New International Version*, Biblica, Inc. (1984, 2011)

NKJV - *New King James Version*, Thomas Nelson, Inc. (1982)

NLT - *New Living Translation*, Tyndale House Foundation (1996, 2007)

NOG - *The Names of God Bible*, Baker Publishing Group (2011)

PHILLIPS - J. B. Phillips, *The New Testament in Modern English* (1958)

TLB - *The Living Bible,* Kenneth Taylor (1971)

VOICE - *The Voice Bible,* Thomas Nelson; Ecclesia Bible Society (2012)

WNT - Richard Francis Weymouth, *Weymouth New Testament* (1903)

ABOUT THE AUTHORS:

Wilma Espaillat English grew up in a bilingual, bicultural family in New York and New Jersey, learning firsthand the significance of hospitality in the Hispanic culture. Today she is a writer, speaker and educator. She's taught a variety of subjects, including Business English, Public Speaking, Spanish, and Ancient World History, at both the college and high school levels. She has written high school curriculum for classes in Multicultural Studies (from a Judeo-Christian worldview) and conducted seminars for civic groups, including law enforcement agencies. She also has taught Bible and Christian Life topics to adults ranging in age from 18 to 80. She is the wife of Tom English.

Tom English grew up in a Southern-fried family in rural Virginia. Today he is a Senior Chemist and Technical Writer for Newport News Shipbuilding. He is also a writer and an award-nominated editor of both fiction and non-fiction. His work has appeared in the print anthologies *Gaslight Arcanum: Uncanny tales of Sherlock Holmes, Challenger Unbound,* and *Bound for Evil: Curious Tales of Books Gone Bad,* among other books and magazines. Like his wife, Wilma, Tom has extensive knowledge in Biblical Studies and has taught many Christian Life classes to singles and "young" married couples ages 18 to 80.

Tom and Wilma invite readers to join them each weekday for new insights, inspiration, and words of encouragement, at their website AngelAtTheDoor.com

ALSO BY TOM & WILMA ENGLISH:
THE HEART OF AN ANGEL:
Becoming God's Messengers of Love and Hospitality to a World in Need!   ISBN: 978-0996693615 • 186 pp • $12.95

ANGEL IN THE KITCHEN:
Truth & Wisdom Inspired by Food, Cooking, Kitchen Tools and Appliances   ISBN: 978-0996693608 • 186 pp • $9.95

DIET FOR DREAMERS:
Inspiration to Feed Your Dreams, Encouragement to Foster Your Creativity   ISBN: 978-0979633577 • 162 pp • $7.95

Ravens' Reads: "Books to feed your spirit!"

ALSO AVAILABLE FROM RAVENS' READS:

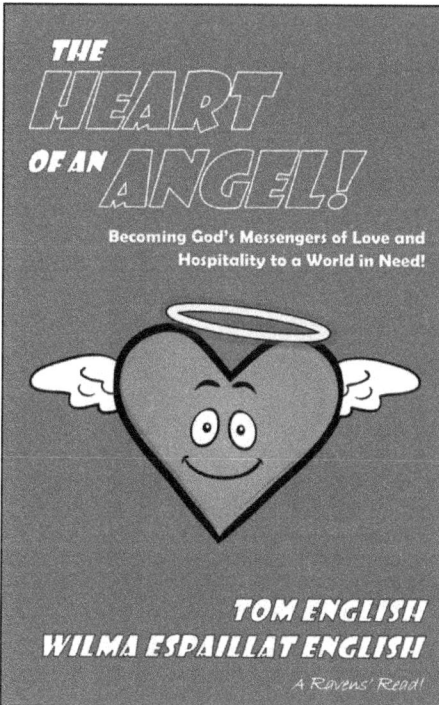

THE

HEART

OF AN ANGEL!

Becoming God's Messengers of Love and
Hospitality to a World in Need!

TOM ENGLISH
WILMA ESPAILLAT ENGLISH

A Ravens' Read!

God has frequently relied on a celebrated company of Heavenly messengers called angels. But in a manner of speaking, we're all called to be God's "Heavenly messengers" here on earth: we all have a story to tell, an experience to relate, a testimony to share; and, like His celestial band of servants, the Creator of the Universe wants each of us to become a Godly emissary of His supernatural love: following in the footsteps of Jesus Christ, through a lifestyle of giving, serving, encouraging, and ... sharing the Words of Life! But something's been holding us back from fully answering the call! We've lost an important truth that expresses the heart and nature of God, and we've abandoned a practice that's vital to peace and unity within our homes and communities, as well as the growth of our churches. It's one of the most misunderstood and neglected Biblical concepts today, and its inexcusable neglect is keeping us from becoming all God intended! God wants us to develop the "heart of an angel"—but how do we accomplish this? Better still, what is the heart of an angel? Join us as we examine the secrets of the heart: learn how to change the world while building meaningful relationships; strengthen your family while becoming more like God; unite your community while impacting eternity; and fulfill the Lord's greatest commandment while "flying" with the angels!

ISBN: 978-0-996693615 • 193 pp • $12.95

SCIENCE FICTION FOR THE WHOLE FAMILY!

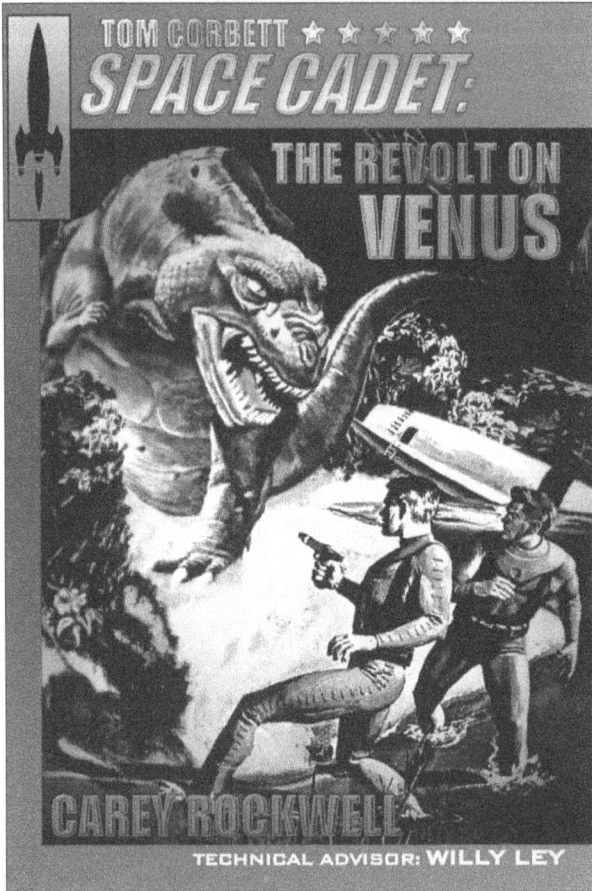

TOM CORBETT, SPACE CADET:
THE REVOLT ON VENUS

On term break from Space Academy, Tom Corbett and Roger Manning accompany their pal Astro to his native planet Venus for a well-deserved rest. There the cadets plan to hunt the biggest game in the star system, but their vacation is soon interrupted when the intrepid crew of the *Polaris* stumble across a secret plot to overthrow the Solar Alliance.

Lost in the Venusian Jungle, unable to contact the Solar Guard, separated from their ship and each other, the hunters have now become the hunted: caught between the heavily armed forces of a would-be tyrant mad for power … and the tyrannosaurus Astro wounded years earlier —thirty tons of terror mad for revenge.   **BOOK 5 IN THE SERIES**

$8.00 ♦ ISBN: 978-0-996693660